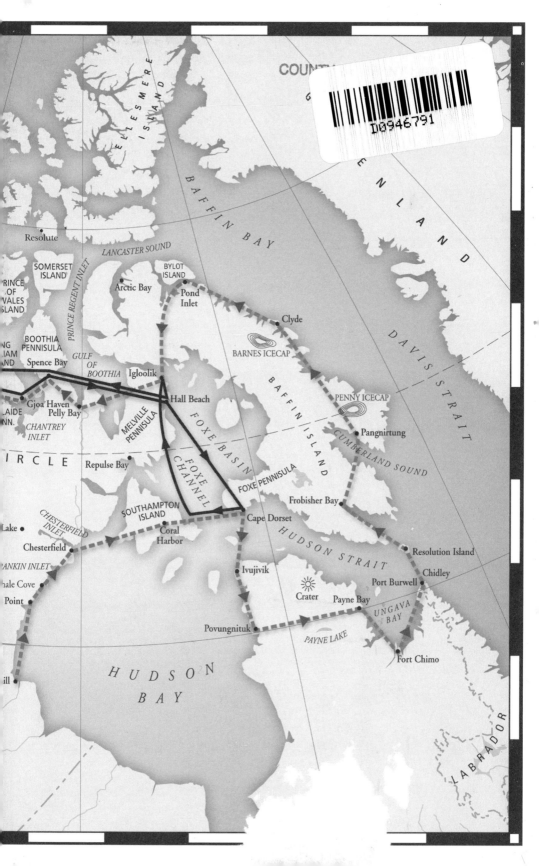

COUNT...

ELLESMERE ISLAND

GREENLAND

BAFFIN BAY

DAVIS STRAIT

Resolute

LANCASTER SOUND

SOMERSET ISLAND

PRINCE OF WALES ISLAND

BOOTHIA PENNISULA

PRINCE REGENT INLET

Arctic Bay

BYLOT ISLAND

Pond Inlet

Clyde

BARNES ICECAP

NG IAM ND

Spence Bay

GULF OF BOOTHIA

Igloolik

PENNY ICECAP

BAFFIN ISLAND

Pangnirtung

LAIDE NN.

Gjoa Haven

Pelly Bay

CHANTREY INLET

Hall Beach

MELVILLE PENNISULA

FOXE BASIN

CUMBERLAND SOUND

I R C L E

Repulse Bay

FOXE CHANNEL

FOXE PENNISULA

Lake

CHESTERFIELD INLET

SOUTHAMPTON ISLAND

Coral Harbor

Cape Dorset

Frobisher Bay

Chesterfield

HUDSON STRAIT

Resolution Island

Chidley

ANKIN INLET

Ivujivik

Port Burwell

hale Cove

Crater

Payne Bay

UNGAVA BAY

Point

Povungnituk

PAYNE LAKE

Fort Chimo

ill

HUDSON BAY

LABRADOR

High Latitudes

High Latitudes:
A Northern Journey

Farley Mowat

KEY PORTER BOOKS

Copyright © 2002 by Farley Mowat

All rights reserved. No part of this work covered by the copyrights hereon may be
reproduced or used in any form or by any means—graphic, electronic or mechanical,
including photocopying, recording, taping or information storage and retrieval sys-
tems—without the prior written permission of the publisher, or in the case of photocopying or other reprographic copying, a license from the Canadian Copyright
Licensing Agency.

National Library of Canada Cataloguing in Publication

Mowat, Farley, 1921-
    High latitudes : a northern journey / Farley Mowat.

Includes index.
ISBN 1-55263-473-6

    1. Mowat, Farley, 1921- —Journeys—Arctic regions. 2. Arctic regions—Description
and travel. 3. Authors, Canadian (English)—Travel—Arctic regions. I. Title.

PS8526.O89Z533 2002   C818'.5409   C2002-902867-1
PR9199.3.M68Z47 2002

ONTARIO ARTS COUNCIL

The publisher gratefully acknowledges the support of the Canada Council for the Arts
and the Ontario Arts Council for its publishing program.

We acknowledge the financial support of the Government of Canada through the Book
Publishing Industry Development Program (BPIDP) for our publishing activities.

Key Porter Books Limited
70 The Esplanade
Toronto, Ontario
Canada M5E 1R2

www.keyporter.com

Cover design: Peter Maher
Electronic formatting: Jean Lightfoot Peters

Printed and bound in Canada

02 03 04 05 06 07 6 5 4 3 2 1

For Jack McClelland who fathered this book, as he has fathered so many others—not only of mine, but of many other writers too. My heartfelt gratitude, old friend.

Contents

Introduction

THINK BACK TO 1952. THE AMERICAN SOUTH WAS STILL segregated, World War II had been over for a mere seven years, McCarthyism was at full boil, women professors were scarce as clowns at a funeral, and there was not yet any rock 'n' roll. That was the year Farley Mowat published his first book, *People of the Deer*, an account of the hard times and injustices suffered by those who lived on the "barren lands" of the Canadian north, and who depended on the cariboo for their existence. *People of the Deer* was not only highly successful as a book, it turned Mowat into an instant and controversial celebrity.

It was also an X in the sand: it marked a crucial turning point in general Canadian awareness. Before it, the only "Eskimos" southern Canadians might recognize were on ice cream bars. Who knew or cared anything about that part of the north? After it, not only was consciousness expanded, conscience was—however sporadically— engaged. *People of the Deer* was to the support for increased autonomy among northern peoples as Rachel Carson's *Silent Spring* was to the environmental movement: a wake-up call, the spark that struck the tinder that ignited the fire from which many subsequent generations of writers and activists have lit their torches, often ignorant of where that spark came from in the first place.

Since *People of the Deer*, Mowat has written more than thirty-five more books. Over the decades, he's been published in forty countries and translated into twenty-five languages, and has been counted among Canada's most widely read writers. Many of his books have reflected his passionate commitment to the ideal of a caring and attentive life within Nature, and his discouragement in the face of the ongoing slaughter and waste carried out by that dominant but often greedy and untidy primate, *Homo sapiens sapiens*. Many of these books have also marked Xs in the sand, and have struck their own igniting sparks: numerous writers on Nature, wolves, wilderness travel, and ecology have acknowledged their debts to him.

His rage can be Swiftean, his humour Puckish, but his compassion for all creatures great and small has been consistent. He's been treated as a revered grandfather, a father against whom one must rebel, a sort of dotty uncle with bright but eccentric ideas who might possibly be making bombs in the garage, an icon to be scribbled on, and as a black-sheep juvenile-delinquent cousin, in trouble again and yet again, but the intensity of the reaction to him merely underlines the strong family connections people feel both with the man himself and with his writing. Love him or resent him, he's now an Ancestral Totem, whether he likes it or not. We might have picked someone less given to howling like a wolf at the dinner table or to doing strange dances in a kilt while making oinking noises, but Canadians have never been too stuck on the idea of inflated notions of stately dignity, so Farley Mowat is right up there on our totem pole. The fact that he's grinning like a goat should fool no one: he has always adopted a prankish public mask, behind which he could live his life as a deeply serious and intensely committed writer.

Now, in *High Latitudes*, he chronicles the journey he took across northern Canada in 1966, by various means of transportation, all of them hazardous. In its origins and intentions, this was a salvation escapade—he hoped to write a book that would let northern people speak for themselves, and that would also give the lie to the current political idea that the north was "a bloody great wasteland" with no people in it, and therefore resource developers could go up there and hack apart and pollute whatever they wanted. That book was not the one that appeared back then, for the reasons Mowat describes. But here it is now, with the original conversations recorded by Farley Mowat during that epic journey.

High Latitudes gives us, with passion and insight, a vertical section of time past—the time that preceded our present. The choices that were made then affect our now, just as the choices we make now will determine the future. I'm sure Farley Mowat hopes that politicians today will be smarter than they were then, though he probably isn't betting on it.

It's both depressing and cheering to note the changes that have taken place since 1966. On the one hand, more damage and devastation, both natural and social, with global warming as a contributing factor. On the other hand, an increased optimism, at least among the people of self-governing Nunavut, recently created in the eastern Artic. Inventiveness and creativity there have been given a big boost. But as Farley Mowat has always known, and as more and more people have come to agree, it's a race against time, and time—not just for the north, but for the planet—is running out.

Margaret Atwood
June 2002

Note

Although it is now considered politically incorrect to refer to Canada's indigenes as "natives," and to people of Euro-immigrant stock as "whites" or "whitemen," these are the names by which they were generally known in 1966 when the events chronicled in this book occurred.

Also it is now *de rigueur* to refer to the people formerly called Eskimo as Inuit. However, in 1966 the term Eskimo was still in general use, not only by non-natives, but by many of the Inuit themselves. I have therefore used *Eskimo* wherever and whenever the context validates that usage.

CHAPTER ONE

Getting

There

IN THE 1960s MY WIFE CLAIRE AND I WERE LIVING ON
the southwest coast of Newfoundland. Home was a fishing village
which could not be reached by road and had no airstrip. Anyone
wanting in or out had to travel by small boat or aboard a little coastal
steamer which called in once or twice a week.

Early in 1966 this not uncongenial isolation was shattered when our
outport was connected by telephone to the outer world. One of the first
calls I received was from Sandy Ross, editor of *Maclean's* magazine in
Toronto.

Sandy was not one for idle chatter.

"How long would it take you to get from wherever-the-hell-you're-at
to Yellowknife in the Northwest Territories?" he demanded.

"God knows, Sandy. Coast boat's not due for a couple of days. Likely
the best part of a week even to get to an airport...but why Yellowknife?"

"Because a charter plane'll be flying a judge and jury out of there in
ten days, heading for some godforsaken hamlet on the Arctic coast to
hold the juiciest northern murder trial of the century. Like you to cover
it for us."

Although I had not been back to Canada's Arctic and subarctic hin-
terland since 1958, it had been my spiritual home since boyhood. I
missed it badly. Which is why, ten days later, I found myself aboard a ski-
equipped DC-3 taking off from Yellowknife for the tiny settlement of
Spence Bay in the central Arctic, where the trial was to be held.

My visit there (it is described in Chapters 18 to 21) turned out to be the preamble to the most extensive of all my journeys to the top of the world.

By 1966 cataclysmic events were engulfing Canada's north. Almost the entire region was undergoing seismic change in consequence of a massive campaign launched by the Conservative government of John Diefenbaker to "enrich the nation by making available the Canadian Arctic's golden cornucopia of minerals, fossil fuels, and other valuable resources."

Dubbed the Northern Vision and heralded as the greatest national initiative since the construction of the transcontinental railways, the Vision's implementation would ensure (or so politicians and business leaders assured us) that the twentieth century would indeed belong to Canada.

Caught up in anticipation of potential wealth, nobody of importance seemed concerned about the possibility of adverse consequences. Suggestions that opening the "golden cornucopia" might bring disasters to the northern world commensurate with those that followed the opening of Pandora's box were ignored.

During my visit to Spence Bay in April of 1966 I came face to face with some dire consequences of "opening up the north" and was told of many others. One of my informants was a long-faced, rather doleful Newfoundlander named Peter Murdoch.

Murdoch was a relatively young man, but an old Arctic hand. Recruited by the Hudson's Bay Company while still in his teens, he had served the Honourable Company for twenty years, during which he had become increasingly unhappy with its treatment of the Inuit. When the Northern Vision swept upon the scene, Murdoch was persuaded it presaged a new deal for northern natives, and so he left the H.B.C. to join the federal Department of Northern Affairs, which had replaced both the company and the Church as the new ruler of the north. When I met him in Yellowknife, he was DNA's regional director for the central Arctic. He was also a thoroughly disillusioned man.

"You won't believe the damage being done," he told me. "It's the old colonial game being replayed with smarter public relations." He even intimated that the government might be deliberately pursuing a policy designed to complete the obliteration of ancestral Indian and Eskimo culture so the next generation of natives would be "totally integrated into the socioeconomic patterns of southern Canada."

By the time I met Murdoch, his disenchantment with the Northern Vision had become so profound he was ready to resign from the department ("before they fire me") in order to foment what was in effect a counter-revolution to protect the Eskimos' way of life, not by trying to isolate them, as some missionaries and romantics would have liked, but by helping them build a parallel civilization to ours. One that would take what it needed from our technology without abandoning their own age-old beliefs and concepts.

Murdoch was a dedicated man. He was also fluent in Inuktitut—the Inuit language—and the possessor of extensive connections in almost every Arctic community. If one wished to understand what was going on in the new north, clearly he would be a good man to have around.

On my way home from Spence Bay to Newfoundland, I stopped off in Toronto to visit my publisher, Jack McClelland. Deeply disturbed by what I had seen and heard during my journey north, I subjected Jack to something of a tirade.

"The vandals are taking over the Arctic, Jack, and they're getting away with it by peddling the myth the whole north is a bloody great Klondike, its frozen guts filled with fabulous wealth. The Arctic's crawling with southern business types who don't give a damn what happens to the land, the people, or the animals, so long as *they* get rich. They're getting away with what amounts to plunder and rapine because most Canadians know nothing about the real north and couldn't care less."

"Well?" Jack asked calmly when I paused for breath.

"Well…maybe it's up to some of us to show Canadians what it's really like up there. That it *isn't* Jack London's Frozen Hell inhabited by a handful of cute little Eskimos in Disneyland igloos. That it's a vibrant, beautiful and *living* world! And it's in trouble!"

Jack poured a large glass of vodka to calm me down. Then he told me about a new publishing project of his: a series of illustrated books designed to familiarize Canadians with their native land.

"Why don't you do the volume about the north?" he asked.

The idea took a moment to sink in.

"But I'd have to travel the whole damned Arctic to do that...and I don't have the time, let alone the money."

"Bullshit, Farley. You've got nothing *but* time. We'll *find* the money."

Such was the genesis of an odyssey which was to take me through much of the enormous and mysterious realm lying north of the sixtieth parallel of latitude: a realm embracing all of the Canadian Arctic together with a vast subarctic sweep of boreal forest—taiga, the Russians call it; massive mountain ranges; and an inland sea whose very existence was virtually unknown to most southerners. It was that portion of Canada's lands and waters over which our species had not yet attained exploitive mastery. Now we were attempting to do just that.*

By early May I had made arrangements for a bush plane to carry me from Churchill north and east through the Arctic island archipelago, then west to the Alaskan border—a journey of more than ten thousand miles that would take me to most inhabited places north of sixty.

I called Pete Murdoch and invited him to join me.

"We'll be an expedition of two. Three for the first bit because my wife has never been north, so she'll come partway. If you'll interpret I'll record what the people have to say about themselves, about what's happening to them and their land. Can't pay anything but I'll provide the wings, and the food and drink. And think of the opportunities you'll have to sow the good seed."

He called back the next day and in the native argot of his home island accepted my offer.

"Yiss, me son. I'll take the berth. When do we sail?"

I was delighted to have him, even though he would be busy with his own agenda organizing a resistance movement among the Inuit. He and I and Claire reached Churchill, our departure point, together.

Squatting at the mouth of the river of the same name on the western shore of Hudson Bay, Churchill billed itself as the Gateway to the Arctic. In truth it was a crapulous-looking collection of mostly wooden

---

* The immediate result was my *Canada North* (The Canadian Illustrated Library, Toronto, 1967), a mainly pictorial and descriptive volume that did not include an account of the actual journey, which is the subject of the present book.

structures sprawled between taiga and open tundra. It was not a prepossessing place; nevertheless Claire was initially entranced. I did not share her enthusiasm. Churchill had served as my jumping-off point for several northern journeys, and I knew it all too well. I thought its unofficial title, Asshole of the Arctic, was more appropriate.

It did at least have a notable situation for it overlooked what is in effect Canada's fourth ocean. This vast body of water embracing Hudson Bay, James Bay, Foxe Basin, Hudson Strait, and Ungava Bay is the world's second-largest inland sea (only slightly inferior in size to the Mediterranean). It has no official name, but I call it the Canadian Sea.

Those who live along its southern reaches are mostly Cree, Algonkian, and Athapascan Indians; those along its northern shores mostly Inuit. Only a smattering of Europeans inhabit its coasts, yet it was one of the first places in the Americas to be visited by them. Viking Norse from Greenland probably entered Hudson Strait as early as A.D. 1000. In all likelihood they were following sea routes pioneered by seamen from the northern British Isles as much as three centuries earlier.*

Churchill's official history begins as early as 1619 when the King of Denmark sent a two-ship expedition under Jens Munk to plant a settlement there. The attempt was a ghastly failure. During the spring of 1620 the smaller of the ships, battered and in sinking condition, staggered back to Denmark bearing Munk and two other survivors. They abandoned the other vessel and sixty-one of their companions dead of starvation and scurvy at the site of the ill-fated settlement.

For almost a century thereafter the Canadian Sea saw only a handful of foreigners, most of them hurried transients seeking gold mines, slaves, or a northwest passage to Cathay, and finding nothing of any worth. However, early in the eighteenth century a group of English entrepreneurs calling themselves the Honourable Company of Adventurers into Hudson Bay began rearing a grandiose stone fortress at the mouth of the Churchill River, from which to "prosecute the fur trade" in the far north.

Ten years in the building, this grim pile (augustly named Prince of

---

* Cf. *Westviking*. McClelland and Stewart, Toronto, 1965, and *The Farfarers*, Key Porter Books, Toronto, 1998, both by Farley Mowat.

Wales Fort) was captured and demolished by the French even before its completion, whereupon the Honourable Company abandoned the ruins in favour of a cluster of log cabins which eventually became the Churchill of our times.

Prince of Wales Fort bears the dubious distinction of having been the first major locus of Western civilization in the north. It is celebrated as such in most history books, although the true nature of that civilization is seldom or never discussed. Samuel Hearne, one of the Honourable Company's most outspoken employees, has left us this taste of what civilized life at Churchill under the fort's then governor, Moses Norton, was like in 1769.

"He kept for his own use five or six of the finest Indian girls....He always kept a box of poison to administer to those who refused him their daughters or their wives....As he advanced in years his jealousy increased and he actually poisoned two of his women because he thought them partial to other men....A few minutes before he expired, happening to see an officer laying hold of the hand of one of his women who was standing by, he bellowed in as loud a voice as his circumstances would admit: "God damn you for a bitch! If I live, I'll knock your brains out!'"

By the late 1920s the crumbling remnants of Prince of Wales Fort represented little more than a shattered dream. But at this juncture someone in Ottawa experienced a foreflash of the Northern Vision and in consequence the Canadian government decided to transform Churchill into an international seaport.

With enormous difficulty, and at horrendous expense, a single-track railway was built through the boreal swamps and forests north of Lake Winnipeg to link Churchill to southern Canada. Completed in 1929, the Muskeg Special (as it came to be called) trundled thousands of tons of building materials to the mouth of the Churchill River for the construction of a Fortress of Commerce, a modern ocean terminal complete with a battery of gigantic concrete silos designed to handle an expected flood of grain bound for European markets from the wheat lands of Alberta, Saskatchewan, and Manitoba. In addition, a grandiose townsite was laid out on the perpetually frozen rock and gravel beside the new port.

My first visit to Churchill was in 1935 when, as a diminutive fourteen-year-old aspiring ornithologist, I accompanied an elderly naturalist uncle north to help him collect birds' eggs.

This was my introduction to that amorphous region where boreal taiga and arctic tundra meet and which the indigenous Chipewyan Indians call Land of Little Sticks. I found it pulsing with breeding waterfowl and other birds, including elegant sandhill cranes; fierce and piratical jaegers; sky-filling flocks of snow and Canada geese; and uncountable multitudes of plovers, curlews, godwits, phalaropes, and tiny sandpipers. Churchill itself was home to a bizarre mix of mysterious barrenland trappers, intrepid fur traders, and more-or-less-bronzed Indians—all of them the stuff of which youthful romance is woven.

By the time of my next visit, in 1947, the aura of frontier romance had dissipated and Churchill had become a shambles. The dream of an ocean port had faded, partly in the face of sabotage by southern shipping interests, and partly because of the fact that not even ice-strengthened vessels could navigate the Canadian Sea for more than a few months of the year. The Townsite (the name resolutely borne by the port city-that-never-was) consisted of a bleak scattering of scrofulous-looking shanties half-buried under enormous snowdrifts.

Yet it was not moribund. The war had planted a military establishment and airport on the nearby tundra and christened it Fort Churchill. The Base, as it was known, had housed, and was still housing, thousands of Canadian and U.S. troops undergoing arctic training. The Townsite, meanwhile, had become a squalid military parasite whose citizenry seemed to consist mostly of bootleggers, hookers, and confidence men.

By the time of our arrival in 1966 a decline in the military presence had withered even this parasitical vitality. With queasy memories of the kind of hospitality afforded by the Townsite in the past, I sought accommodations on what remained of the Base, only to be told that men and women, even if duly married, were not allowed to sleep together there.

We chose to risk the Townsite, where Claire and I found ourselves two army cots in a threadbare flophouse passing as a hotel.

Despite the waning of its military star, the Townsite was experiencing a boom. The federal government, hot in pursuit of its newest chimera—the Northern Vision—had brought a massive new presence to Churchill. Outposts of the Departments of Northern Affairs, Indian Affairs, Public Works, Transportation, Health, and Justice were producing a fungoid growth that some disaffected locals were already referring to as Fortress Ottawa.

The paramount influence of the Department of Northern Affairs was attested to by clusters of prefabricated building that appeared to be kith and kin to Fort Churchill, but spiritual kin to ancient Prince of Wales Fort. They were called Camp 10 and Camp 20.

We had expected to meet our chartered plane and crew at Churchill. They had not yet arrived so we went sightseeing. We first visited Camp 20, which was billed as a "holding facility" for Eskimos in transit between their far-flung Arctic homes and hospitals and other institutions in the south. A harried young social worker from Montreal showed us around what seemed remarkably like an enclosure for displaced persons. He explained that many of the "clients" were being returned to the Arctic after as much as two years in tuberculosis sanatoria, other hospitals, detox centres, and even prisons.

"We're supposed to keep them here 'til we can teach them how to become white men. How to get a job and live the good life. Only," he added with a mirthless grin, "it don't work out that way. What this place actually is, is a dumping ground for people with problems.... Frankly it's a sink of drinking, whoring, and general disintegration, and we don't know what the hell to do about it. Right now we've got ninety-three people here. How many have jobs? Two. One's a sweeper at the grain elevator. The other's a hooker."

Camp 10, which was similar in its institutional construction and appearance, was intended to provide "residential transition facilities" for families of Chipewyan Indians who had been brought in off the land.

The Indian agent turned out to be another unusually outspoken government employee.

"The only hope for these people is to get them back *out* on the land as far away from Churchill as possible. They were pressured to come in here so their kids could go to school and so they'd be easier to administer. Well, there's sweet f.a. for them to *do* here. No hunting grounds. No work. Just lots of booze and the scum of white society to teach them tricks."

We also took a guarded look at an area known as The Flats because it sprawled on a portion of the harbour's muddy tidal flats. Here about a hundred treaty and non-treaty Indians subsisted in shacks which would have made many southern slums seem palatial.

By this time the bloom was off the rose for Claire. She had seen too much of Churchill in too short a time. I tried to lift her spirits by pointing out that the place was an anomaly and by promising that, as we travelled on, things would improve.

Returning to the hotel, we were delighted to be greeted by two young men who introduced themselves as the pilot and engineer of our chartered plane. Although they had only just arrived, they told us they would be ready to begin our flight early next morning. Weather, of course, permitting.

Doug Lamb, the pilot, was a stocky, round-faced, ruddy-complexioned twenty-six-year-old. Roy Boyce, the engineer, was about Doug's age but lean and lanky, looking like the proverbial prairie farm boy, which is what he had been until seduced by the magic of airplanes. Both were shy, but had an aura of competence about them.

Doug had a surprise for us. He explained that the de Havilland Beaver airplane I had chartered had become unavailable due, as he delicately put it, to "kissing a floating log" during an attempted takeoff.

"But our bad luck's your good luck. Instead of the Beaver, you've got our Otter. It's a lot bigger and got longer range. Just had an engine overhaul too, and she's yours for the same price as the Beaver."

Next morning dawned fair for flying. An old truck trundled us and our gear to Churchill's float-plane base on a tundra pond a few miles out of town. Here we were introduced to our Pegasus: a hulking great creature painted fire-engine red with her insignia, CF-DCL, emblazoned in white on wings and fuselage.

Although of the same lineage as the Beaver (perhaps the most famous of all bush planes), CF-DCL was almost half again as big. Roy was inordinately proud of her.

"She'll do 120 miles an hour and cruise at a hundred, even dragging them christly big pontoons under her belly. Loaded light, the way we'll be, she's got a range of five hundred miles. Can land or take off from a good-sized puddle. Rough and tough. Built like a two-ton truck."

Claire, Pete, and I were to share the roomy cabin with a forty-five-gallon reserve drum of aviation gasoline (filling stations in the Arctic are few and far between); several cases of engine oil; boxes of spare parts; food; and survival gear, including sleeping bags, cooking utensils, a rifle, and a tent. I supervised the loading of a case of rum, something even harder to procure north of sixty than avgas.

Clad in dungarees, denim jackets, and red baseball caps, Doug and Roy stowed the gear, and then, with exaggerated courtesy, handed Claire up the boarding ladder.

"Cabin service ain't up to much, ma'am," Roy apologized, "but if you need a bottle opener or a wrench, just call on me. If it's the ladies' room you want, there's a bucket in back."

Claire's nervousness about flying in a bush plane was so evident that Pete undertook to soothe her.

"This is really the best way to get around in the north, you know. Of course you've got to be prepared to spend time on the ground. Maybe a lot of time. Maybe a long way from anywhere. So they take precautions. We can camp out for a month if we have to."

His intentions were good, but he signally failed to ease Claire's apprehensions. Nor was she soothed when the six-hundred-horsepower Wasp engine burst savagely into life. It howled like an outraged dragon as we began our takeoff run.

DCL lifted off above Churchill's fallen fortresses into a pellucid sky and headed north.

Bay of
Whales

O N THIS DAY WE WOULD BE FLYING (AS ON ALL
other days) by what is known as VFR—Visual Flying Rules. In
other words our Otter possessed no equipment for instrument flying. Preferred conditions ought to be, in pilot's lingo, CAVU—
ceiling and visibility unlimited. And this is how they were when our big,
scarlet dragonfly made a climbing turn to the northward before levelling off at eight hundred feet above the broad estuary of the Churchill
River.

The tide was out and the shallows were mottled with pods of white
whales—belugas—who use river estuaries as their nurseries. These
giant arctic porpoises (some measuring twenty feet in length) drifted
like smoky ghosts among wavering clumps of purple kelp. Claire was so
enraptured by them, and especially by the porcelain-coloured calves
nuzzling their mothers' flanks, that she momentarily forgot she was suspended in space in the bowels of a raving red machine.

This was a day of days. To the eastward the Canadian Sea shimmered
under a serene and cloudless sky. To the west the tundra prairies (mis-
named "barren lands") rolled in swirling patterns of muskeg brown and
swampy green. Flecked and pocked with innumerable lakes and ponds
and fissured by the quicksilver gleam of streams and rivers, they
appeared to consist as much of water as of land.

This low-lying coastal world was awash with life. Shivers of shore-
birds flickered along the mud flats. Fleets of ducks shared the shoal
waters at the mouths of rivers with pods of white whales.

Claire shouted in my ear: "...ought to call Hudson Bay the Bay of Whales...how beautiful they are!"

"Not just whales," I bellowed back. "Look!" and pointed westward where the sodden plains were whitened by flocks of snow geese waddling across the tundra like a multitude of pinheaded sheep. This being the moulting season most were flightless, but a few were airborne and some even seemed inclined to dispute our passage. Doug meekly altered course to let these have the right-of-way.

The sixtieth degree of north latitude passed under us unremarked. We had been airborne for two hours without seeing any sign of human beings when Doug drew our attention to a glint of reflected sunlight on the low coast far ahead. This, he informed us over the intercom headphones, was the tin roof of the Roman Catholic church at Eskimo Point, our first port of call.

I had visited Eskimo Point several times before and had written extensively about it so, on this occasion, I planned only a brief refuelling stop.*

On my last visit, in 1958, the settlement had been dominated by the Hudson's Bay Company compound (easily identifiable by its white-painted walls and garish red roofs); a Royal Canadian Mounted Police barracks; a squat and weather-worn Roman Catholic church; and an even smaller and shabbier church (hardly more than a chapel) of the Anglican faith. For the rest, Eskimo Point had consisted of a handful of shacks.

In 1966 the symbols of the Old Empires still held pride of place but were clearly being challenged. We landed to find ourselves sharing the harbour with the HBC supply ship *Fort Severn*. She was unloading not only a year's requirements of goods for the Company store, but also mountains of construction materials consigned to the Department of Northern Affairs.

In eight short years Eskimo Point had burgeoned from a simple trading post with a resident population of only four or five native families,

* *People of the Deer*, McClelland and Stewart, Toronto, 1951; *The Desperate People*, McClelland and Stewart, Toronto, 1959; and *Walking on the Land*, Key Porter Books, Toronto, 2000; all by Farley Mowat, deal with people and events at Eskimo Point, and in southern and central Keewatin.

to a settlement of 460 people, most of them brought in from camps once scattered across much of interior and coastal Keewatin.

The few shacks and tents of my earlier visits had mostly been replaced by prefabricated plywood "native housing" which, as Claire noted, looked like rows of oversized cereal cartons. The shoreline was cluttered with stacks of timber; freight containers; serried ranks of steel drums (some containing gasoline and some diesel oil to fuel an electric generating station in the making); and other matériel associated with a major construction project.

Most of the residents were on the beach unloading barges from the ship. Although we were anxious to refuel and be on our way, Claire and I managed a brief visit with a friend from my earlier days.

A rather saturnine-looking youngish man with heavy black-rimmed glasses, Armand Tagoona had recently become the first Eskimo to be ordained a priest in the Anglican Church. He met us on the shore and, while Doug and Roy hand-pumped gas into the Otter's tanks, the Reverend Armand took us to his "rectory" for tea.

Armand's three-room cabin housed his wife, nine children, and several other relatives. In true Eskimo fashion it also served as a general drop-in centre. Coherent conversation was almost out of the question, but I recorded some of Armand's reactions to the revolution taking place around him.

Everything change too fast now. It's pretty hard, you know, because there's a big difference the way whites and Eskimos thinking. Whites look all the time ahead, but Eskimos mostly think and talk about the past. Never talking about the future more than a day or two away....Life for them is right now; but looking back too.

People here liking to think about the past because it was better for them than now. Wasn't always good, but we forget the bad parts. And the future looking pretty scary. A friend of mine say: "Why should I think about the future? I'm not a prophet. I can't tell what the future is."

When I ask the people where they rather be, what they rather be doing, they say they rather be where they used to be, but when I ask them, Why don't you go back there where you want to be, they say, "How can I? I have no more dogs, no gear; all got left behind on the country." I ask, Why you moving in here anyway? They say, "Police moved us." Why? "Because police say we always hungry." Were you? "Sometimes, when we got no ammunition, but usually lots of caribou and fish around. We only hungry when had no gear to fish or hunt with. If the police just give ammunition and nets we be happier to stay in our own places."

I asked Armand if he would prefer living the way his forebears had. He laughed softly.

To be perfectly honest, no. But all my life I work and live with whites, you know. But again, I did have three years living on the land as real Eskimo, and they were happiest years I ever had. Free to do what you want….

I don't know about the future…we looking to white people to tell us what to do. People are just waiting. They afraid to move back onto the country even to hunt. They afraid if they stay away too long a man would be missing the white man's job he was told was coming.…Probably that job never come anyway, but the man still hoping. This was the reason he was stay on here.…

He still hoping.

We took our departure from Eskimo Point bound for a brand-new settlement called Whale Cove. As we flew northward, the land's overlying skin of muskeg shrank to reveal the granitic bones of an elder earth beneath. Beyond the mouth of Dawson Inlet the country became a maze of wrinkled rock ridges with a shoreline dotted by barren islets and stony reefs. It looked singularly inhospitable, but white whales were numerous, and the reefs smoked with dense flocks of arctic terns.

In mid-afternoon the horizon ahead resolved itself into a fifteen- or twenty-mile scimitar of granite curving south and east into the dark waters of the Bay. This was Term Point, with Whale Cove at its eastern tip.

Whale Cove was named during the nineteenth century by Yankee and Scots whalers who sometimes used it as a summer station for flensing and trying-out the blubber of the giant of the Arctic seas—the bowhead, or Greenland whale. After the whalers had effectively exterminated the bowheads, they turned their attention to vast herds of walrus, but these did not last long, and shortly after the turn of the century the last whalers departed from the Canadian Sea.

Whale Cove was so distant from the caribou grounds and good fishing lakes and rivers of the mainland that native people had never made more than passing use of it. It would probably have continued forever free of human settlement had it not caught the attention of DNA planners in distant Ottawa.

In the mid-1950s DNA decided to construct a new kind of arctic community, one that would serve both as a rehabilitation centre and as a model for a series of new settlements where the Inuit ("refugees from the Stone Age," one of the planners called them) could absorb and be absorbed into southern civilization.

The site for the prototype was chosen, not by consulting the people destined to live there, or by old arctic hands with local knowledge, but by looking at a map while taking into account such vital factors as "infrastructure maintenance," "external communication and access" (particularly to and from Ottawa), and "transportation facilities." So Whale Cove was selected as the right place to build a New Jerusalem of the North.

At Eskimo Point in 1958 I had talked with the gung-ho ex-army officer in charge of launching the project. Now my companions and I were about to see how the great experiment had fared.

Even on this superbly beautiful summer day Term Point was about as desolate a place as one would care to see: a grey jumble of frost- and ice-shattered rocks terminating in a tiny crab-claw indentation hardly adequate for sheltering canoes.

This was Whale Cove. As we roared low above it, I noted the wreck of a landing barge, and a frieze of wood, metal, and plastic flotsam along the shore—debris from a failed attempt to land cargo from an ocean-going freighter. Half a dozen temporary-looking sheds of the kind one sees on construction sites were scattered about amid disordered piles of building materials. There were a dozen or so canvas wall tents and two rows of prefab cabins of the type we had begun referring to as corn-flakes boxes.

The model town we had anticipated not being in evidence, we turned our attention to the small harbour. A crimson flood was spreading fanwise across it from the inner beach. Not until DCL's floats were thumping through foaming red water did we realize we had landed in a tide of blood streaming seaward from a row of beached white whales.

We anchored a hundred yards out. A dungaree-clad Eskimo youth driving an outboard-powered, twenty-two-foot canoe roared alongside to ferry us to the beach, where we were greeted by a shambling giant whose long blond hair and pale blue eyes gave him the look of a vagrant

Viking. He was the administrator in charge of the new community of Whale Cove.

"Welcome!" he shouted. "My name is Finn. We have for you fresh muktuk!"

A trestle table on the shingle beach behind him was smothered in inch-thick slabs of white whale skin and fat. Eskimo women were slicing the slabs into oleaginous strips and flinging them into plastic buckets.

We had barely gained the shore when Finn seized a strip and thrust it, all slithery and glistening, into Claire's hands. Always the trooper, she took it bravely enough, but it was only with considerable encouragement from Pete and me that she could be persuaded to taste this famous arctic delicacy. Raw muktuk, she reported, has a buttery flavour and slides down very easily.

Finn congratulated her. "You have just eaten some of the new white gold of the Arctic. Maybe it is going to make the Eskimos rich so they can live like white men."

Dark blood was continuing to ooze from seven great cadavers stranded in a ragged row along the beach, their flukes slowly rising and falling in the surge. The largest was about fifteen feet long and weighed perhaps three tons. It might have been carved from alabaster, except that its throat had been cut, exposing a crimson cavern. Men and boys swarmed over the whales, stripping off the muktuk. When that task was completed, the flayed carcasses would be abandoned to the rising tide. Few Eskimos here still kept dogs so very little of the meat was wanted. Muktuk alone was the reason for this slaughter.

The clock had come full circle in the Bay of Whales. The mighty bowheads had enriched humankind until extinction came upon them. Now it appeared to be the belugas' turn.

Earlier attempts had been made to turn white whales into money. The Hudson's Bay Company had employed Eskimos to kill and render thousands of them for their oil, but that fishery had not proved to be sufficiently profitable to maintain. Recently a Churchill businessman had tried using beluga to lure wealthy Canadian and American sportsmen north with the promise that they could roar around the estuary in powerboats and shoot white whales to their hearts' content. But Edward Schreyer, the NDP premier of Manitoba, had put a stop to that.

It had been left to the economic experts of DNA's Industrial Division to come up with the ultimate proposal for turning white whales into cash.

Aggressive and imaginative marketing, they proclaimed, would convince the gourmet carriage trade that muktuk from arctic beluga was as rare, as delectable, and as socially *au fait* as caviar from Caspian Sea beluga. Presumably no one would care (if indeed anyone noticed) that the arctic beluga was a whale, and the other was a sturgeon.

The transmutation of beluga into gold was to be Whale Cove's first great industrial achievement. Finn was happy to show us what was being done to further that end.

"We fish with nets," he explained, "big-mesh nets. When the whales get twined up they cannot get back to the surface to breathe so they drown. We have nineteen nets out right now and three big boats working them. Some people also shoot the whales from their canoes. A few even still harpoon them, but that is old-fashioned and catches too few. Already this year we take about 250 whales. Right now most of the muktuk goes to our cannery at Rankin, but soon we have an even bigger cannery and freezer right here. You must see our factory at Rankin. It is amazing."

In due course we visited the plant at Rankin Inlet, site of a defunct nickel mine some forty-five miles north of Whale Cove. Indeed, it *was* amazing: a large metal-sheathed building filled with stainless-steel industrial cooking and preserving equipment, run by an enthusiastic and imaginative German chef named Eric who took Claire and me on a tour of the premises. Nineteen Eskimos, mostly women, were busy at assembly lines producing such delicacies as jellied beluga tongue; muktuk in several guises, both cooked and frozen; tiny whale meatballs for cocktail snacks; whale salami; creamed blubber as a spread for canapés; whale heart in aspic; whale liver paste; and a spread made of smoked whale flipper.

Eric proudly told us he expected to produce three hundred thousand cans of beluga specialties for the World's Fair, which was to be held in Montreal the following year.

"We will make a culinary breakthrough there," he said happily. "And not *only* whales. We make fish delicacies too. We even can the eyes of arctic char, deep-fried in batter. You will be surprised how good they are."

He may have been joking about the eyes, but he told us he had already shipped ninety thousand cans of char products, together with a ton of smoked char, and another ton frozen, to Montreal. "Soon we will double that. Triple that. Already we experiment also with seals. And there are also many other fishes in Hudson Bay. Then there is caribou—reindeer we call it at home. We will be able to make many good things with caribou."

Although a determined exploitation of local animals was being touted as one of the paths to economic salvation for northern natives, it did not yet seem to be yielding significant results at Whale Cove, whose fishermen were getting only ten dollars each for beluga and were selling arctic char—a red-fleshed, salmon-like fish of superb flavour—for about five cents a pound, after bringing it as much as fifty miles by small boat from the rivers where it was caught. It did not appear that the native fishers were in the way of becoming rich.

I was concerned about the sustainability of this "rational utilization of natural resources," which, it was hoped, could be implemented all across the north. I discussed my fears with two government biologists associated with the new enterprise. My doubts about such massive "harvesting" were swept aside with the assurance that there were far more char in arctic rivers than could be caught, and that arctic saltwater fish stocks were essentially untouched and inexhaustible. White whales, I was told, were "probably over-abundant, and the stocks need to be culled for their own good." One biologist even predicted that the caribou herds, which had been dwindling for fifty years due mainly to over-hunting, would be restored by "new management techniques" and their meat would then be able to support a specialty export market worth "many millions of dollars annually."

When I relayed the gist of this conversation to Peter Murdoch, he responded with a sardonic grin:

"If you believe that crap, you'll believe whales can fly. You know as well as I do arctic wildlife can't even begin to support this kind of exploitation. It's pie in the sky. Meat pie, if you will. It can't last. While it does it *may* make a few people wealthy, but I guarantee you they won't be Eskimos."

Finn himself thought that perhaps the Inuit of Whale Cove were not yet ideal material for transforming the Northern Vision into a reality. The population consisted of 184 men, women, and children, all of whom had been transported here from their ancestral homes by government ukase. They belonged to five different groups with little in common except that all were of an inland culture almost totally predicated on caribou. They had virtually no knowledge of the sea, or of how to make a living from it. It was one of Finn's tasks to show them how this could be done.

"I do not find it an easy thing," he told us as we walked through his new "town" of warehouses and cornflakes boxes. "Young people can maybe learn, but older people, no. We will have to find something different for them. We are trying arts and crafts."

He led us into a shanty in which half a dozen middle-aged men were working in desultory fashion carving small soapstone objects: polar bears, seals, ptarmigan. The work was rough and the images crude. I said as much when we were outside again.

Finn smiled. "*They* think it is foolishness. But the Department says we must do it. So we pay these men for it and they come here like it is a nice little club, and smoke a lot and talk a lot, and carve a little."

Finn knew of my long involvement with the inland people who called themselves Ihalmiut and who had originally lived at the headwaters of the Kazan River, deep in the interior. Now he led us toward a pair of tents pitched near one of the prefab boxes.

"Here is some of the people you wrote about. I'm sorry they are not doing so well. We try our best...but they do not even want to live in the houses we build for them."

There were six people in the two tents—two women, two young children, and two men, Mikki and Belikari, both of whom I had known in the late 1940s. All six were dressed in dirty white men's clothing. The women smiled at us and the children gaped. The men averted their eyes. They recognized me; but it was some time before they would talk, and when they did it was with reluctance.

"It is over for us," Mikki explained softly. "Nobody lives in our country now. We are alive in a strange place. No caribou here. We cannot hunt here. The white men give us food so we don't starve. Maybe our kids will get used to it. I would like to go back to my country where I was born. Where the Old People are buried. And *tuktu*—the caribou. They are our life."

The white residents of Whale Cove were a mechanic whose job it was to keep the diesel electric generator throbbing; two elementary school teachers and their wives (who had gone "outside" for the summer); Finn himself; and *three* missionaries.

The latter were all of fundamentalist persuasions. I met only one, an American representing Intercontinental Missions Inc.—a name he seemed not to find either distressing or amusing. He was well-intentioned, but interested only in souls.

Finn regarded the missionaries with good-humoured contempt.

"There is no Roman Catholic or Anglican priest here yet so these other fellows come hurrying to be first. So far I think they have just one convert among them."

As he'd got to know us a bit, Finn had relaxed his guard, sometimes ignoring the party line.

"The Eskimos here can have a pretty good life if they take what we can give and mix it with what they had. It's not the policy, but I encourage them to spend as much time as they can out on the land: go to fishing camps, sealing stations, caribou hunting places, go trapping for foxes. Of course, they know if they just stay here in Whale Cove they have security, specially in wintertime. And if they get really sick a plane will fly them to hospital at Churchill. The children can go to school and learn what they have to do if they are going to live like us.

"But you know, maybe one of the best things we can do for them is something Eskimos just take to naturally. That is the co-op movement. It is not a popular idea with the big chiefs in Ottawa, but there are some people in the Department quietly trying to push it, from the bottom, if you know what I mean. And from what I see, it is being a great success. You go and talk to Luke Okowlik. He's manager of our Issatik Co-op."

Luke was a small, shy, gentle man of about thirty who looked sixteen. We drank tea in the back of his makeshift store while he talked surprisingly freely and in fluent English.

Issatik's a producer and consumer co-op. I guess when it started up here in 1962 I had a lot of trouble because I never run any store before and I get into a lot of difficulties with the paperwork. Anyhow, I learn and everybody help so we get along.

It's a funny thing. When we first heard the idea of a co-op store here there was a lot of people said we should stick to the Hudson's Bay Company because they been in the north so long. It took a while for people to realize they was better off with their own store. Now they all come around and nobody would want to go back to the old-time way of dealing.

We sell pretty near everything now. Dry goods, groceries, and hardware. Mostly groceries because that's what we need most. This is a temporary DNA building we're in now, but we bought the Hudson's Bay post at Tavanni sixty miles south of here. We took it down last summer and the men moved it up here in winter over the ice. We're putting it back up now, so it'll be finished this autumn.

You want to know where money is coming from to buy the stuff we need? Little bit from the whale fishing; some from char fishing; but the most is what we get off the land, and that's white fox. Whale Cove people trapped eight hundred fox skins one good year. We ship it right from the store here to the auction in Montreal, so all the money the people earned come back to them.

When the people asked me to help start up the co-op here I was pretty scared at first. But I really like the idea of running the store for ourselves, and selling our fur for ourselves. Now we'd all like to see more Eskimos running things our way. Not having white people telling them what to do. And we'd like to have our own administrators because that's the only way we'll get ahead.

I don't think we should try and be just like the whites. Our older people mostly prefer to live their own way, living off the land. They miss getting caribou meat and seal meat and fish for themselves and their families. But young people, they like the idea to work for wages. Problem is, there isn't much work for them. If I have sons I hope they will be able to get jobs up here in the north. All the same, we'd like to see people still living off the land too.

I really don't know what the answer is, but one thing I can tell you. People sure like having our own co-op here.

CHAPTER THREE

SNAFU

WE PARTED COMPANY WITH CLAIRE AT RANKIN Inlet: she to return home while DCL bore the rest of us on into the north. I hadn't planned on visiting the nearby community of Chesterfield this trip, intending to overfly it en route to Coral Harbour on Southampton Island. However, a teacher stranded at Rankin whose pregnant wife was anxiously awaiting him at Chesterfield prevailed upon us to give him a lift.

It was a transcendental day, succulently warm under a high, wide sky in which a pair of rough-legged hawks drifted like motes in outer space. A flight of a mere sixty miles across a rocky plateau deeply etched with glacial scoria brought us over Chesterfield Inlet thrusting almost two hundred miles into the barrens to the westward. The settlement at the inlet's mouth consisted principally of a Roman Catholic residential school, students' residence, hospital, church, and an imitation bishop's "palace." It was essentially a mission bastion.

We would have come down in the harbour but a singularly low tide had exposed such a jumble of rocks that Doug elected to land on a small tundra pond a mile behind the settlement. It proved to be almost *too* small, and DCL nearly ran up on a *chevaux de frise* of boulders along the far shore.

We had expected to remain only long enough to disembark our passenger, and Doug was running up the engine for takeoff when the radio warned us that heavy fog was engulfing Coral Harbour, so it seemed wiser to stay put for a while.

We scrambled ashore where Roy brewed up tea and warmed some stew on a little fire of dwarf willow twigs. We were entertained by a scurry of Parry's ground squirrels, inquisitive little beasties related to the prairie gopher, that stood bolt upright in their marmalade-coloured coats and whistled their shrill alarm at us—*sic-sic-sic*.

A peaceful hour went by, then Coral radio reported the fog was dissipating. However, our pilot had by now concluded the pond was too small to permit a fully laden takeoff, so he dispatched Pete, Roy, and me to the sea beach in front of the settlement, taking with us as much heavy gear as we could handle. There we were to await DCL's arrival. *If* Doug succeeded in extricating her from her pond.

Word of what was up quickly got around and we three were joined on the beach by most of the population. The mood was hushed. Even the children were subdued. When the audience heard the distant roar of the Wasp engine revving up to full throttle, people exchanged anxious glances. Two nuns rather furtively made the sign of the cross. When the noise diminished instead of culminating in an almighty bang, everyone relaxed.

Minutes later the Otter thundered triumphantly overhead and made a stylish splashdown in the harbour. Far *out* in the harbour, for the tide was still quite low. Nobody offered the use of a canoe so we had to roll up our pants, shoulder our packs, and wade for it. Now the audience livened up. There was even some fitful cheering when Pete stumbled into an underwater hole and went down to his armpits.

We followed the mainland coast northward, flying low over a complex of bald islands, deep inlets, coastal ponds, and ice-blue lakes. Our passage disturbed colonies of arctic terns, which rose below us like puffs of glittering confetti. Seals swivelled their heads and gazed upward for a moment before smoothly submerging. Pods of belugas manoeuvred majestically in the shallows at the mouths of Winchester Inlet and Daly Bay. The vista to the west was of an endless expanse of seemingly lifeless, glacier-scoured rock and bog.

Passing Cape Fullerton, we flew over many raised beaches dotted with stone tent-circles and ancient house pits, testimony that the adjacent waters must once have provided a living for many human beings. That had been long ago. Now we saw no signs of human life, and only an occasional seal and a few eider ducks were visible in the fringing waters of Roes Welcome Sound, which separates the mainland from Southampton Island.

Before turning east to cross the sound we climbed high so that, in the event of engine failure, we would have a longer glide potential. Fifty miles wide where we crossed it, the sound was shallow and filled with reefs clearly visible below the surface.

Southampton Island is a tundra triangle roughly two hundred miles per side, much of it emerged from undersea only during the past few thousand years. Our first view as we descended toward it was of a succession of sprawling, sandy terraces, each formed by an ancient beach marking a stage in the island's post-glacial emergence. Between the terraces lay broad strips of muskeg strikingly patterned with frost polygons and streaked with linear ponds. Tens of thousands of geese, both snows and Canadas, together with innumerable brants and ducks of several species, flew, swam, and waddled about below us. Our passage did not seem to disturb them overmuch. Perhaps their numbers gave them confidence. Few were airborne since most of the adults were still in moult and young birds-of-the-year had not yet become practised fliers.

Southwestern Southampton Island is one of the world's great wildfowl breeding grounds, a bird haven of nearly four thousand square miles. In 1966 ornithologists investigating it were setting something of a precedent by involving local people in the studies. The Canadian Wildlife Service had hired two Inuit brothers from Coral Harbour as field workers. Thomas Atalik, a round-faced smiling man with heavily pockmarked cheeks, told me how every summer he and his brother, David, with seven or eight relatives and friends, journeyed in open whaleboats to the estuary of the Boas River, taking with them tents and all the requisite gear for living off the land in the ancestral freedom of camp life while at the same time working for wages.

Every day, weather permitting, a straggling procession of men, women, and children would walk several miles inland. After a leisurely lunch of bannock and tea, they would spread out in a half-moon, separated from one another by a few hundred feet. Then they would amble slowly toward one of several wire-mesh corrals previously erected along the bank of the Boas River. Laughing, singing, and shouting boisterously, they became gooseherds, shepherding an ever-increasing flock of flightless geese before them.

As the cackling mob of geese neared the steep riverbank, the birds were funnelled between extended arms of fencing, into a corral. Here they milled about until Thomas or David caught them and fixed a numbered aluminum band around each one's leg. They were then turned loose to trek back inland at their leisure, complete their moult, and, in due course, fly off to the distant south to spend the winter.

The Wildlife Service hoped some of the banded birds would be shot by hunters in the south and the bands returned, thereby shedding light on migration patterns and other arcane scientific mysteries. The Inuit believed there might be more to it than that. When I asked Thomas what he thought about goose banding, he caught David's eye and both began to smile.

"Well," he said slyly, "must be good idea, because white man do it. But maybe is a trick geese play on white man. When goose gets nice shiny ring on leg, must be easy to find husband or wife then. I never see goose with ring it don't have big family."

Flying low over the braided channel of Boas River we came upon a different kind of bird—the charred remains of a four-engined transport which had crashed and burned during construction of the DEW Line (Distant Early Warning Line), a string of massive U.S. radar installations spanning the Arctic from Baffin Bay to the Bering Sea intended to provide a first line of defence against Russian bombers should these attempt to attack the United States by flying across the polar basin. The DEW Line had yet to claim an enemy plane but over a hundred U.S. and Canadian aircraft had crashed while employed in its construction and maintenance. At least nine men had been incinerated in the crash at Boas River.

A sprawling desert eastward of the Boas looked like part of the Sahara. Hardly any sign of life enlivened its vast expanse of sand and gravel which, until relatively recently, had been seabed.

To the east of the desert, on the southern coast, lay Coral Harbour—so called because of fragments of fossilized red coral found along its shores. We landed in a snug cove dominated by the Hudson's

Bay Company compound. This was a village unto itself, boasting an array of eight spic-and-span, red-and-white buildings including a big store, a bigger warehouse, and two neat bungalows for the manager and for his clerk.

The supply ship *Pierre Radisson* lay at anchor in the cove, her landing craft delivering crates, cartons, and barrels to a dilapidated dock where the cargo was being seized upon by Inuit men, women, and children and carried piecemeal up a long slope to the Company warehouse. They were a motley crowd, mostly dressed in scraps of military uniforms or shoddy store clothing, although some of the women wore traditionally styled parkas cut from cotton cloth instead of caribou skins.

A grinning Inuk in a small outboard came alongside DCL and ferried us ashore, where we were accosted by a grim-faced white man who identified himself as the area administrator. His manner made it clear he considered himself to be at least the equivalent of a district commissioner in Britain's palmy days of Empire. It was also clear that he did not approve of us. However, hospitality in the north being sacrosanct, he was unable to avoid asking us home for lunch of anaemic sandwiches and tea served by a pallid wife.

Home was a veritable mansion. Four-square, flat-roofed, and two storeys high, it suggested a block-house fort. In fact, the dour Hudson's Bay Company post manager stigmatized it as "yon bluidy castle." It was certainly the most impressive residence I ever saw north of sixty.

Official hospitality did not extend beyond the tea and sandwiches. No accommodation was offered. Happily, the administrator's Eskimo assistant proved more forthcoming. Once we were out of sight and hearing of his boss, Jonee Attuk kindly made us free of an empty construction bunkhouse. He also let us in on the name by which the administrator was known to the Eskimos of Coral Harbour. They called him *Kuujangajuq*—the upside-down-person—apparently because his ideas were mostly topsy-turvy.

Jonee showed us around. The older part of the settlement was so littered with debris as to more nearly resemble an urban dump than a habitation site. Jonee explained that during the war, and for some years after, Coral had hosted a U.S. military base. When the Americans finally departed, they simply abandoned their buildings together with much of their equipment and supplies. Local people scavenged plywood, lumber, sheet metal, and anything else they thought might someday come in handy. Much of what they hauled home they subsequently discarded around their scattered shacks, forming middens of junk to which had been added seal and walrus bones, broken bottles, tin cans, and quantities of nameless garbage.

By 2001 the site of this "urban dump" had become one of Coral Harbour's (renamed Salliq) tourist attractions, and was actually a registered archaeological site from which it is forbidden to remove "artifacts." The site is called Snafu, and even Salliq's current residents believe this to be a corruption of an Inuit name. They do not suspect it is really a World War II phrase meaning Situation Normal—All Fucked Up.

Only in the immediate vicinity of the administrator's castle was there a semblance of order. Here nine plywood boxes regimented in three tight rows had recently been erected as part of a centralized housing program. These frail structures were already beginning to disintegrate and, one could confidently predict, would soon be indistinguishable from the rest of the shanty town.

At the time of our visit, Coral was nominally home to 64 Inuit families numbering 225 individuals. However, so Jonee assured me, more than half of the island's inhabitants still lived as they had always done, dispersed in out-camps across the length and breadth of the island. This did not suit the authorities. DNA policy required all of Southampton's people to live at Coral Harbour where they would rent cornflakes boxes at "a nominal fee." A new "infrastructure" was being put in place to deal with their needs. In addition to the resident representatives of the Old Empires and a Department of Transport radio station, it would include a nursing station, schools, a clutch of Northern Affairs administrative staff and arctic experts, and an RCMP detachment.

The prospect did not rouse Jonee to enthusiasm.

"Too many white boss here now!" he told us feelingly.

Curious as to how the whites of the old regime were reacting to the winds of change I called on the Anglican minister, the Reverend Fred Burningham, who invited me in for a cup of tea or, if I preferred, something stronger.

A rangy, thirty-six-year-old Brit, Burningham was temporarily batching it in a snug bungalow close to his plain little church while his wife was home in England having a baby. He was lonely and anxious to talk.

I asked him how he felt about his work.

How do I feel? Well, sometimes I feel I'm neither fish nor fowl here. My sympathies lie with the old-style Eskimos, which doesn't endear me to most of the other white people. But the fact is, I am white and though after six years in the country I speak the native tongue rather well, the Eskimos don't really welcome me into their minds or their lives. So it's rather like living in double Coventry. I really do miss my wife. She's the one person I can unburden myself to.

Southampton is a bit of an oasis in the north these days, with lots of wildlife still. Its people can pretty well support themselves trapping foxes on the land and hunting seals at the floe edge and it's a wonderful place for hunting polar bears. Walrus hunting is also very good in the summer.

So people are able to earn a fair amount trading furs and skins with the Hudson's Bay chap here. He's the only trader on the island. At the same time they can supply themselves with plenty of country food. Their income depends, of course, on the current price of furs. If the ladies in the south are looking for short-haired furs like mink this winter, then it's hard luck for the Eskimos who only have fox furs to sell.

When Europeans first came to Hudson Bay this island was populated by people who called themselves Sadliermiut. Archaeologists think they could have been survivors of a really ancient culture, but they were still a viable people in the latter part of the nineteenth century when they first met white people.

These were whalers; some from Scotland and England, and some from the eastern seaboard of the United States. They were after the big bowhead whales. The whalers found they could use the Sadliermiut to help them hunt, harpooning whales from rowing boats very similar to some you can still see in the harbour here. In fact, the local people have kept the tradition of those whaleboats alive long after they have forgotten about whaling itself.

Contact with the whalers was rough on the Sadliermiut. During the winter of 1902 the natives seem to have caught some kind of intestinal disease from overwintering sailors. By the spring of 1903 all the Sadliermiut were dead except one woman and four children. It is ironic, I suppose, but the whales were soon destroyed too; so the Sadliermiut and the whales went out together.

For many years the island was pretty well abandoned because of what had happened to the Sadliermiut. Eskimos from the mainland didn't want to live here. Then, in the 1920s, the Hudson's Bay Company decided to build a post and import Eskimos from other places.

There's only the one settlement, at Coral, but the Eskimos range the whole island, right up to Duke of York Bay in the north. The fact is most of them prefer to be out in the camps and away from here, only coming in occasionally to buy what they need at the Company's store.

The people are strong in their wish to go on living their lives on the land. They have a particularly strong feeling about that and about being Eskimo. They don't really seem to want to become white men. They seem to almost glory in the differences between them and white men. I think, in a way, they are conscious of being superior, knowing they can live here on their own, but that the reverse isn't really true.

I hear that in many other communities now the government is encouraging handicraft shops, and all sorts of programs so the local people can earn a living without going back to the land. That doesn't seem to be happening here. The people just aren't interested.

They don't like doing anything that interferes with the seasonal routine of living off the country. Right now, for instance, most of them are in out-camps hunting seals from their whaleboats. They are also taking big Peterhead boats out to more distant places like Coats Island to hunt walrus.

They will hunt polar bears there if they find any, although the bear hunt doesn't really begin until the snow comes on the ground and the Eskimos can get their dog teams going again. The bears come inland then—at least the females do—to den for the winter.

As winter progresses, the men go fox trapping, which is the chief winter occupation. There is also a certain amount of seal hunting done at the edge of the ice floes and then, in spring when the white fox season begins to fade out, there's another go at the bears which are coming out of their dens and making for the sea. Following that, people go back to hunting seals. And then, of course, there are the geese and ducks coming in, and they can be hunted all summer long.

So that's about the cycle, as it is now and probably always was, even in Sadliermiut times.

Apart from foxes, it really is a sea economy. There are no big land mammals here—no musk ox and no caribou. There were caribou once but they were hunted out.

Of course some men rather like to be employed by the whites, but only on their own terms and only when they want to be. Underneath everything is the need to prove themselves good hunters, which is a lot more important than being able to drive a bulldozer or a garbage truck. One young fellow who just came back after being at school in Churchill for ten months and getting his Grade 8 certificate told me the thing he was most proud of was that he went out last week with his dad and got a seal.

The future of the young people is the thorniest problem of all. Health conditions are better than they were and a lot of children are being born, thirty-five in Coral Harbour already this year. At this rate of growth it's obvious the land will not be able to support everybody the way it used to.

There is a great division developing between the younger generation and the older ones. I think we are going to get the same sort of situation here they've got in most of the islands off the western coast of Scotland, where there were once flourishing communities of sheep farmers and fishermen. Now the call of wage employment has depopulated those islands of young people and the race is dying out. I do honestly feel this is probably going to happen here. I don't like to think what will happen to the people who remain.

The most difficult thing for me is having to decide what I should do to help them. I see my task as trying to strengthen a spiritual base from which they can accept or reject the things that are coming to them by way of education, and the whole flux of the twentieth-century world which is sweeping over the Arctic. I don't want to see them swept away by it. They have to believe that if they want to stand up and say they don't like it, then we will have to listen. Well, I say we will have to but, of course, the truth is that we never have listened to people who were different from ourselves and I am very much afraid we may never do so.

Fred Burningham had calls to make that afternoon. He invited me to accompany him to the tidal flats along the harbour shore where some of his parishioners lived in tents.

One tent housed an emaciated, but cheerful, middle-aged woman with two pretty daughters aged eight and ten. The husband and father had died of tuberculosis a few years earlier, and the mother was recuperating from the same disease after spending a desolate two years in a Winnipeg hospital. Now she was getting to know her children again.

She lay on a blue woollen bedspread flung over a polar bear hide serving as a mattress. The girls hustled about making tea on a roaring gasoline pressure stove and bringing the priest and me chunks of dried char and soda biscuits to nibble on. The sun had broken through and a warm golden light flooded the tent, bringing a glow to the faces of the three Inuit. Whatever their past had been, they seemed happy now.

"In a week these two girls will be sent south to a residential school," Fred told me as we walked back toward the village proper. "The family's been together for just two months. Now it'll be split up again: the children gone and the mother living with a brother-in-law's family.

"You see these people caught in the middle of change. Half one thing, half another. The young people may weather that change but it's tearing the old people apart."

We walked on in silence for a while and then he added: "I wish to Heaven I knew what should be done. I certainly wish I knew...."

CHAPTER FOUR

The New Stone Age

LOW OVERCAST AND A DRIBBLE OF CHILL RAIN GREETED me as I walked down to the Otter, moored at the HBC dock so Doug and Roy could fill her tanks from a row of bright red drums of high-octane gas. The reek of petrol fumes mingling with the stench from rotting seal carcasses on Coral Harbour's beach reinforced my desire to be on our way to Cape Dorset, our next port of call.

Dorset clings to the southwestern corner of massive Baffin Island. It is famed as the place where the first artifacts of the ancient pre-Eskimoan culture which now bears the Dorset name were discovered. It is also the birthplace of modern Inuit art. Dorset was high on my list of places to visit, but Doug was not sanguine about our chances of getting there on this particular day.

"Pea-soup fog offshore, rain overhead, and ice pans underneath," he warned gloomily.

Nevertheless, we took off and at three hundred feet entered a grey void. Nothing was to be seen beyond the Plexiglas windows so Doug descended until we were once again in touch with the land, if dimly so. Then he followed the shore of the inlet which cradles Coral Harbour, while looking for a possible hole in the cloud ceiling pressing down upon us.

The sandy beaches so close below were not attractive, being encrusted with the rusting remnants of hundreds of forty-five-gallon fuel drums, mute testimony to the profligacy of the American (and Canadian) military occupation of the north.

THE NEW STONE AGE

For decades almost all diesel, gasoline, and kerosene consumed in the Arctic had been shipped north in steel drums. Once emptied, these were then mostly discarded into the sea, or dumped upon the land, whichever was most convenient. Before our journey ended, we would see uncounted thousands of them. Graveyards of corroding steel drums almost surrounded some settlements and military installations. Others ringed lakes and lagoons, coating the waters with an oily sheen.

Unable to find a hole in the leaden ceiling, Doug decided to bite the bullet. DCL climbed steeply and the world vanished until we emerged into clear air and bright sunlight at five thousand feet. Doug set a compass course for Dorset, and after an hour the cloud below us began to thin until we could catch glimpses of pancake ice floes drifting in the metallic-green waters of Foxe Channel.

The sky continued to clear, revealing Baffin's massive Foxe Peninsula ahead. Soon we were approaching what remains of the Kingait Mountains: a range so ground down by time and glaciers that only stubs endure.

We skirted this imposing coast until Cape Dorset itself came into view thrusting south into Hudson Strait. A sheltered bay with a sprinkle of human habitations lay behind it, bathed in blazing sunlight. The settlement, straggling haphazardly along a strip of sandy shoreline, resembled flotsam washed up by some particularly high tide.

We taxied ashore, to be met by Dorset's DNA administrator, a friendly fellow whose svelte young wife offered us good cheer in a prefab log bungalow hung with lithographs done by the local people. We were soon joined by Terry Ryan, manager of the West Baffin Eskimo Co-operative.

A lean, intense man in his early thirties, Terry was accustomed to conducting guided tours of his bailiwick. He led us off briskly to visit the co-op's print, silk-screen, and carving shops where mostly middle-aged or elderly Eskimo artisans were exercising skills that were bringing them world fame. A boisterous lot, they exchanged ribald greetings with Pete, whom some had known in his earlier guise as a Hudson's Bay man.

Leaving my crew to shop for souvenirs, I followed Ryan up a steep slope behind the settlement to his eyrie—an A-frame chalet crouched

on a narrow ledge and surrounded by a profligate growth of purple sax-
ifrage in full bloom.

Terry had designed and built this house for himself and his wife, a
nurse who was currently "outside." He had sited it to catch maximum
sunlight through its big, triple-paned windows. The building required
far less heating oil than the standard Department of Northern Affairs
prefab bungalows which were then springing up across the north. I
asked Terry if the government's designers had taken note of the superi-
ority of his A-frame style. He laughed.

"They don't like it. It wasn't drawn up in some architect's office.
There's been no rush to copy it, except by a couple of Eskimo families
who claim *I* copied *them*. And so I did in a way, because their conical
skin tents are hard to beat for comfort and convenience. My place has a
similar profile."

Having treated me to the luxury of a hot bath, Terry made a pitcher
of Moose Milk (Demerara rum, canned milk, and maple syrup), and I
settled down to listen to his story of how a new stone age was returning
to the Arctic.

*In my last year at the College of Art in Toronto, George Pepper, a painter of the
old school, got me fascinated with the idea of the north and I decided I had to go
see what it was like.*

*My first attempt was back in '54, but nobody in the north had work for an
artist so I took a course in meteorology and went to work on a weather base on
north Baffin Island.*

*I first saw Dorset in 1958, coming south aboard the government ship
C.D. Howe. The settlement here was much smaller then, and the people
were wonderfully independent and extremely friendly and I guess I fell in love
with them.*

*In 1960 I managed to convince DNA to hire me and send me to Dorset for two
months filling in for James Houston, the guy who started the art program here and
built the first print shop.*

*When I got here I found a great many Eskimo drawings in the old building Jim
had been using as a shop. They were unbelievably good! I'd no idea Eskimos could
express themselves so damn well. I decided I wanted to stick around. When my two
months were up the members of the co-op, which was then very small, asked me if
I'd stay on and manage it for them as their employee. Of course I said yes.*

34

The co-op now employs fourteen people. It's of the consumer-producer kind. All salaries are paid by it—nothing comes from the government. We are autonomous, with our own board, our own directors, our own president, all of them Eskimos, and all policy is set right here in Dorset.

The crazy part is that I came here as an artist but I've become so involved with the co-op I hardly ever get time to paint. I've become a weekend painter. I figure if I'm going to help these people I've got to go whole hog. And having seen the talent among the Eskimos develop and grow, I've come to believe art could be vital in bridging the gap between their old way of life and a modern one.

Working in stone comes naturally to these people. Wood is something they're not really very accustomed to because there's not much of it in the Arctic. They work freely with stone. The Eskimo carver doesn't feel it's an alien material since his people have worked with it for thousands of years.

We get soapstone from our own quarry, about 160 miles from here down the coast and bring it back in our own boats.

Since the people are used to working in stone—a hard medium—I thought I'd introduce copper for printmaking and we tried it in 1961. The first print we pulled was done by an old man called Kiskou. Copper was an instant success. I think at that time if we'd introduced softer materials like linoleum or silk-screening, which we use now, they wouldn't have been comfortable with them.

Until recently marketing has been our bottleneck. However, there's now a marketing body down south called the Canadian Arctic Producers Limited. It's run by the Co-operative Union of Canada, and it's been a terrific help.

The graphic medium is now the big thing—much bigger than carving. There was no tradition of graphic art in Eskimo culture, except perhaps for some drawing on ivory. The first graphic medium introduced here, by Houston, was the soapstone block which is, of course, similar to a woodcut or a linocut and uses the same basic principles. Graphics seemed to really fire the imagination of the people and now it seems there's no stopping them.

Our co-op has four workshops. One does the rough cutting of stone blocks into sculpture-sized pieces, another inks plates, while a third works on the development of new fabric designs. We do silkscreen printing in the fourth.

Most of the stone carving and fabric making is actually done at home. In fact, really, there is not an awful lot of primary work done at the shops. People prefer to work at home.

It's quite astonishing what the income to the co-op is now. Our annual graphic *production grosses up to $90,000 and we sell about $60,000 worth of carvings. It's really making a tremendous difference to our economy, and I believe could to the economy of the whole north.*

Some people have suggested the arts and crafts stuff up here is a flash in the pan that'll soon swamp its market potential. But they've been saying that since '48, when the first attempts were made to encourage it, and this is fifteen years later and the market gets bigger and bigger. The thing is that the work produced by most Eskimos is not intended to be commercial. They do what they do because they love doing it and this is the true basis for producing art. As long as it has this content I think it will continue to be saleable.

The funny thing is there doesn't seem to be any jealousy between those who produce really extraordinary work and those whose stuff is run-of-the-mill. It seems to be still the way it was in the past: the co-operative way, share and share alike. If the carvings of one man earn a lot more than those of another, he has no objection to all the money being pooled and divided on a basis of need. This wouldn't go down very well in the south but then, thank God, this is still the north.

Despite the fact that the main effort of the co-op here is seen by outsiders as producing art for southern consumption, that is not its primary role. Our co-op concerns itself with community activity of every sort. It is involved in fishing, trapping, handicrafts such as women's sewing, and tourism. You could think of the art production as a kind of catalyst. The money from it makes the co-op independent of the traders and other outside businessmen and, to some degree, independent of government support and control as well, so they have freedom to develop their culture and society in their own way. It's my feeling that co-ops like this could be the answer to the whole problem of the transition from the traditional Eskimo way of life to a modern version. The co-operative idea comes as naturally to Eskimos as breathing. It's how they have managed to stay alive for thousands of years.

The problem is, though, that co-ops aren't popular in capitalist-run societies and, by the same token, aren't popular with our governments. I believe co-ops actually would be the key to a successful and fairly painless transition from the old traditional Eskimo way of life to the modern world, but it seems impossible to persuade the powers this is the route to go. There's a few people in DNA, mostly in fairly junior positions, who agree. Unfortunately they're in the minority and they don't have any real power of decision. In a way, the success we've had here at Dorset is politically bad for the co-op movement because it has shown how successful a co-op can be in helping people to help themselves.

As has been the case with almost all northern settlements, Dorset was established to advance "white" interests. In 1913 the HBC built a post here to capture the Inuit trade from the southwest portion of Baffin Island.

Initially the new post was a great financial success, though it threatened to become a liability when World War I destroyed the market for white fox fur, which is still the sustaining element of the arctic fur trade. However, fox again became fashionable after the war and trade picked up. The HBC factor at Dorset eventually had an Eskimo "clientele" extending as far to the east as Lake Harbour and south across Hudson Strait to northern Ungava. The numbers of people coming in to trade soon attracted a mission, then an RCMP post. By 1966 Dorset had become the nominal "home" of most of the 450 Inuit in the region. Although, as with Southampton Island, many still lived in camps for part of the year, getting much of their livelihood from the country, increasing numbers were moving to Dorset to live there more or less permanently, earning their livelihoods as artists and artisans.

Dorset was booming.

The foreshore was piled high with recently arrived materials and equipment, including two bulldozers for the construction of an all-season landing strip. Prefab houses, mostly of the one- or two-room variety, were displacing makeshift shanties. There was a proliferation of Ski-Doos—and a corresponding paucity of dogs. A new school, teachers' houses, nursing station, and RCMP post added weight to the white quarter, but the centre of Dorset's vitality was the disorderly cluster of buildings housing the activities of the co-op.

This was Dorset's heart, and it was beating strongly. In the co-op retail store (which was as well stocked as any store I saw in the north) I met a group of remarkable young men. They were vocal (almost belligerent) in their espousal of Eskimo rights. Such behaviour seemed atypical, but these youths could not have cared less. As one eighteen-year-old Grade 12 graduate boldly put it: "You white men made us do what you want in our own country for a long time. Well, now we're going to do what *we* want, the way we used to before you people came around."

Although this was radical stuff, the young men were not hostile. They insisted on buying me unwanted soft drinks while they earnestly proclaimed that the *kablunait* had had his day.

The white man has certainly had a long day in the north—and a long night too. Hudson Strait and south Baffin Eskimos have been in more or less regular contact with Europeans for three centuries, and in occasional contact for perhaps as long as a thousand years. There is no doubt but that there has been a considerable infusion of blood from traders, explorers, whalers, and missionaries. One of the young Eskimo nationalists in the store was a grandson of Captain Joseph Elzear Bernier, French-Canadian commander of a government survey vessel in arctic waters in the early part of the century. A second was the son of Leo Manning, a legendary Hudson's Bay Company factor. A third would not have drawn a second glance on the streets of any of Scotland's once-famous whaling ports.

The implications of their mixed ancestry seemed entirely lost on these young men. As far as they were concerned, they were *Inuit*—and that was that.

Shortly before leaving Dorset I attended one of the north's most cherished social events, held in the home of an old-time employee of the Company. It involved males (no women, be it noted) representative of the old arctic empires: police, church, and trader. As was usual with such gatherings, this one was characterized by lurid and often libellous descriptions of and comments about the habits, characters, and morals of other white northerners. Some of the tales were funny. Many were bawdy to the point of obscenity. The point and purpose of most was to take the mickey out of contemporaries who did not happen to be present, but especially to ridicule and denigrate the activities of recent arrivals from the south who were committed to altering the long-established relationship between whites and natives.

Because Terry Ryan was an outsider and seen as being heavily biased in favour of the natives, he was not treated kindly *in absentia*. I suspect I may only have escaped equally derogatory treatment because, pending the arrival of the first supply ship of the season, there was a critical shortage of alcohol in Dorset—a shortage which a bottle of my rum did much to alleviate.

In the small hours of the morning the critic's circle was disrupted by a sonorous whistle blast. The room emptied hurriedly as everyone

headed for the shore to welcome the *Pierre Radisson*, which was majestically steaming into the harbour bearing in her holds many of the supplies
upon which Dorset would rely during the long winter soon to come.

Unloading began almost as soon as the vessel's anchor was down.
The shore swarmed with Eskimos of all ages, drawn as much by the
excitement of this annual event as by the few dollars some of them
would earn as stevedores.

Much had altered in the Arctic I had known off and on for thirty
years, but "ship time" clearly retained its pride of place as the paramount
event in the year's long round.

CHAPTER FIVE

Under Two
Flags

T HE NEXT LEG OF OUR JOURNEY WAS SUPPOSED TO
take us south across Hudson Strait to the small settlement of
Sugluk to refuel before making a long southeasterly traverse of
the Ungava peninsula to Payne Bay.

Payne Bay was a primary objective, not because of the people who
currently lived there, but because of those who had lived there in the
distant past. In 1957 archaeologists had made a puzzling discovery on the
small island of Pamiok at the mouth of a river estuary on Ungava Bay.
The find was described as "a huge rectangular structure measuring 85
feet by 20 feet…the walls, which are collapsed, being made of stones."
The scanty report made no attempt to identify the builders but the
description sounded to me sufficiently like a Norse longhouse foundation to whet my curiosity. Then, a month before our 1966 journey I
learned that archaeologist Thomas Lee of Quebec's Laval University
would be digging the Pamiok site that very summer. I hoped to see for
myself what Lee uncovered.

Although the skies were clear on the morning of our departure from
Dorset, we did not head directly for Sugluk, 150 miles to the southeast
across the wide and turbulent waters of Hudson Strait. Instead, Doug
elected to island-hop, flying first to Salisbury Island in the middle of the
Strait, thence to Nottingham Island, and so to the mainland Ungava
coast.

We took off over the rusting remnants of the legendary Hudson's
Bay Company supply ship *Nascopie* and of a nondescript little freighter,

both of which had gutted themselves on reefs at the harbour entrance.

An hour later we were over uninhabited Salisbury, a forty-mile-long monolith somewhat resembling a titanic aircraft carrier and looking just as hostile.

Nottingham Island proved more welcoming. Fifty or sixty walrus were sunbathing on one of its stony beaches. Copper-coloured under the summer sun, they bore a marked resemblance to a party of corpulent human tourists.

With the worst of the open-water crossing behind us, Doug took us down for a closer look at the sunbathers. They were so somnolent they hardly deigned to raise their heavy heads as we thundered by. Although on this day they had Nottingham's beaches to themselves, many old tent rings bespoke earlier times when these same shores probably ran red with walrus blood.

Cape Wolstenholme, Ungava's northeastern cape, materialized on the horizon and drew us on. Then a radio report crackled in our earphones. Heavy fog was rolling westward along Hudson Strait threatening to blanket Sugluk.

Away went our plans to refuel there. We held a brief conference over the intercom and decided to try Ivugivik, a little place just south of Cape Wolstenholme and one of such insignificance that it did not even appear on my map. If we could top up our tanks there we could head cross-country to Payne Bay, overflying a seldom-seen, mile-wide meteor crater en route.

The majestic table mountain called Wolstenholme is flanked by the thousand-foot-high precipices of the twin Digges Islands. Our low flight past these bastion rocks caused mass panic among hundreds of thousands of nesting seabirds. Battalions of guillemots, regiments of fulmars, and legions of kittiwakes streamed off the cliffs in living cascades. As we banked away from the guano-whitened crags, we could see hundreds of harp seals porpoising through waters thickly rafted with sea fowl. This was clearly a place where life abounded.

Ivugivik lay only a few miles south of the cape but was so inconspicuous and well hidden we were almost directly over it before we saw it. A handful of shanties and tents fronted on a small beach in a cove backed by a forbidding ring of sheer-sided hills. We landed in the cove and taxied to the gravel beach where the four or five dozen residents had gathered to receive us.

Clad in an incongruous mixture of store-bought clothing and caribou-skin dress, they formed a motley crowd. A jet-bearded young white man stepped forward from among them and introduced himself.

"Karl Mailhot. *Je suis de Montréal.* I represent here *le gouvernement de Québec* and I make you welcome."

The Department of Northern Affairs, all-powerful throughout the rest of the north, was *not* the kingpin here. In 1912 Ottawa had given the portion of the Northwest Territories now called Ungava to the province of Quebec in an act of political appeasement. Quebec had duly added this vast new region to its provincial map, but had otherwise paid little attention to it until the boom in northern resource exploitation began. Now Quebec was making her presence felt. Although the Ungava Inuit legally remained under Ottawa's protection, Northern Affairs was being aggressively displaced by a French-speaking bureaucracy. Ivugivik turned out to a beachhead of this new invasion.

A tour of the community under Mailhot's enthusiastic guidance did not take long. Apart from a newly built one-room school and a tiny store, there were ten or twelve well-worn wall tents and a few driftwood shacks, which appeared to have sprouted spontaneously from the flotsam and jetsam strewn around the shores of the little harbour. Three battered motorboats lay on the beach, backed by drums of gasoline. These metal penguins garbed in regal red and sober black gladdened our pilot's heart for they included several drums of aviation gas.

Wooden racks stood all about thickly hung with split arctic char drying in wind and sun. Almost every shack had a frieze of dead seabirds hanging from its eaves, ripening, as it were. I was delighted to see, smell, and hear many dogs. Their presence assured me that the snowmobile had not yet conquered Ivugivik. I was not so happy to see the mangled wreckage of a Beechcraft which, a few months earlier, had attempted an emergency landing on the beach.

Mailhot proudly escorted Pete and me to his tiny but spotless office-cum-living quarters above which flew, not the red and white flag of Canada, but a very large specimen of Quebec's blue and white fleur-de-lis.

Noticing my interest in the flag, Mailhot laughed.

"Times change, eh, *mon ami?*"

He took my arm and ushered us into his lair, where he brewed excellent coffee while talking a mile a minute about his job.

Ivugivik, she is the northeasternmost Eskimo community in Nouveau Québec. She's one of the smallest outposts so she is still looking a little bit like the Eskimo land of yesterday. Ivugivik is very isolated and so she keeps her history. What the people like is the life of hunting and fishing. They don't think much of a lot of things white men bring. Like houses. Maybe they are not so far wrong. The wooden house is not so warm as an igloo in winter. It's the same for a rifle. It brings problems. A rifle means they can kill seal at a thousand feet, when before they were only able to kill by getting close. So now they can kill more seals than they may really need, and lose a lot of them too so seals get scarce.

All the same, this is one of the best places in all Nouveau Québec for fishing and hunting. Here people can catch everything from white foxes to arctic char, and even walrus.

You know, the change to administration by Quebec is new. When it first happen the Eskimos were unhappy because French-speaking people means Catholic to them and English means Protestant, and most Eskimos are Protestant and speak English so they don't like to come under Quebec.

But they like the co-op we bring. Quebec wants lots of co-ops. We think Eskimos should run everything themselves that they can. There was a Hudson's Bay Company post here until last September but there's no room for two stores so we tell the Hudson's Bay Company to leave. Voilà! Now there is just one!

Mailhot had to break off to meet a radio schedule. Doug and Roy were busy topping up DCL's tanks so Pete and I went wandering and were invited into the shack of a handsome young Eskimo somewhat improbably named Peter English. He was married to a very pregnant and hospitable woman who smilingly fed us big bowls of oily, pungent soup made from the blood and fat of a square-flipper seal her husband had killed on a recent hunting trip to the Digges Islands. It was powerful stuff. I eased it down with chunks of bannock made by Peter's fourteen-year-old sister, Annie.

Annie was diminutive and shy. She would not be parted from a young guillemot her brother had brought her from Digges as a pet. The bird, which was *not* house-broken, spent most of its time in Annie's lap.

Her devotion to it was not unusual. Eskimo girls tend to be extraordinarily attached to young animals.

Born and raised in Ivugivik, Peter English had been one of DNA's young hopefuls. At the age of sixteen he had been flown to Churchill and enrolled in a technical school where he had demonstrated the mechanical aptitudes with which most Inuit men are endowed. After two years there he had been sent to Camp Borden in faraway southern Ontario to learn the operation and maintenance of heavy construction equipment.

He did so well that by 1964 he was ready to begin working as a drilling machine helper at a gold mine in Yellowknife. Then he was seriously injured.

"Steel cable break, you know. Fly back and hit me. Now I got plastic top over brain." With some pride he added, "Guess I only Eskimo got plastic skull."

Upon being discharged from hospital he had been offered a chance to retrain as a mechanic, but refused outright. "I tell those DNA fellows I go back home now. You fly me back home because I never going away from there again.

"Very happy here. Hunt every time I want. Got lots good meat. Trap fox for buy co-op stuff. Got good wife. You guys can keep what you got down south; me, I going keep what *I* got right here."

When Murdoch asked him what he thought about the change in administration in Ungava, Peter replied in Inuktitut.

"You know, English *kablunait* came to our country long, long ago, and ever since they have told us what they wanted us to do. Now French *kablunait* are coming into our country and we don't see much difference. They speak French and go to the Catholic church, but they tell us what to do just the same. They are still *kablunait*—and we are still Inuit.

"Some Inuit may change to be like them. Not me. I will never change now. I tried that. Now I will be Inuk until somebody piles stones over me out on the country some place. Inuk—that's who I am."

Our visit was cut short by Roy's arrival at the door. The radio was reporting better weather.

"Fog's lifting," Roy said. "Skipper thinks we should be able to make Payne Bay *if* we leave right now."

We had been airborne barely fifteen minutes when a new weather report came through. The western coast of Ungava Bay was now fog-bound. Once more we conferred.

"Can't go east," Doug told us. "And if we try going back north to Dorset the goddamn fog'll likely catch us before we get there. About all we can do is head south to Povungnituk—it's the nearest settlement."

And so we flew south along the east coast of Hudson Bay under a blazing sun and a flawless summer sky. The rolling, sometimes boggy and sometimes rocky tundra to port glowed with an almost incandescent mixture of earth colours that moved Peter Murdoch to introspection.

He passed me a note.

Only Europeans would have called this the Barrenlands. Shows you how blind we've been. And are.

CHAPTER SIX

Duel at Povungnituk

SOME SEVENTY MILES SOUTH OF IVUGIVIK WE CAME TO the great coastal indentation of Kovic Bay. When I glimpsed something white near its foot, Doug put DCL's nose down and we turned back to circle three tents pitched beside a rapids-riven river. Flame-hued char fillets were drying in the sun upon willow bushes behind the tents. Several Eskimos were standing knee-deep in the river, which had been barred off with stones placed to channel the run of fish. The fishers beckoned with trident-pronged spears, indicating that fresh char awaited if we would land. Alas, there was no place DCL could put down so she waggled her wings and we flew on.

We crossed Mosquito Bay, into whose head four rivers flow through deep canyons between parallel granite ridges. The visual effect is as if some titanic monster had slashed the coast with an armoured paw. Eskimos at Povungnituk would later tell me this was where the mighty ancestor of *nanuk*—the white bear—had come ashore to sharpen his claws.

The day was growing old by the time the gleam of a major river ahead of us signalled our approach to P.O.V., as Povungnituk was familiarly called. The settlement, which bore an unhappy resemblance to an industrial construction site, sprawled on an ancient raised beach along the north side of the estuary. It was a modern, almost instant, creation, though it had deep roots. Three thousand years ago people of the Dorset culture had pitched their pyramidal tents on its raised beach, anchoring them against the gales with heavy glacial boulders. Thule people inheriting the site had made use of the same boulders to hold down their own big circular tents. And Inuit descendants of Thule had continued to use the stone circles into our time.

The manifold attractions of the place included a river hosting an enormous run of char which was navigable for small boats far inland to prime caribou country. The extensive estuary offered good sealing and was a major birthing place for white whales. These attractions had made the region a popular summer residence since dim antiquity, but there had been no permanent occupation until the mid-1920s when the HBC built a post to trade with Inuit living along the four hundred miles of coast between Cape Wolstenholme in the north and Cape Harrison to the south. The Company post had also exploited the beluga, hiring Eskimos to do the killing. Such large numbers of whales were slaughtered for their sparse yield of oil that their rotting carcasses, encrusting the shores of the estuary, discouraged people from camping near what they began calling Povungnituk—the Place That Stinks.

Twenty-five to thirty discrete Inuit camps had been scattered throughout the region before the post opened. Each had consisted of several families living in skin tents in summer and snow houses in winter. As the seasons changed, people moved about within their traditional local territories, taking advantage of the ebb and flow of animal life across the land and in the waters.

They soon began visiting the trading post but, until relatively recently, only the few who were employed as "servants of the Company," lived at P.O.V. itself.

Early in the 1950s the pattern underwent radical change.

Pat Furneaux, P.O.V.'s bluff and cheerful DNA administrator, described what happened.

Father André Steinmann was the first white resident here other than the Company post manager. He showed up in 1950, though nobody could figure out why he came because he was R.C. and all the eastern Hudson Bay Eskimos were Anglicans, even if they only saw a clergyman once a year.

Well, Steinmann built a church. Nice one too, though even today he hasn't got more than four or five families of parishioners. About then was when DNA began getting involved. In 1957 we built a one-room federal day school. Other classrooms were added as camp people started staying all winter at P.O.V. so their kids could go to school. I was posted here in 1960 when the department really began building a permanent settlement instead of a place the Eskimos would visit once or twice a year.

In 1960 there were still seven big camps out on the country. There's none now. All the northeastern Hudson Bay Eskimos live right here—all 562 of them. Nearly everyone lives in a house now, too. They didn't come here attracted by a mine, a DEW Line site, or some military base. They came because of the nursing station, the school, and all the things the federal government could do for them—like subsidized housing, social benefits, and that sort of thing. But it was mainly the prospects of an education for their kids that drew them in.

So now, for the first time in their history, these people are enjoying real community benefits. For example, we all draw our water from the river. Well, this spring something went wrong with it. Pretty soon everyone was suffering from dysentery. It persisted for some time and, you know, it kind of bound us all together because it was shared all through the community.

There's some old-timers that'll maybe tell you there never would have been an epidemic if the people had all still been living out on the land. Maybe not. But the clear fact is that when a medical problem struck, everybody was here in one place so they could benefit from centralization.

Most of the whites here now, two missionaries, DNA staff, teachers, Quebec provincial staff, even the Company people, are pretty well dedicated to helping the Eskimos move into the modern world. And the Eskimos are very receptive. The children going to school, for instance, seem anxious to learn the disciplines they'll need to live in the twentieth century and the twenty-first.

I think it's inevitable the Eskimos, as a remote, isolated people, will be integrated—I don't like the word assimilated—into our world. We all live in this world so the Eskimo has to become part of it.

At the moment we've got a real cash economy going here for the first time. But, you know, in the long run there may not be enough economic reason for P.O.V. to continue. It may be kind of a halfway station. Its economy really rests on subsidies from governments. So sooner or later we will likely have to find other places for these people to go…or they will have to find them for themselves. They will likely have to go south if they can't find work in northern development, and down south is where I believe the future for Eskimos lies. What we're doing up here now is opening the doorway into the real world for them.

A skiff belonging to the Roman Catholic mission came out to the anchorage to ferry us ashore, and the first person we met when we landed was Father André Steinmann, O.M.I.

There was no nonsense about this stocky, black-bearded Oblate missionary. He knew of my criticisms in my book *People of the Deer* of the way the missions had behaved in the north. Standing bareheaded on the beach, arms akimbo, he told me unsmilingly that I should get back in my plane and go to the devil. However, he added, if I insisted on staying I had better come to his house and have some dinner.

The four of us went off with him to his spartan dwelling where his housekeeper fed us caribou stew washed down with communion wine made from raisins. When we were replete, Steinmann pushed back his chair, stood up, and leaned belligerently toward me.

"So!" he bellowed. "I give you my hospitality, eh? Now you will give me satisfaction!"

With which he reached into a wall cupboard and hauled out a .45-calibre revolver and a snow knife as long as a machete. He banged them down in front of me.

"You are my guest so you have the choice of weapons."

I glanced at the revolver. It was fully loaded. The snow knife was razor-sharp. I looked hopefully to my companions for confirmation that this was a joke. None of them was smiling. In fact, Doug and Roy seemed poised to leap from their chairs and flee out of the line of fire.

Pete, however, had met the Father before.

"If there's something to settle between you two," he said soothingly, "we'll do it civilized fashion. I'll get a bottle of rum, then we'll see which of the two of you can drink the other under the table."

Father Steinmann hesitated for just a second then burst out with a great, booming laugh:

"Done, by God!"

So began a sometimes heated and not always rational verbal exchange which lasted until the handsome housekeeper shooed us out into the brisk early morning air so she could cook breakfast unimpeded.

We continued our conversation over coffee, though in a more subdued manner, for the record.

FM: *Father, you're probably the only priest in the north who hasn't got a congregation. When you came here it was an Anglican stronghold. It still is. So why did you come and why stay?*

AS: Because my bishop tells me to.

FM: *And what have you done since you arrived?*

AS: Well, I've tried to love the people here, to help them. I took care of sick people. I started to teach the youngsters and helped them improve themselves.

FM: *And?*

AS: And I started a co-op. I wanted the people to be their own masters and to do that you have to run your own affairs. Everybody else was being the masters of the Eskimo destiny so I thought maybe they should have a chance. But I guess the biggest thing was, after I'd been here quite a while, I had to stop and think what purpose I really was serving. Had I come in to destroy something the Eskimos had had in their past? Or was I here to try and do something useful for their future?

FM: *Let's talk about that. What future do the Eskimos have?*

AS: It's partly in their hands. But the Eskimo has to have a chance to think for himself. The trouble is he is dictated to, and if he's not a victim of paternalism, it comes pretty close to that. We whites lack humility. We have our western way of thinking, and we impose it on other people as has been done in every colony in every age. For instance, I hear whites say Eskimos have no civilization because they still eat on the floor. Well, the Japanese sit on the floor to eat, and they have a civilization much older than ours. We western people come to the Eskimos with the idea we know the right way to do everything. I think we have to learn maybe they have ways to do things just as good as us, if not better. Eskimos say we treat them as if nothing they have is any good. One old fellow once showed me a little bit of dust on a table and said, "Look, that's about what you think we are." Then he pushed it off the table with his finger.

All the same the Eskimo has to change. Western civilization is here to stay. It's for sure some Eskimos will assimilate, but maybe some will not. Maybe some small villages in remote places could be like fishing villages in your Newfoundland where some are moving out and being assimilated by the big civilization, and some are still remaining behind. Surely there is room for everybody.

FM: *Or maybe we might do like the Russians? Help the native peoples develop the north themselves. They'd still have to deal with southern culture, but at least they'd have some control over what happens. But education seems to be the thorniest subject here right now. What most needs doing about that?*

AS: *First off, whites coming into the country should have to learn the Eskimo language before they begin teaching the children. Another thing, there is too big a difference between the way of life of whites and the local people. When we decided to put the people in houses we should have given them the same kind of houses the teachers and the administrators are getting. We should have brought something much better than the plywood boxes we give them. And we never taught them how to live in houses. We give a house, say eighteen feet by twelve feet, where you have six children, the father and the mother, and maybe the aunt and uncle, and an old lady or two extra to live in the damn thing. Well, for God's sake, I defy any white person to try and make a life in a house like that.*

But you were asking about education. The schooling system here is not what I call education at all. It's instruction. To me, education is learning how to conduct yourself, how to balance the human faculties—intelligence, willpower, passion, all those things—so you are able to live in some kind of harmony with your fellow beings. But it seems obvious to me that all we are offering the Eskimos is technical training. What they're getting isn't related to the life they once led here and will be little use to them trying to lead a new kind of life outside. Sure, they can be drivers of trucks, maybe, haulers of garbage, that sort of thing, but the so-called education they're getting will fit them for nothing better.

There's also a problem with the teachers. Too many who come here are very nice people but they come for the adventure or the extra money. They think it's great fun to spend a couple of years living with Eskimos in the wilderness, then they have enough adventure and enough money and they go back south again. They don't really contribute anything, and there is no understanding between them and the people they teach. There are, of course, some good and dedicated people who really come here to help the Eskimos but they usually become so frustrated by the system they can't stand it and eventually leave.

Another thing is the schools here have no contact whatever with the adults in Eskimo families. There is the language barrier, of course, but even those whites who manage to bridge it still only have sentimental, not what I call harmonic, contacts. There are some white people who nicely receive an Eskimo in their home if they like him or feel affection for him. This is not leading to a deep contact with people. You could call it patronizing contact. It flatters the sentimentality of both whites and Eskimos but does not bring them close together at any deep level.

FM: *Why do you think there is so much emphasis on education?*

AS: *In Ottawa I once talked to the man in charge of Eskimo education. I asked* him to tell me what the government wants to achieve in educating the Eskimos. Here's what he told me:

"Father, policy is based on what very high people in government want. They think the north is going to suddenly open up for development and exploitation of mines and other resources. They calculate that ten thousand jobs are going to need to be filled in the north within the next few years, and they want Eskimos to be ready to fill those jobs."

Those people in Ottawa think it will be hard to get many whites to go north and live in such hard conditions and such distant places.

FM: I've heard from a deputy minister of the Department of Northern Affairs that those ten thousand jobs will be available within five years and will be the salvation of the younger Eskimos. Only, what's going to happen to the older ones, and to those who've lost touch with the old ways but haven't any real training for the new?

AS: If I had an answer to that one I'd be glad to give it, but I think you have to ask Ottawa, and if you believe what they say then you might be more foolish than I think you are. I think it is genocide, murder of a culture. I think, too, it is a stupid thing to do. In my belief, we should be making every effort to preserve the Eskimo culture, to properly help them preserve it for their good and for ours. They have been living in this country for thousands of years under conditions which are very difficult. Nevertheless, they laugh and live in peace and with joy. Their philosophy is one which shouldn't disappear. The day is coming maybe when we will need to be able to live like that for our own survival.

Eskimos believe you cannot make the elemental forces do everything you want; that you are too small; that you have to be patient; that what you don't do today, for God's sake, to hell with it then, you can do it tomorrow. There is another day after today. We rush recklessly around trying to finish everything fast. The Eskimo stays calm. Don't rush it, for God's sake, he says. He believes that if you try to force things you might finish up under the ice.

White people say Eskimos don't respect children and old people and can be cruel and have bad morals. For God's sake, they have the most wonderful respect for old people! If an old man has the guts to say, "Let me die so the young can survive in this time of hunger," that is nobility. That is not immoral. And if sometimes a little girl had to be smothered, it wasn't because they wanted to kill her, it was because there was not enough food for her to survive. It was more of a sacrifice made by love. When they make sacrifice of this kind, we call it suicide or *murder and say it is wrong, because we don't know what we're talking about. We need to re-learn the importance of devotion to friends, hospitality, patience, self-sacrifice. I myself have learned all this from the Eskimos. I was a hot-head when I was younger. I was going to reform the world, the Pope, the King, and everything. But when I had lived with the Eskimos long enough to learn to live like them, things began to change for me. I could see myself in perspective in the world, and I could see all life around me in perspective, and it all seemed to belong in one reality. But the civilization we have built up is so artificial. After a few years up here, when you go back to the south, by Jove, the whole civilization you see looks so crazy you can't believe people would live like that on purpose.*

I think it's vitally important for human beings to retain physical and psychic contact with nature. And to live under conditions of some natural adversity. We say in French, "On ne font pas les hommes avec du sucre ou du nougat." You don't make human beings with sugar and candies. To form a man you need to put him sometimes to struggle with natural conditions. The Eskimo is a man formed by natural conditions. He doesn't oppose the elements; he learns to adapt himself to them. He learns to become part of the world he lives in.

The struggles he had made him a survivor. Now this is a new kind of situation we make for him. This is one he cannot deal with naturally and already you can see the breakdown taking place. It looks as if we are forcing him into a kind of physical security that may really be the kiss of death. Could we be doing that to ourselves as well?

I woke early the next morning. The sun, which, this far north, hardly set before rising again, had brought us a superb northern day: cool enough so a sweater was welcome yet warm enough to encourage a quartet of children to wade about in a backwater of the river chasing rock sculpins and sticklebacks. Beyond them the broad, estuarine valley channelled the crystalline waters of Povungnituk River through myriad braided rivulets to the sea.

After a meal of fried goose breasts and bannock, Father André took me on a jaunt upriver in his outboard-driven skiff. We skittered through the shallows accompanied by schools of grayling whose iridescent dorsal fins sliced the surface like those of miniature sharks. We also shared the river with hundreds of merganser ducks busy stuffing themselves with fish fry.

We passed forty or fifty dogs marooned in small groups on barren little islands. They watched in immobility, half-starved mendicants exiled for the summer by order of the settlement's administration and fed only if, and when, their owners remembered them.

André shook his head as we passed one forlorn pack whose members appeared to be little more than bones covered in matted fur.

"Camp Eskimos used to look after their dogs real good—nearly as good as themselves. They needed those dogs. Now many in P.O.V. have Ski-Doos. Twenty new Ski-Doos came in on the boat this summer. These poor dogs, I think soon they will all be gone…with much else."

Seven or eight miles upstream the river widened into a lake-like expansion, and we went ashore to a place where people had been catching char for more than three thousand years. A dry, grassy swale beside a stretch of rapids at the lake's exit was strewn with circles of lichen-covered rocks that once had anchored long-vanished tents. The hills behind this pleasant little vale were stippled with *inuksuak*—little stone "semblances of men"—some of whose ancient builders doubtless lay close by beneath mounds of stones.

We stopped to look at some of the old graves. Two were considerably larger than the rest.

"Supposed to be Tunit buried there," André told me. "You know about the Tunit, eh?"

I nodded. Tunit loom large in Eskimo tales. They were reputedly big, awkward, but not very bright people who occupied the Arctic until the Thule people chased them out—or did them in.

"I've heard about them. Were they real do you think, or are they myths?"

"Come," said André. "I will show you what people here call the Place They Fought the Tunit."

He led me through a haze of mosquitos up a gentle slope to a level piece of tundra where two waist-high upright stones presided over twin T-shaped depressions in the mosses. Each of these was about fifteen feet long.

"Eskimos say their forefathers and Tunit used to come here to fight a kind of duel. Each man had a bow and arrows. Each would run back and forth across the top of his T, and each time he passed the long arm he could shoot an arrow at the other fellow. Eskimos were the best shots, but you had to hit a Tunit in the belly to make him die.

"A wounded Tunit might run off across the tundra to that hill you see five miles north, with his guts hanging out of the wound. If he made it there his people would sew him up and he might live to fight again. Not many Tunit could do that though, and after a while none was left in the country. Then the Eskimos had it all to themselves.

"You ask were the Tunit real? I think they were. I think they were the people archaeologists call Dorset. Real people, but all gone now."

On our way back to P.O.V. André steered the boat into a narrow-mouthed inlet of the estuary that dried out at low tide. This, he told me, was once a famous place for catching white whales.

"People would go out in kayaks at high water and herd whales into this little bay then bar it off with their boats 'til the tide fell and some of the whales stranded. In old times they were satisfied to kill just what they needed, but then the traders came here and began buying whale oil, and after that was a terrible slaughter. Now there are almost no more white whales left on this coast. This year the people see only three and never got one."

One afternoon André and I visited a man called John P.O.V., a grizzled ancient with an enormous grin who had received his honorific surname (before our coming the Inuit did not use surnames) because he was the oldest, and had been the most influential camp "boss" or leader in the region. He had performed legendary feats, once leading a group of hunters *in kayaks* to the Ottawa islands, seventy-five miles offshore, to hunt walrus. These hunters had been so successful that when they returned to the mainland they had to hire a schooner to go and get their catch.

John was still nimble, but his old wife was so crippled by arthritis she had to make her way about on hands and knees. Since coming off the land the couple had been living in a two-room DNA-supplied house. It was spotlessly clean despite the presence of a partly skinned seal on the floor of the main room, and of unnumbered neighbourhood children who clearly viewed the building as a playground.

Mrs. P.O.V. (I failed to get her first name) scuttled about serving tea and hardtack biscuits, without which no northern social occasion could be considered a success. She also provided us with entertainment. Somewhere she had acquired an old-fashioned wind-up gramophone and a single well-worn record. This she played nonstop while we slurped our tea and tried to talk against a background of "Mary Had a Little Lamb," "Little Jack Horner," and sundry other nursery rhymes screeching at maximum volume.

"When John and his camp first came to live in P.O.V.," André told me later, "he didn't know what to do with himself. They didn't need a boss any more, you see. We whites were the bosses now. He didn't like it here anyway, and one day he told me it was time for him to go walk in the country.

"You know what that means? It means time for a man who is no longer any use to himself or his people to go away and die.

"I told him, 'No, John. Your people still need you. Maybe they don't know it yet, but if you leave them it would be like taking the spark plug out of an outboard motor.'

"I don't know if he believed me or not but, you see, he is still here, and I am very glad for that. It is from him I have learned a great deal about what it means to be an Eskimo."

The young Anglican minister invited me to a youth gathering in his shiny new parish hall. The gathering included most of the hundred or so teenagers in the settlement. There was no doubt where *their* interests lay. Rock and roll, Coca-Cola, Elizabeth Arden, and Smilin' Johnny were among the watchwords of the evening.

Smilin' Johnny was a cowboy guitarist and singer whom the Anglican minister had arranged to have flown to P.O.V. the previous summer to give a concert. Johnny's travel costs and fee had almost drained the community's coffers, but not its appetite for his wares. He was scheduled to return to P.O.V. in a week's time, and the four of us were urgently invited to contribute to his second coming.

"We do everything we can to bring the south to these kids so when they go south themselves it'll be familiar to them," the young minister explained. "You'll be doing them a great big favour if you help us pay for Smilin' Johnny."

That night I lay awake on a camp bed in the loft of the Catholic mission thinking about the differing visions of the Eskimos' future I had encountered in P.O.V. From away upriver came the dismal discord of howling, hungry dogs.

I was jolted awake early next morning by Roy firing DCL's engine up to a full-throated roar in a static test. It was time to go.

I wondered how long it might be before the Inuit would also have to leave Povungnituk.

CHAPTER SEVEN

The

Maverick

THE DAY OF OUR DEPARTURE FROM P.O.V. DAWNED overcast with an easterly wind predicted to reach gale force before midday. The Povungnituk estuary was already white-capped as DCL took off and resolutely pointed her blunt nose to the eastward.

Once upon a time the Ungava interior had been corrugated by ranges of towering mountains. Over the aeons these had been reduced to a rolling plateau paved with some of the oldest rock on earth and now chiefly the domain of some of the oldest plants: mosses and lichens.

North of the tree line the Ungava Peninsula encompasses some sixty thousand square miles of primordial rock indented by lakes and roaring rivers. Although the native peoples who not long ago roamed its vast spaces have now mostly abandoned the interior, it remains home to the world's greatest caribou herds. Wintering in the boreal forests to the south, about a quarter of a million caribou spend their summers drifting across the peninsular plateau. Their ancient and ongoing presence is writ large in an intricate pattern of trails etched deep into muskegs and bogs and even into the living rock itself.

As DCL laboured eastward, the land rose and the relief became bolder. We began seeing patches of snow and ice in the deeper ravines. Caribou trails were everywhere, forming an all-encompassing tracery. At this season, most of the animals themselves were still well to the north, but when we were halfway across the peninsula we came upon a herd of several hundred bucks whose wide-spreading antlers were still in velvet.

The headwind had by now reached the predicted gale strength, reducing our speed over the ground to not much better than a fast gallop. In order to avoid the full force of the wind we had descended to an altitude of only a few hundred feet, and our sudden and thunderous appearance sent the caribou fleeing fan-wise across the tundra as if DCL were a gigantic hawk and they a mob of frightened lemmings.

We lumbered on and the hours passed all too slowly. Roy's eyes seemed glued to the fuel gauges. An inveterate gum-chewer, he chewed more and more ferociously as the needles flickered inexorably downward. At last we came over a broad, deep valley through which flowed a major river.

"The Payne!" Doug shouted triumphantly as he sideslipped DCL into the valley, levelling off just above the rapids-strewn surface of the river.

Now, as we sped downstream, we were protected from the worst of the gale. It was an odd sensation to look outward and *upward* at high riverbanks slipping swiftly by.

At this juncture something flashed past close to our port wingtip. I had the impression of a cross ten or fifteen feet high, but glimpsed it only for an instant before it vanished astern.

We flew on at deck level until the river debouched into Payne Bay. The red roofs and white walls of a clutch of HBC buildings came into view in a little cove and, beyond them, twenty or thirty shacks and wall tents. Doug wasted no time getting down. Within seconds DCL's pontoons were pounding hard in three-foot waves.

A living gale howled through the struts and the Otter jerked and lunged at the end of her anchor line. Then, seemingly out of nowhere, a big, seagoing canoe came pounding alongside. A spray-soaked Eskimo at the tiller of a sputtering outboard beckoned urgently.

The canoe belonged to the post manager, a young Newfoundlander only recently promoted from the rank of clerk. He was delighted to welcome visitors to his lonely outpost.

"Some quiet here, me sons. Nobody around but natives. Only other white man come this way for weeks is a quare feller out on Pamiok Island digging up bones."

"Is the quare feller's name Thomas Lee?" I asked.

"Yiss, bye, that's it. He don't smoke and he don't drink and I don't say he'd give a look if a girl hoisted her skirt. But old *bones*! Me *son*, he'll walk miles for dey!"

The man I sought was camped on a bald scrap of rock in Ungava Bay some twenty-five miles from the settlement. There was no possibility of landing a plane there while the gale raged so I arranged to borrow the company's canoe and its driver, a middle-aged man named Zachareesi.

The tidal range in Ungava Bay is of the order of twenty feet. When Zachareesi and I set out through the estuary's confusion of channels, reefs, and islets, the tide was falling as much as two inches a minute. The post manager had warned me of the necessity of quickly getting clear of Payne Bay or risk finding ourselves marooned in a morass of mud and broken rocks until the rise of the next tide.

Fog had begun rolling in from seaward. The murk thickened as Zachareesi fish-tailed the big canoe through a maelstrom of currents pouring past and over unseen rocks, "smelling his way" toward the northern headland of the estuary.

After about an hour he pointed to the left. There, wavering in the gloom, was a dim shape. The fog swirled away momentarily to reveal a stone tower roughly twice the height of a man. Zachareesi announced we had reached Tuvalik Point and were free of the tormented estuarine waters of Payne Bay.

We went ashore and had a smoke while I examined the tower. It was built of flat stones carefully fitted together without mortar to form a remarkably symmetrical cylinder nearly five feet in diameter. Apparently it had once stood as much as twelve feet high, but had lost some of its upper-level stones, which now lay scattered at its foot.

When I asked Zachareesi who had built this imposing beacon he waved his stubby pipe toward the north and replied succinctly.

"Old-time people. Not Eskimo."

The canoe was in danger of being left high and dry by the receding waters so we pushed off and in due course reached Pamiok Island.

Seen through a scud of driving mist and rain, this barren mound of sea-racked rock facing the swirling gales and fogs of Ungava Bay could hardly have looked less inviting. However, first appearances were deceptive. Situated close to the mouth of a major river leading into the interior caribou country, adjacent to coastal bird islands, walrus haul-outs, and excellent sealing grounds, it had been favoured as a seasonal home by countless generations of human beings. We found it inhabited by only two people: Thomas Lee and his teenage son, Robert. Their home consisted of a wall tent and a squat storage tent struggling to keep their grip on the ground in the teeth of the gale pelting in over the icy waters of this great eastern arm of the Canadian Sea.

Born in a fishing village on the shores of Lake Ontario, Lee had spent much of his youth collecting Indian "relics" and dreaming about life in Canada before the arrival of Europeans. When World War II erupted, he volunteered for service in the army and served overseas. Returning to Canada in 1945, he set about chasing his youthful dreams by becoming an archaeologist.

By 1950 he was ready to go to work for Canada's National Museum. Here he soon showed himself to be a maverick for whom doctrinaire conclusions posed irresistible challenges. Some of his associates judged him to be politically naive, but his work was of the highest quality.

Now Lee waded out through a slimy fringe of kelp to help us land on Pamiok's stony shore. At fifty-one years of age, he somewhat resembled a burly barrenland grizzly bear graced with a round and ruddy human face and a Roman nose. He was not a man to waste time. I had barely introduced myself before he was leading me off to see the sights of Pamiok Island.

I recorded my reactions on tape that night. They have already been published in my earlier book *The Farfarers*, but I repeat them here because I do not think I can better them.

We came to a bunch of knee-high mounds of stones. "Tombs," Lee told me cheerfully. "Look inside." I bent down at one, peered through a crevice, and saw a jumble of human bones but no skull. "I've collected the skull," said Lee. "Perhaps it's Eskimo, but I doubt it. I've collected five skulls altogether and at least two are more European than Eskimoan. The others look in between."

Almost every little hollow or more-or-less-level bit of ground on the island seems to have its stone tent ring, some of them as much as twenty feet in diameter.

Near the east end of the island we came to three cairns, cylindrical and each about six feet high. They didn't look anything like the Eskimo inuksuak *I've seen all over the Arctic. I made the point to Lee and he agreed: "Yes, too big. Too regular.*

Too well made. Not Eskimoan at all. And the thickness of the lichen growth on them makes them far too old to belong to the historic period. I've found thirteen towers like these, mostly bigger, generally ten to twelve feet tall and five feet in diameter, south and north of the Payne. The Eskimos tell me there are more at Diana Bay to the north, and in Leaf Basin to the south."

We trudged back along the shore. The tide had fallen so much that the sea was now only distantly visible across a vast, glistening plain of jumbled rocks, boulders, and mud. Lee pointed to a sort of broad pathway or ramp running seaward from the high-tide line. Somebody must have put in a hell of a lot of work clearing it of the worst of its jagged rocks. Again Lee ruled out natives: "No Eskimo would go to that much trouble to make a landing for kayaks and canoes. This was a haul-out for big boats."

By now I was rain-soaked below the waist and sweat-soaked under my parka. Whatever else he may be, Lee is a bloody dynamo. He trotted me behind a ridge of frost-shattered rock to show me the site he was currently digging.

Not very impressive. A muddy rectangle about forty-five feet long by maybe fifteen wide, with turf, moss, and stones stripped away to a depth of a few inches, at which point the diggers had hit bedrock. I could just make out the remains of some low stone walls. Lee waited about ten seconds for questions, then beat me to the punch.

"This is some sort of longhouse. Not the kind Indians built in the south, but its own kind. There are three like it on Pamiok—two this size and one much larger. The Eskimos say there's several more north of here. Nothing like them has ever been described in Canadian archaeology.

"I've traced the outline of this one. It's somewhat boat-shaped, with slightly curved sides but rounded ends. The walls were of stone and turf, and they were low—four feet at most. I've found little in the way of artifacts except a lot of Dorset-culture litharge [scraps and flakes of flint], much of it on top of rotted turf from fallen walls. Dorsets may have camped here after this longhouse was abandoned. But then again, it may have been built on an ancient Dorset site. Whatever. There is nothing to suggest they themselves built it."

He led me up an easy slope and I almost stumbled over the ruin before I saw what he wanted to show me next—the big house. Boulders, tumbled every which way, blended so well with the mess of other rocks that it needed to be pointed out to me. Then I was able to make out the shape of what looked like a tomb for Gargantua. It was at least eighty feet long, nearly twenty wide, and bloody massive!

In some places the walls still stood three feet high but were mostly broken down, their boulders rolled into the central space. Lee guessed some might weigh a thousand pounds. All were coated with a layer of lichens that must have taken hundreds of years to accumulate.

Looking across this enormous jumble, Lee summed up his thoughts: "Difficult to believe this was built by any Eskimoan people. What earthly reason would they have had? Eskimos may have sometimes pitched their tents inside these longhouses, and Dorset and Thule-culture people probably did the same. But I doubt they built them."

"Then who did?"

He smiled quizzically. "Well, now, Mr. Mowat, I suppose that's for you to ask and me to find out. At this stage a cautious professional wouldn't say. But I don't think you'll be surprised if I predict they'll turn out to be European. Possibly Norse."

Driving rain sent us to shelter in the cook-cum-work tent where young Robert had a Coleman stove roaring and a pot of canned beans simmering. Though Tom said he was a teetotaller, having an avid listener may have got to him. He accepted a noggin of rum in his tea. It really loosened him up.

"My colleagues could give me a rough time about this, you know. Orthodox dogma says there were no Europeans in the Canadian Arctic before Columbian times. But I can't imagine native people building the longhouses, or the towers. For one thing, there's almost no wood up here, so how would natives have roofed the longhouses? Europeans could have brought joists and rafters in their ships. A lot of other things are hard to explain.

"For instance, four years ago DNA tried to introduce a project here for the Eskimos to collect eider-down from the coastal islands. Eskimos never collected down in any serious way in the past. Had no use for it. But when the DNA chaps went out to the islands to check on the duck population they found hundreds of neatly built, three-sided, stone-roofed little shelters each just big enough for an eider to nest under. The shelters were heavily moss-grown and clearly ancient. The thing is: exactly the same sort of nest shelters were built in prehistoric times in Iceland and Shetland by people collecting eider-down, and are still being built and used there to this day.

"There's a deal more evidence of anomaly. I wish you could see what I found at Payne Lake. Right in the middle of Ungava is the site of an entire village I'm sure isn't Indian, Dorset, Thule, or Eskimo."

DCL costs $300 every hour of flying time, but what the hell? There might never *be another chance like this. I asked Lee if he would guide us to his Payne Lake site next day. He was happy as a kid at the prospect. Now it's 3:00 a.m. and I'm in a borrowed sleeping bag in the store tent. But I can't seem to sleep. Bloody Norsemen rattling their bones outside....*

Tom had us up at 5 a.m., fed on instant oatmeal (without milk or sugar), and into the canoe and away by six. This time the tide was with us and we made fast progress though we were forced to make a detour to avoid some seal hunters. They were presumably shooting at seals but ricochets from their 30-30 rifles whined close enough to give me the feeling of again being under fire in wartime Italy.

The post manager later told me the near misses might not have been entirely accidental.

"The natives don't like Lee digging up graves and carrying away the head bones. He should look to hisself."

We took off and headed up the Payne River valley, flying at deck level in order to get a better look at the "cross" I had glimpsed on the way east.

Lee, who had examined it on the ground, described it as a standing stone, or stela, nine feet tall, weighing in the neighbourhood of two tons. Balanced upon the top was a stone crossbar. This, in turn, was surmounted by a granite block set slightly off centre.

The visual effect of this cruciform structure was stunningly enigmatic. But if one had happened to be ascending the river in search of a Christian community supposed to be somewhere in the interior, it would unmistakably have directed the searcher to the first of a series of four tower beacons that mark the route to Payne Lake.

Payne Lake stretches almost eighty miles from east to west. Near its eastern end it constricts at a narrows only a few hundred feet wide. In early autumn the Ungava caribou begin drifting south and are deflected eastward by the barrier of Payne Lake. By the time they reach the narrows, they have coalesced into an aggregation so vast that, after the herds have swum across, the shores of the Payne River for miles downstream are felted with a yard-wide pad of shed hair.

As many as a hundred thousand caribou pass through this natural defile every year. And here, in ancient times (and well into modern ones), they were met by hunters for whom caribou was the staff of life.

Lee first came to Payne Lake in 1964 to investigate a Dorset caribou-hunting site on the north shore of the narrows. Late that summer, his field work mostly done, he chanced upon a canoe abandoned by some airborne prospectors. A bear had ripped its canvas covering but Lee repaired the damage with surgical tape and launched himself on a reconnaissance of the lake's southern shore.

There he discovered the village to which he was now guiding us.

As we flew low along the south shore of the lake we surprised a large black bear not far from an upturned red canoe. The animal reared up in alarm, and Lee laughed, then yelled in my ear.

"There's the canoe...maybe that's the same old character who belted it in '64....Look! There's the village!"

Disappointingly little of it was to be seen from the air—some rectangular discoloured patches of ground about the size of small kitchen gardens, and a few piles of stones. We landed well out in the lake and could not taxi close to shore because of off-lying rocks. Someone suggested Roy swim in and fetch the canoe. "What about that goddamn bear?" he asked. Doug reassured him. "Strip off. He sees you bare-assed naked, he'll run a mile."

Once we had all waded ashore Lee trotted us briskly around the site, making sure we experienced every nuance of the place.

When he first came upon it, he told me, nothing had been visible except five shallow depressions along a six-hundred-foot strip of foreshore. These had been vaguely outlined by low grassy ridges from which occasional large stones protruded.

"They reminded me of tumbled-in cellar pits in a long-abandoned village street somewhere down south, so regularly laid out I could hardly credit their presence here in the middle of the Ungava tundra. Such regularity did not accord with any northern native culture."

Two seasons spent excavating the site only strengthened first impressions. Removal of turf and of a thin layer of stony soil revealed long and relatively narrow house floors sometimes paved with size-selected stone cobbles from the beach. The rock-ballasted turf walls had long since collapsed.

Unlike the usual run of native structures, the floors of these were almost totally devoid of artifacts, of debris from toolmaking, or of domestic garbage.

"It was as if," Lee marvelled, "they had been swept clean by fussy *hausfraus*. No bones. The only traces of charcoal came from fires probably left by casual Thule or Dorset visitors who camped on the site later on. Such visitors had also used stones out of the house walls to make meat caches nearby and to anchor their tents."

Among the structures damaged or destroyed by later comers were the remains of three tower beacons.

Dating the houses by radioactive carbon-14 testing proved impossible because there was insufficient organic matter in them. However, later-day visitors had used stones from one house to make a tent ring, and Lee found a firepit inside this ring containing sufficient charcoal for testing. It dated to circa 1390, thereby establishing that the longhouse from which the stones had come must have existed before that date. Lee concluded that the five houses (which, he estimated, could have accommodated sixty or seventy people), might have been built as early as A.D. 1000.

One house seemed to have been special. Lee lingered over it.

"It's forty-six feet long and sixteen wide, and in the southwest corner there's a six-foot extension that looks uncommonly like a porch. Just beyond the porch, on the inside wall, you can see the foundation of a built-in wall fireplace.

"So far as I know, this is the first such wall fireplace ever found in the eastern Arctic. I know of nothing similar built by native peoples. I can't associate it with anything but Europeans.

"Facing it you see another remarkable feature: a carefully laid floor of flat stones forming a semicircle five feet wide. It's my impression that people might have put caribou skins down on that paving so they could sit around the fire in comfort while discussing their affairs, telling stories, or just enjoying the warmth.

"And that's not all. At the far end of the main room we have two semicircular walls, two feet apart, with the enclosed interior space also very neatly paved with stones. The whole arrangement is extraordinarily reminiscent of ambulatories in early Christian churches in northwestern Europe.

"There are other things. When I excavated at the Dorset sites across the lake, I found evidence for the frequent use of *metal* tools, but apart from scraps of soft native copper the Dorsets are not supposed to have had access to metals. Where did those folk get theirs if not from people of a metal-using culture?

"Come along and I'll show you something else behind the house sites in the middle of the village. See? That's a dam. We excavated part of it, and it's carefully built of rocks and clay. It's four feet high and forty long and backs up a pond behind the village. Mainly it serves to tame a stream that would otherwise flood the low area where the village stands during spring thaw or after any really heavy rain. Now, tell me please, can you imagine Eskimos going to all that trouble? I think they would have just moved their tents.

"Imagine what it might have been like living here. Uncounted caribou to hunt at the crossing so you could easily put up a winter's supply of meat, fat for light and fuel, skins for clothing, and the like. The rapids at the exit of the lake jump with char in season. The lake itself is an inexhaustible storehouse of fish. Two prospectors who were here when I was in 1965 caught forty lake trout in one evening, most of them over ten pounds weight. If you lived here you could fish all winter through the ice.

"This place would have been a northern garden of Eden. It still is, though now there's nobody but that old bear to take advantage of it."

Lee spent eight seasons between 1964 and 1975 digging at Payne Lake, Payne Bay, and along the adjacent coasts of Ungava Bay. During the winters he wrote and published voluminous and meticulously detailed reports of his fieldwork. These were pointedly ignored by most of his peers, who were aghast at Lee's fearless (some called it feckless) questioning of archaeological dogmas.

One of the few who was in sympathy with Lee put it this way: "Tom was the cat that got loose in the archaeological pigeon loft. He became a non-person professionally, largely because of his conviction that Europeans had been active in the Canadian Arctic for a lot longer than was officially recognized."

The upshot was that Lee ran out of institutional support for his work in Ungava.

Ostracized by his peers, denied funding, physically impaired by years of hardship in the field, Lee could no longer carry on his northern researches so, in the summer of 1982, he determined to return to one of his earliest digs—a site called Sheguinandah on Manitoulin Island in Lake Huron.

Here in the 1950s, while employed by the National Museum of Canada, Lee had unearthed abundant lithic evidence indicating a human presence extending as much as fifteen thousand years into the past. Such an early date for man anywhere in the Americas was not then acceptable so Lee's extensive collection of artifacts, together with his reports pertaining to Sheguinandah, were quietly consigned to limbo.

But times change. Many archaeologists now accept the probability, if not the certainty, that man has been in the Americas for as much as twenty or thirty thousand years.

Lee returned to Sheguinandah in 1982 hoping to substantiate his earlier findings there.

A week after pitching his tent on the ancient flint knapping site he had discovered thirty years earlier, the maverick was dead of a massive heart attack.

CHAPTER EIGHT

Skipper Jimmie

I WAS NOW READY TO RETURN TO BAFFIN ISLAND. TO GET there we had the choice of tracing the coast north from Payne Bay followed by an open-water flight of ninety miles across Hudson Strait, or we could follow the coast south around the bottom of Ungava Bay, fly north up the east coast, and take a departure from the northern tip of Labrador, where offshore islands reduced the over-water crossing to fifty miles.

Doug was the captain. "We'll take the long way round," he told us firmly, "'Cause that's the shortest way across Hudson Strait."

Flying south down Ungava Bay's west coast we looked at several other places Lee suspected of having hosted early European visitors. One was Ivik Island, near the mouth of Payne Bay. Ivik's four-hundred-foot-high dome was dominated by a trio of stone beacons, the largest thirteen feet high and six in diameter. The three towers made an arresting spectacle even when seen from the air. They are visible as sea-marks from thirty miles offshore.

We circled low over Ivik then headed south. The tide was out and the coast was a forbidding spectacle, bordered in some places for as much as six miles to seaward by a morass of mud and boulders.

An hour's flight brought us to Leaf Inlet, a spectacular fiord thrusting nearly fifty miles southwest into the land. Leaf Inlet boasts some of the highest tides on earth. Jimmy Ford, whom we would meet in Fort Chimo, described seeing a spring tide there in excess of sixty feet.

"And when she turned, the water come out of Leaf Narrows foaming like a fountain and running at fifteen knots or more. You could hear her roaring miles away."

We dropped down for a look at the barren Gyrfalcon Islands just off the mouth of the Inlet. Here, in 1965, Lee had briefly visited ruins similar to those at Payne Lake village, but stormy weather had forced a retreat before he could do any digging. He had asked me to photograph the site from the air, but we failed to find it.

Not far south of Leaf Inlet we crossed that amorphous boundary officially called timberline, or tree line. It is not a "line." Rather it is a fluctuant battleground between tundra and taiga. The taiga advances its outriders of dwarfed and twisted conifers to the north. The tundra retaliates by stretching fingers of moss and lichens south into the realm of trees.

At noon we reached the broad, brown Koksoak River at the foot of Ungava Bay, and soon thereafter made a landing on the small lake which served Fort Chimo as a seaplane base.

Sprawled along the west bank of the Koksoak, Chimo consisted mostly of shabby cabins and shanties scattered every which way across a sandy plain dotted with scrub spruce. A few gimcrack warehouses and bunkhouses testified to the ephemeral presence of mining companies prospecting the Ungava Peninsula. Dusty roads and tracks traced seemingly aimless patterns through the thin taiga surrounding the settlement. Oil drums and abandoned vehicles littered a sandy landscape. In the midst of this desolation DNA had built an "Eskimo village" consisting of two rows of prefabs that from a distance resembled discarded freight cars fallen from the skies.

We bummed a ride to town with a scruffy, middle-aged white man driving a truck for one of the mining companies. He told us the population consisted of about 450 Eskimos—"Huskies," he called them—150 mostly transient whites, and one lone Cree Indian.

"Things ain't so good as during the war when the Yanks had an airbase here. Christ! You could get *anything* then. But some young Husky squaws will still lay you for five bucks."

He also told us that beer, flown in from Montreal nine hundred miles to the south, retailed for ten dollars a case of twenty-four cans, but was usually in short supply. However, despite the presence of a large detachment of Quebec Provincial Police, several "blind pigs" provided backup. "The cops don't give a shit," our driver told us, "so long as they get theirs."

Chimo bore most of the stigmata of the traditional North American frontier settlement and had about the same appeal. "Want to go on the town tonight?" I asked Pete Murdoch.

He grimaced and replied, "Let's find my old friend Jimmy Ford instead."

Born in 1900 in the Labrador outport of Nain, Jimmy Ford was the product of two centuries of intimate liaison between Labrador Eskimos and Newfoundland fishermen. He had spent most of his life in the service of the Hudson's Bay Company and was one of the last of the old breed of "Company Men." Now retired, he lived in a snug and friendly little house that turned its back on the scruffy town to overlook the broad river and the unspoiled taiga beyond. A small, lean man, Jimmy welcomed us into his home where, because of a spell of terrible weather, we ended up staying for the best part of the next two days, seldom venturing out of doors except to use an outhouse whose twin seats were luxuriantly upholstered with black bear fur.

In the snuggery of his kitchen, Jimmy talked of a lost world while his very large Eskimo wife, Maggie, cooked up a storm of caribou, char, salmon, ptarmigan, moose, and assorted other northern delights.

"I been tryin' forty year to put meat on that old man's bones," she snorted, with a nod at her husband. "I see what can I do with you young pups."

We stuffed ourselves, and listened raptly as Jimmy reminisced.

Us Fords was always rolling stones. I weren't no different. Afore I were ten I were goin' down the Labrador all the way to Cape Chidley with my old granddad in his little schooner to trade with the natives there. When I were fourteen I shipped on a Newfoundland fishing schooner to St. John's. I had kin there, and lived with them for a while and they laid it to me to go to school. But one summer morn I see a Portugee square-rigger comin' in through the Narrows and I was bloomin' well lost. When she sailed, I were aboard of she.

Two years later I got into an old tramp steamer with a hellion for a skipper. I jumped ship in New York and went to work diggin' subway tunnels. I didn't take to the place. Rock under me and rock-hard hearts above. A pretty woman kept me there awhile but one day I decided, bejesus, there's more to life than pretty women. So I headed north.

Back on the Labrador in 1924 I heard the Hudson's Bay Company was lookin' for hands so I joined as an apprentice clerk. I was sent to Chimo first off. All there was here then was the Company and a few cabins scattered in the woods.

The Company had been boss in this country for a hundred years, but after the First World War a French outfit, Revillon Frères, moved in. Competition was fierce. We'd build a post—they'd build one alongside—and so on. There was a lot of native camps around the coasts of Ungava Bay those times, so both Revillon and us would send native traders out to work the camps. One day the factor here at Chimo, a big Scot, says to me, "Jimmy, they Frenchmen to the west is getting too much fur. So you go on up to Payne Bay and build a post that'll cut 'em off." He give me one of the Company natives and an old open sailboat, some grub and trade goods, and sent us on our way.

I built the bloomin' post, and bejesus if next year Revillon didn't stick one right across the cove from me. Their manager and me fought it out for the next ten year, then the Company bought Revillon out.

For the most part it were a lonely kind of life. You didn't see that much of the natives. They'd come in when they needed stuff, but mostly they lived out on the land. They didn't want much in the way of luxuries. Ammunition, fish-hooks, tobacco, tea, flour, things like that, was our stock in trade. If we was expecting a specially good white-fox year I might get in a couple of gramophones, and I always kept a stock of good woollen dress material and head scarfs. That's what the women wanted. 'Twas stuff like that as softened Maggie up when I asked her to be mine.

I never sat around the Post too much. I'd dog-sled out to trade with native camps in winter, sometimes a hundred miles away. Summertime, I was mostly on the water. Every spring we went to Akpatok Island out in the middle of Ungava Bay to hunt walrus for dog feed, and polar bears; then it was out among the Plover Islands for seals, and eider ducks and eggs.

There was hundreds of thousands of eider ducks out there them times. You didn't need a gun to get all you wanted. You could corner them in a cove with a kayak, and they was so fat they couldn't fly, and you could kill all you bloomin' well needed with your paddle. Today you got to be lucky to get a meal.

Same with the fish. Used to be so much char in the Payne you could bloomin' near walk across on their backs. In two days a native family could catch enough to last the year for them and their dogs. Nowadays you might get enough for a good feed. Salmon is the same. Salmon used to rip into the rivers in the south end of the bay so thick I've seen men throwing 'em ashore with their bare hands. The Company used to salt and barrel 'em by the bloomin' ton and ship 'em to England. Nowadays you catch a couple salmon and you can waltz around Chimo like you was the biggest jeezly fisherman on earth. Don't know where they've all got to.

I done a deal of sailing on the Bay. Some years that was the biggest part of my work. Until after the last war they was only one supply ship a year. Everything for all other posts around the Bay was dumped off at Chimo and had to be distributed by Peterhead boat. That got to be pretty well my full-time job during the summers. I'd supply all the other posts from Chimo, but leave Payne 'til the last so's I could end up home for the winter.

Now, you know, Ungava Bay can be a rough old lady. She's shoal, so she can build up the hell of a sea in no time at all. Near the end of September in '43 I come down to Chimo with an Eskimo crew to pick up my last load for Payne. Most of it was firewood because the Company didn't supply oil for fuel and there's no trees north of Leaf River. Fellows from the tundra posts had to come down into timber and cut their own, and I'd haul it home for them in the Company's Peterhead.

Well, this load was my own winter wood, and it was a jeezly big load. We filled the Peterhead to the hatches then piled logs three feet high onto her deck, and them stickin' out over each side a couple of feet. All you could see was a pile of logs with a mast stickin' out at one end, and the wheelhouse at the other.

First day out of Chimo it was calm and our engine, a two-cylinder 16-horsepower make-and-break, pushed us along as far as the Gyrfalcons. There were another, smaller boat keeping company with us, and she was slower so we hung back for her.

Next morning a bit of a breeze sprung up from nor'east. By nightfall it was a hard punch, blowin' maybe thirty knots and cold as the mill-tail of hell. We lost track of the other boat so about midnight we turned about and come back looking for her, but it was a howler by then and black as the inside of a whale's gut. We never saw her. She drove ashore near Hopes Advance Bay and beat herself to pieces, drownding the two young native fellows as was aboard of her.

When it got light enough to see through the muck, I held in for shore, thankin' God it were high tide. We took shelter behind a little island and put down two anchors. Both of them dragged, so we started the engine and hauled in as close to

73

the clifty lee side of the island as we dared. There the anchors took hold and we thought we was all right. But it kept on blowin' and after a while the seas started to break right over the island, which was maybe seventy feet high, and pour right down on top of us.

When we sailed from Chimo we never battened down the hatches, figuring the weight of the logs on deck would be enough to keep them tight. But it weren't enough! Water come pouring into the hull. We tried to pump her out, but the pumps clogged up with bark and ice and wood chips. We couldn't get to clear the jeezly suctions without we threw the deck load overboard first. But that was our winter fuel and we bloomin' well didn't want to let that go.

We couldn't get clear under power either because by now them anchors had got such a grip we couldn't budge 'em. Thank God they held, because there was nothing to the leeward of us but a smother of white water breaking over rocks. A seal could never have lived in it. Then, about noon the second day, one anchor chain parted. About ten minutes later the other one let go.

Well now we was in a jeezly fix! The water had got so high into her it'd filled the exhaust pipe so the engine wouldn't start. At that time we had about an eighty-knot wind, too strong for sail to stand. But we was driving down onto them rocks. We had to get steerage way. We started hauling up the staysail, triple reefed, but it blew right out of the bloomin' bolt ropes and disappeared.

The only thing left then was to try the mainsail. We wrapped it with a coil of rope wound around sail and boom and gaff, just leavin' a little slack. Then we hoisted the whole mess a couple of feet up the mast. And she blew out!

Just then the wind shifted into the north and that saved us because now we was drivin' along parallel to the shore, but the tide was falling and pretty soon there'd be no water left under our keel. We finally got some scraps of canvas tied into the riggin', and the wind was so strong that little bit give us some steerage, and we began to claw off a little from the shore. It seemed like we might get clear, except that dead ahead was a bloomin' big stony bluff juttin' half a mile out into the bay.

But we never struck it. The seas was so big when they hit the bluff, the backwash away from it would carry us back out. We wasn't much better than a log by now: half-full of water, couldn't steer, couldn't anchor, and couldn't go nowhere but where wind and sea fetched us.

My crew was two boys—two brothers, age sixteen and eighteen—and their old daddy who was a cripple with only one leg. They took it all very good. They didn't say anything, but I don't doubt they thought the more. We'd been soaking wet for a long time, and it was around freezing, but we hardly felt the cold for wondering what was going to happen to us next.

What happened was the backwash carried us around the point of the bluff and we drove down on a row of bloomin' reefs that was breaking white. Our starboard side come down on the first one, and bejesus if the backwash didn't wash us off. Same thing happened on the next reef. Our old boat was some strong—she struck three times and never stove a plank.

There was just one more reef now between us and deep water. It was about a mile long and breaking high in the air, white as snow and roaring like a bunch of bulls. I never thought we'd get across it but somehow or other the old boat found a way.

Then we drove off into deep water. The wind had come westerly so we got out a bale of relief blankets—wore-out army blankets they was, sent up by the government to give to the natives—and wrapped ourselves up in a ball in the wheelhouse. The windows was beat out, but the roof still held, and we knew the boat couldn't sink under us because she was too full of wood.

During the night the wind went right around into the sou'west, so we was drifting nor'east out across the bay. About three o'clock next morning we got our next big worry. We was driving down on a monstrous big iceberg. We come almighty close to it, but the backwash threw us off again and we blew clear.

By midday we were driving past the cliffs of Akpatok Island and what we would have give to get ashore there! But we just blew on by. Next day the wind hauled back into the west and that evening we could see Resolution Island up ahead. Now we was in the mouth of Hudson Strait, and pretty soon looked to be out in the North Atlantic. That would have been the end of us. We had to try and get ashore on Resolution.

There was a couple of tarpaulins aboard so we tied them together somehow and rigged a sort of staysail. The wind had fallen out a lot, so we was able to keep the tarps drawing and get steerage way at last. I pointed her for Resolution, then I thought, That's the wrong way home. The wind was coming northerly again, so we brought her round and headed back for Payne, about 150 miles away.

Now we decided to see what we could do with the bits and pieces of the blowed-out mainsail. I had no sail needles, but the old cripple did, in a little tin box tied around his neck. The four of us stitched half a day and made a sail of sorts.

The ship was so waterlogged she would hardly move. The suction of one pump had cleared itself so, while the boys pumped, I got down into the half-flooded engine room and cut away the exhaust pipe with a hacksaw so the water could drain out of the engine. It took a jeezly long time, but at the end of it I got the engine fired up and running. Then we cleared the power-driven pump and got it workin' too.

Thing was, by then we didn't know where we was at. Had no compass aboard and, of course, no charts. We just kept pounding westerly until finally we raised Cape Hopes Advance at the northwest tip of Ungava Bay. I was going to try getting into Diana Bay near there, but then I thought we was getting close to home so let's bloomin' well go home; so down the coast we steered.

We was within twenty miles of Payne Bay when the storm come back. It come on so wicked I knew we wouldn't ride it out at sea this time. I hauled her in for Dry Bay where there was a good little natural harbour, but you could only get into it at high tide and we'd been at sea so long we'd lost track of the tides. We had no choice anyway. It was take her in, or she'd take us down.

After a while we saw a crowd of natives on shore. We bore down, and they was all women—their men was away hunting caribou. They waved us on, pointing left or right, and piloted us into the snuggest little cove with a V-shaped notch in the rock just the right size for a Peterhead. We nosed the old girl into it, and you could just about hear her sigh of relief.

Not much more to tell. The women said there were an old anchor layin' on the shore ten miles away, so we walked over and carried it back. It only weighed about a hundred pounds, but was better than nothing. We patched some of the holes in the old girl's sides and, when the storm was over and the tide was high again, launched her off. Late that same day we anchored off Payne River post. We was home. And what a fuss the people made about it! The women wailed and yelled and took on so bad I almost put to sea again.

That was one jeezly storm. Seven boats lost in Ungava Bay, and a lot of good men with them. The government radio station at Cape Hopes Advance logged winds of 135 miles per hour until their wind gauge blew away.

The seas was so bad the ducks and seals couldn't handle it. There was times we had hundreds of eiders and dozens of seals right up against the vessel's side, looking for a lee so they could breathe. Every now and again a big sea would lift up the boat and she'd just slide over the lot of them. They'd come up to windward, then scramble like bejesus to get back on the lee side again. Lots of eiders washed right aboard, and one jar seal spilled right into the wheelhouse. I like duck and seal meat, but never had the heart to kill any one of them poor things.

Before I left Payne for Chimo to get the wood, my helper, Bill Calder, was putting new red roll roofing on the store and on the house. When we got back after the storm I noticed the roofs were white. I asked Bill why he'd whitewashed the roofs and he said he hadn't. "How come they're white, then?" He said it was salt. The seas coming over the point was so jeezly big the spray slathered the Company buildings on the far side of the cove until the roofs was turned as white as a virgin's heart. And that's the bloomin' truth!

Jimmy had an abiding curiosity and possessed a wealth of knowledge about the Ungava country. He knew the whereabouts of dozens of old "ruins," some of which he had seen for himself; others he had heard about from his Eskimo friends and relatives. He was also a repository of native folklore, including tales about the Tunit—and one about another alien people. The latter were said to have come to the country in very big *umiaks* (skin boats) and to have lived along the west Ungava coast from Leaf Basin north to Hudson Strait. They were the people who reputedly built the big stone houses Tom Lee called longhouses, as well as the great stone beacons.

According to Jimmy they may have built other things as well.

In the old times fox wasn't worth the powder to blow it to hell as far as the natives was concerned. Too small to make much meat, and the skins was too soft to stand up to hard wear. But somebody was after foxes in a big way long before we traders come along. Whoever they was caught foxes in stone towers, the same shape as the big ones you've seen, but less than half the size, and hollow in the middle with a hole at the top just big enough for a fox to squeeze through. If you put bait in the bottom Mr. Fox would jump in but couldn't climb back out. I know those old stone fox traps work because I've tried out some of them. Of course, steel traps and snares is a deal easier. Since the natives began trappin' white fox for trade, they've always used steel traps and snares. So who in bejeez made them hundreds of stone fox traps all along the west shore of the bay?

Then there's them bloomin' eider duck houses on all the islands along the west side of the bay. Hundreds and hundreds of them on the Plover Islands. But I never heard of a native taking the trouble to build one. I don't believe whoever built all them duck houses was just after eggs. I think they was after eiderdown, something the old-time natives never bothered about.

A real old woman from Diana Bay once told me a story. She died thirty years ago, but she said her grandmother heard from her grandmother about foreign people that lived along the west coast of the bay. And when the strangers went away, the old lady said the natives was real sorry to see them go. I hear Mr. Tom Lee thinks it could be as those people come from Europe. Maybe so. Our folks come over here from Europe. Some in boats no bigger than a Peterhead. What was to stop earlier fellows from making the trip?

CHAPTER NINE

Paradise
Lost

OUR DETOUR AROUND UNGAVA BAY HAD TAKEN US
south to the latitude of Churchill. Now we had to regain
nearly two hundred miles of lost northing between us and
Port Burwell on Killinek Island, our jumping-off point for recrossing
Hudson Strait.

The forecast on the morning of our departure from Chimo could
hardly have been better: light westerly winds and ceiling and visibility
unlimited (CAVU) all the way to Killinek. In fact, however, Chimo was
smothered in a thick grey murk, and when Doug called around on his
radio he found the coasts of Ungava Bay fogged in almost everywhere.

We stayed put until nearly noon, by which time our patience had
run out. Claiming he detected some lightening in the gloom, Doug
fired up the Wasp and we took off. Finding ourselves forced to fly at
about three hundred feet in order to keep in touch with the ground, we
were about to give up and retreat to Chimo's cold comforts when Doug
spied a "hole" in the dour overcast. DCL climbed steeply into it to
emerge some minutes later in a flawless azure dome flooded with bril-
liant sunlight.

The gods were kind. Two hours into the flight the undercast began
shredding away to reveal the saurian spine of Labrador's Torngat
Mountains encrusted with small glaciers and patches of perpetual snow.

As DCL grumbled northward, the Labrador peninsula grew ever
narrower until we were able to look right across it to the vast sun-
silvered plain of the North Atlantic Ocean.

Losing altitude as we closed with the island of Killinek, which forms the northern tip of Labrador, we sideslipped into a steep fiord and came to rest in Mission Harbour, adjacent to Port Burwell.

Before the Otter's propeller had stopped turning, Sam Ransom's motorboat was alongside.

A fisherman from an outport on the north shore of the Gulf of St. Lawrence, Sam was a bright-eyed, dark-skinned youth of twenty-two with a beguiling old-world manner. Although he never quite pulled his forelock or ducked his head, he made a point of addressing each of us as "sorr."

Sam ferried us ashore to a newly erected DNA bungalow where we met Sarah Ransom, his bride of six months, a shy but smiling young woman also from the North Shore, who served us hot biscuits and coffee and was patient when I asked vapid questions.

"How do you like living way up here?"

"Well, sorr. 'Tis just like back home, you see. Rocks, cold water, a long and starmy winter, but a store of good folk to keep you company."

The good folk of Port Burwell consisted of 115 Eskimos, together with Sam and Sarah. Temporarily absent was Newfoundlander Fred Brushett, Sam's boss and the architect of a remarkable attempt to help the natives of northern Labrador continue living in their own world while accommodating themselves to ours.

The most northerly useable harbour in Labrador, Port Burwell had offered refuge to far-faring Newfoundland fishing schooners long before the HBC built a trading post there in 1905. At about that same time the Moravian Brethren, who considered Labrador to be one of their mission fiefdoms, built what was to be their most remote outpost at nearby Mission Harbour. The years between then and 1919 were prosperous ones for these newcomers. Thereafter the place declined rapidly until, by the beginning of World War II, Killinek stood abandoned by whites.

Their departure did not leave the land uninhabited. The mountainous northern third of the great peninsula had harboured human beings since soon after the end of the last ice age, and it continued to do so. The region abounded with animal life. Thousands of walrus poured past its shores bound into and out of Hudson Strait. So did whales, both great and small. Enormous schools of cod fed in its plankton-rich surround-ing waters. Harp seals streamed past in millions on their long annual migrations between the Gulf of St. Lawrence and high arctic seas.

Four thousand years ago archaic Indians were exploiting the fecun-dity of the waters bordering the northern portion of the peninsula. They were succeeded by the Dorset culture, then by Thule, and finally by modern Inuit. At one time or another this portion of Labrador sup-ported some of the most vigorous native communities in the north.

The twentieth century brought change for the worse. Decimated by epidemics (especially by the terrible influenza pandemic of 1919), many of the surviving Inuit drifted south to the theocratic Moravian commu-nities of Hebron and Nain; but a few intransigent pagans remained in the far north, doggedly persevering in the old ways. Only a handful of them were left when, in 1961, Fred Brushett came among them.

Brushett's father and grandfather had both spent most of their lives "prosecuting the summer cod fishery down on the Labrador." Although that fabulous fishery was effectively over by the time Fred was old enough to take part in it, cod fishing was in his blood. As Sam Ransom admiringly put it: "Mr. Brushett's born to it like a fish hisself."

In 1960, Brushett was hired by DNA to see what could be done for, and about, the remaining Eskimos living in and around Port Burwell.

Sam gave us this account of a man he clearly regarded as a paragon of all the virtues—and whom he never referred to by his first name.

Mr. Brushett is a man as thinks about other folk more'n hisself. He belongs to a small place, same as me, and knows we got to stick together and work together to get along. The natives, they think that way too. They've had real hard times for quite a while now because they got so much into the way of trade that when the traders pulled out they didn't know which way to turn.

Mr. Brushett figured they could turn back to the sea. 'Twouldn't be nothing new for them because they'd always caught seals and fish for their own selves, and he figured they could just as easy catch them for others. So that was his idea: to get a little commercial fishery going at Burwell. That way the people could go on living the way they wanted and not have to move to Nain where most of the Labrador natives lives now on welfare.

That was four year ago. Him and another Newfoundlander, Mr. Max Budgel, got things going so good that natives started coming back to Killinek. Some come from as far off as Payne Bay, some from Nain. Word was that people could make a living here. Mr. Brushett saw to it they got the gear they needed: cod traps, gill nets, and trap boats. Him and the natives built a little fish plant, sort of a pilot plant, where the girls and women learned to fillet and pack fish for the market. They built a walk-in freezer to hold the fish until a ship could pick it up.

The government supplied a lot of the gear but it was the people did the work, and Mr. Brushett as showed them how. They was glad to do it...happy doing it. Two years ago Mr. Brushett brought up a forty-eight-foot longliner, and they took her out to see was there any halibut, and filled her up every trip they made. They filleted and froze that too.

Then they struck a reef. They was told they couldn't sell their fish down south because it hadn't been inspected where it was caught. Even Mr. Brushett couldn't get the government to send an inspector here. So that looked very bad. Then Mr. Brushett had another idea. Why not sell the fish in the north? To places like Frobisher Bay, and the new mines, and government places, and the military and the DEW Line—places where all the grub had to be brought in from far away?

That's where he's off to now. Travelling about in the north to sell Burwell's frozen cod and halibut, and char too if that's what people wants.

Another thing he did, he hired me to come up here and show the natives how to catch seals with nets and seal traps. There's a big market overseas for the skins, and you can bottle [can] the meat. Us North Shore people've been netting and trapping seals for hunnerts of years, which is what the most of us made our living at. Mr. Brushett figured it would work here too.

I come down north last year with a seal trap in a thirty-five-foot longliner. Took me and a buddy three weeks and we had some real good storms and some big lot of ice. Last fall the natives and me set out the seal trap and some nets and killed nine hunnert seals. The natives'd never killed so many as a hunnert in a season before that. When news of how well we done got out, more families come to Burwell to try their luck.

The government sent supplies so we could build sixteen native houses, a school, a warehouse, and the like. You can see for yourself how it's comin' on to be a regular little town. And the best of it is, the people run it pretty well theyselves. It's a co-op from the word go. Mr. Brushett is going to be moved on next year, so he asked me to stay and keep an eye on things. My woman and me. And we'll do it. This is going to be a good place to live and raise kids. And, you can say, we owes it all to Mr. Brushett....

While Sarah Ransom cooked supper—seal flipper pie was the entrée—I went sightseeing. Everything was new, except the worn-down roots of mountains surrounding the twin harbours.

It was a colourful scene. Anchored perkily in midstream close to where DCL squatted like an immense damselfly, the longliners *Killinek* and *Kyolik* gleamed in fresh coats of blue and white paint. The shore of a cove on the north side was chock-a-block with scarlet fuel drums brought in by the annual supply ship, waiting to be hauled up above high-tide line. Along a stony shelf just above the landwash (it was one of the few level places available) ran a row of recently erected, pastel-painted plywood houses, still so new they had not yet begun to look like abandoned packing cases.

A gleaming, metal-sheathed shed housed the fish "plant," within which eight grinning girls and young women were filleting the day's catch of nearly a thousand pounds of cod. The plant boss, an Eskimo little older than Sam Ransom, proudly showed me the freezer, already so full it could hardly hold any more.

Sam later confessed that he had had to dump many tons of older pack because no buyer had been found.

"We hopes that won't happen again. It's a right shame because we can deliver the finest kind of frozen pack to Frobisher with our own boat, instead of them having to buy fish shipped from St. John's to Montreal then flown all the way up to Frobisher. You could eat gold pretty near as cheap."

I was struck by the tempo of this settlement. Everyone, old and young, seemed to be going somewhere, doing something. Saws rasped to an obligato of hammer blows as walls of new houses literally rose before my eyes. A clashing rumble came from the landwash where youngsters were fishing oil drums out of the water and rolling them up the stony beach. As I watched, two trap boats steamed into harbour propelled by old-fashioned make-and-break engines popping away like giant firecrackers.

Burwell was far and away the liveliest place I had so far encountered on my current travels. It seemed to throb with vigour.

I was cheered too by the presence of a multitude of sled dogs. Snowmobiles could not negotiate the maze of mountain stubs that make up the northern portion of the Labrador peninsula—but dogs could. Prick-eared, of every hue, well-fed and friendly, they had the freedom of the settlement and revelled in it. And, Sam pointed out, "We don't have no call here for a sewery or a garbage collector. The dogs does it, and a sight better than some places I been at down south. And they keeps the white bears away—we gets a lot of they."

If life seemed good for the human inhabitants of Mission Harbour, it was clearly paradisal for the dogs.

I would have been delighted to remain at Burwell for days (or weeks), but that could not be. Hudson Strait is notorious for its fog, especially during easterly weather, and a depression was blowing in from the Atlantic. Doug was anxious to put the strait behind us.

As DCL lifted out of Mission Harbour I had no suspicion that within a dozen years the dreams and hopes of Fred Brushett, Sam and Sarah Ransom, and of the more than a hundred Inuit who had joined them in the belief they would be able to secure a new future for themselves would end in desolation.

In 1977 senior bureaucrats of the Department of Northern Affairs decided Port Burwell was not "cost effective" and therefore would have to be closed and its people relocated. Some would be sent south to Nain where they would come under the jurisdiction of the province of Newfoundland and Labrador and would join several hundred other Inuit who had been "centralized" there and who were, for the most part, without any sufficient means of earning a living and so almost totally dependent on relief.

The majority of the Killinek islanders were to be deported to a remote post at George River on the southeastern coast of Ungava Bay, where they would come under the jurisdiction of Quebec. In both cases they would cease to be the direct responsibility of the federal government.

None of the victims of this clearance scheme were given any choice. They protested vigorously that they were well-fed, happy, and comfortable at Killinek and wished to remain there. A (junior) departmental staffer in Ottawa even came to their support by pointing out that Burwell's fishery was proving so productive it was attracting increasing numbers of draggers and longliners from Newfoundland. They were ignored.

Port Burwell was shut down in 1978. Today Killinek Island is bereft of human residents. It is visited by Newfoundland vessels engaged in the lucrative gill-net fishery for turbot and halibut, seeking shelter from foul weather in Port Burwell and Mission harbours. Crew members go ashore and amuse themselves rummaging through the remains of the abandoned settlement.

These transients pay little heed to a notice hand-printed in English, French, and Inuktitut, tacked beside the gaping doorway of what remains of the little packing plant built by Brushett and his native companions.

Notice to Visitors to Killinek

We, the Inuit of Killinek, were forced to abandon our community on Killinek Island in 1978. Many of us now live in Kangiqsualujjuaq [George River] but still return to hunt and fish on the island. Since the community was abandoned some visitors have broken and damaged the buildings that are left and have shown little respect....We ask all visitors to respect Killinek. Do not damage it any more.

CHAPTER TEN

Simonee

S EEKING ALTITUDE FOR THE FIFTY-MILE CROSSING TO
Baffin Island, DCL climbed steeply away from Killinek above the
Button Islands; known to the Inuit as the Stepping Stones.

This was a good year for icebergs, and a rising tide was propelling an
armada of them into Hudson Strait. Most were of the towering, cathe-
dral-spired variety, but one was a tabular monster nearly a mile long and
half as broad. Its relatively flat surface cradled a sapphire-hued meltwater lake which Doug reckoned might be long enough to set DCL
down upon. The opportunity to become the first pilot to land a float-
equipped Otter on an iceberg must have tempted him, but he forbore.

As we flew north at ten thousand feet, an elephantine presence
began to loom over the horizon ahead. This was the southeastern
peninsula of Baffin Island, called Meta Incognita—regions unknown—
by the buccaneering Englishman, Martin Frobisher, who came upon it
in 1576.

Our landfall was the craggy mass of Resolution Island at the eastern
tip of Meta Incognita. As we approached it, Doug began letting down.
Flying at a comfortable altitude of two or three thousand feet we
opened Frobisher Bay and set a northwesterly course along its southern
shore.

Apart from occasional overwintering whalers, Frobisher Bay had
remained a generally uncontested domain of the Inuit until 1942, when
white men established their first permanent settlement there. These
latecomers were not seeking fur, gold, or whales. They were looking for

a place to build an airfield to service military aircraft being ferried to Europe via Baffin Island, Greenland, and Iceland.

They found a suitable site near the foot of the bay, and construction began. The work involved hundreds of aircraft, scores of ships, and thousands of white men. The result was a sprawling melange of military structures, a huge landing field, and a "town" named Frobisher Bay, which was usually called Frobisher or simply Frobe. Renamed Iqaluit, it is now the capital of the new territory of Nunavut.

After the war Frobisher continued to grow—first as a base from which nuclear bombers of the U.S. Strategic Air Force could threaten Russia with atomic annihilation, then as the eastern Arctic centre for the DEW Line radar system. For a time it also served as a refuelling base for commercial piston-engined planes flying Great Circle routes between Europe and North America.

During construction of the base hundreds of Inuit from Baffin Island and other parts of the eastern Arctic were inveigled into coming to Frobisher, which became something of a boom town. In the mid-fifties, the apostles of the Northern Vision concluded it should become Canada's first true city of the north.

Architects were duly commissioned and plans drawn up for a mini-metropolis complete with high-rise apartments and business complexes, all to be sheltered under an enormous plastic dome.

This bubble soon burst. Following the diabolical perfection of the intercontinental guided missile, Frobisher's huge USAF base became obsolete. Most military forces were withdrawn while at the same time the ascendancy of jet-powered commercial aircraft which did not require refuelling between continents rendered the great airport complex on south Baffin Island virtually redundant.

No portion of Frobisher's population was more vulnerable to the loss of its economic *raison d'être* than the Inuit who had been suborned into exchanging a semi-nomadic, hunter-gatherer way of life for an approximation of our industrial urban culture. Now what were they to do? Emigration to southern Canada was no option since they had neither the language nor the requisite skills to compete there with a burgeoning flow of immigrants from Europe and Asia. They became a displaced people in their own land.

When we arrived, the population consisted of five hundred whites, most of them transients, and eleven hundred Eskimos. Practically the only employment stemmed directly or indirectly from government. All key jobs and most minor ones, together with almost all "entrepreneurial opportunities," were in the hands of whites.

Government administrators, technicians, and educators occupied some of the giant buildings abandoned by the U.S. military. Of the several "private sector" businesses only one, Inuk Limited, was run by Eskimos.

Frobisher natives told me, with cutting irony, that it was not *they* who needed government so much as it was government who needed *them*— to sustain and justify the employment of scores of white administrators, teachers, scientists, technicians, policemen, social workers, and the like.

Most of my time here was spent visiting a new settlement under construction four miles outside "town." Apex Hill, as it was called, was being built by DNA specifically for Eskimos. It was, in effect, a formal exercise in segregation, a fact of which most of its inhabitants seemed perfectly well aware.

At Apex I was the guest of a heavy-set, pockmarked, forty-eight-year-old named Simonee. He and his family lived in a two-bedroom house several cuts above the new housing being made available to Eskimos in most outlying communities. Here several of Simonee's friends joined us to talk about northern life and problems. Or, rather, they talked while I listened.

Simonee was the chief spokesman.

My name Simonee—E-275. You know, every Eskimo got to wear a dog tag with a number on it round his neck because white men, they can't tell the difference who we are by just looking at us. We can tell different white men, though. They smell different....

Was born in camp near Lake Harbour. Learned to be hunter when I was a kid, just like everyone. Hunt seals, sometimes walrus, caribou. One time I shoot a polar bear when I was fourteen, but was really my brother killed it because he was better shooter.

Two, three times a year we go to Lake Harbour and trade with Hudson Bay, and visit lots of people come from all along the coast. Pretty good life. But then my two sisters got sent out to school in the south, then my dad and mother both get sick with TB and flown out south somewhere. My mother die there. Only Father come back.

In our camp we hear about big war going on. When we go to Lake Harbour, manager say lots of Eskimos work for Americans now in Frobisher and lots of chances for young fellows like me. He say I should go too. So I go there and work three years peeling spuds at the base, then five years as carpenter. After that I work for DNA as interpreter. Never had no school, just learned English by myself.

Now I work for me, my family, my own people. Not too much future for us here though. Lots of my friends worry about no future for our kids, so we try to do something white man's way. We start Inuk Limited. We collect money from all Eskimos in Frobisher and buy an old bus and start a bus line from the base out to Apex. Then we get work repairing some DNA buildings; then buy two trucks and try get contract for garbage in Frobisher. But white company come in from Montreal and get that contract. Then we get a janitor contract, but another white company come north and we got to share those jobs. The way it is, the whites in that company look after office and supplies and we look after the work. One white fellow tells me: "We get the cream; you guys get the milk." Something like that, eh?

We want to get into co-op housing, but white big shots don't like co-ops. So I don't know if we ever get it. We like to start other co-ops for making work, because not much work here, you know. Some of us think about go back to old ways. Live on the land part of the year, and maybe work part in Frobe. Government say no. Say kids got to go to school, and if we go live on the land they going to take our kids away and send them south to school again like they used to do. Well, we have enough of that. Everyone here have brothers, sisters, sent away one time to school outside, or got sent away themselves. No damn good! Break up families. Can't talk to each other afterwards. Bad things happen to kids. Nobody want that any more.

We don't understand what happening. We learn to work machinery easy! We got lots men can operate heavy machinery, any kind machinery. And fix them too. Do it good as any white man. But we don't get those jobs. White men come in from south, and work for a year maybe, then go. They very rough with machines, smash them up good sometimes. We could run that stuff better, but the bosses don't want it.

There's nothing an Eskimo can't do with his hands. Carpentry. Machines. Electric. Build houses, boats, anything you want. Houses, now. Why are they send prefab houses all the way north? If they send wood and nails and stuff, we make them houses for ourselves.

DNA talk plenty about Inuit being own bosses. When is that, eh? Times when we live in the north before any white people, we were the bosses. We know what we need and how to get it. We learned a lot in all them years our people lived in the north before you fellows come. We can learn whatever new we need, but we should decide what we want to learn. And what we want to change. And how fast we change.

One time used to be only one sort of people here. Nobody have much more than everybody else so we get along good, helping each other. Happy times together. Now is two peoples. Whites and Inuit. Whites got most of everything. Maybe you going to take all of everything? Inuit better be careful; only maybe is too late already.

Frobisher was the first community we had visited where a significant number of Eskimos seemed to suspect it might be too late. An aura of something approaching despair pervaded the place. Passive despair. Nobody was starving—the welfare system saw to that—but almost nobody was engaged in useful or satisfying work.

One of the things people *did* do was drink.

On Friday and Saturday nights drunkenness was rampant—not that it was absent at other times. Family Allowance (child support) cheques and welfare payments seemed to be spent as much on alcohol as on food, clothing, or shelter. In the depths of winter people froze to death because they were drunk. Fights had become so frequent the police seldom even attempted to act as peacemakers.

When I went to the liquor store to replenish our own supplies, I was told the stock on hand was being flown up from Montreal and commanded a premium price. However, the supply ship *Radisson* was due in next day with a consignment of *40 tons of liquor*, the bulk of which, so the white manager of the store told me, would go down Eskimo throats.

"They don't know how to drink, is the trouble. Goddamn lushes, some of 'em. But what can you do? This here's a goddamn welfare town but I guess they got the right to buy the stuff just like anybody else.

"Can't take a man's rights away from him, can you?"

CHAPTER ELEVEN

Something Else to Do

ALTHOUGH WE USUALLY ARRIVED AT OUR destinations unannounced, Pangnirtung was an exception. Simonee knew a white man there he felt we should meet and he called him by radio to tell him we were on the way.

South Baffin Island is nearly split asunder by mighty Cumberland Sound, which strikes northwest for more than two hundred miles. The sound's southern shore is fringed by hundreds of islands while its northern one is walled by mountains and glaciers. In 1966 it was home to about six hundred Inuit but had only one settlement—Pangnirtung, familiarly known as Pang.

On the morning of our flight to Pang, clouds obscured the world but as we approached Cumberland Sound they dissolved.

Magnificent mountains loomed fifty miles ahead of us across a cerulean expanse of sea. Their splendid peaks fringed a dazzling ice field which filled the entire northern horizon. Serpentine rivers of ice flowing imperceptibly down from its glittering heights were swallowed by black-bellied canyons spewing glacial fragments into the sound.

One of these canyons was Pangnirtung Fiord, its mouth guarded by a pair of four-thousand-foot capes. We flew between these and could see far ahead what looked like a handful of confetti scattered at the base of a rock slab six thousand feet high.

As we drew closer, we could distinguish a Hudson's Bay Company compound with its regimented cluster of red-roofed buildings. Nearby was an RCMP barracks overhung by a very large Canadian flag. A mission compound enclosed a small hospital, a large church, and a school.

These were the three pillars of the Old Empire of the North, but they were being eclipsed by a powerful newcomer. On high ground overlooking the bastions of the Old Order, a sprawl of recently built oil storage tanks, garages, construction sheds, a diesel-electric generating station, and a neat row of suburban-style, prefabricated buildings testified to the presence of a new arbiter of northern destiny.

The objects or, as it may be, the subjects of all this new activity were living in thirty-seven well-worn wall tents, and twelve of the now achingly familiar plywood boxes. The latter had been painted vivid kindergarten colours which were already blending into the dun-coloured landscape under the influence of oil-dripping seal skins nailed to the walls, and fish nets, dog harness, partly dried fish, and blackened chunks of walrus meat flung onto their roofs. No sign was needed to identify this section of Pang as the Native Village.

What appeared to be the entire population was at the shore as DCL edged in to a makeshift dock. The people were not, however, typically Inuit in appearance. Aquiline noses, blue and hazel eyes, and fair hair testified to earlier visits of Scots and English whalers for whom the sound had been a famous and lucrative whaling ground during the late nineteenth and early twentieth centuries.

However, only one bona fide "white man" was present. He was a youngish, slightly built fellow wearing a screaming crimson sweater and wielding a double-bladed kayak paddle as if it were a spear.

"I'm Peyton," he yelled, brandishing his makeshift weapon. "Heard you were coming. Did you bring a bottle?"

Escorted by twenty or thirty brightly clad men, women, and children (the women mostly dressed in traditionally cut cotton anoraks), we followed Ross Peyton to his neatly built little house on the fringe of the native community. Here we gave him gifts, and he responded by talking at length about his life at Pang.

I belong to Norton Sound on the north coast of Newfoundland. We fished there, mostly cod. Wintertimes we went into the woods and cut pulp for the big paper companies. That was pure slavery and I made up my mind to get clear of it. When I heard the Hudson's Bay Company was looking for men, I signed on.

That was 1950. They sent me to apprentice here at Pang. I suppose you could say I fell in love with the place, but more so with the native people. They weren't that much different from Newfoundland outport folk. They worked hard, and they liked to get together to have a "time." What made them happy was to run a nice camp and, if you were a man, keep it well supplied with meat. Women got as much pleasure out of seeing the seal skins were well prepared, and making clothing. Especially skin boots. Boots were extra special. If you paid a compliment to the boots a fellow was wearing and his wife heard, she would just about die with pleasure.

When I first came here all the people were in camps out on the land. Spread all around Cumberland Sound, but mostly out toward the mouth where the most seals, walrus, whales, and bears are. Summertime they'd come in to Pang by boat to visit and buy stuff at the Company store.

It wasn't very often people went wanting. For the most part they had plenty of meat, fat, skins, and furs. If a family run into bad luck and was going short, somebody would be sure to help them out.

The first part of my job was to learn the language. To do that I went out to the camps and lived with the people. There'd be maybe twenty to thirty in a camp, three or four families working and living together. And playing together, too. I don't remember ever getting much sleep in the camps. We'd sit around drinking tea and talking and laughing and eating all night and half the next day until someone might yell there was white whales in the cove, then all hands would go running for guns and boats. If we got one, that night there'd be another big feed, and they'd keep up the good time 'til next day rolled around.

The one thing about them different from anywhere else I ever been, was the pleasure they got out of giving pleasure. They really did! When I got to be manager here, men would bring in their fox furs and bear skins and seal skins and lay them on the floor in front of me. Then they'd watch my face. If I smiled, if I was pleased, they'd bust right out laughing with joy. Didn't matter about what they'd get in exchange. What mattered was they'd brought something that made me happy. You can imagine there was more than a few traders would take advantage of that.

In 1953 the Company moved me to Frobisher and I was back in white man's country. The place was roaring. Must have been three or four thousand whites there working on DEW Line sites, the base, whatever. I got a promotion and better pay, and got married, and everything looked rosy—but for one thing.

I didn't like what I could see happening to the Eskimos. They were down at the *bottom of the heap in Frobisher instead of on top of the hill like when they were out in the country. A lot of the whites that come in there then was the roughest kind. There was a lot of Yanks who treated Eskimos like they was niggers down south. Some Canadians was no better. It sickened me. Booze and whoring was just tearing the Eskimos up into pieces. Then about 1958 the government got into the act. Going to save the Eskimos.*

They started hauling people in off the land, sending the kids out of the country for a white man's education, and generally screwing up whatever was left of Eskimo life.

In 1962 there was an outbreak of distemper in the dogs. You get that every ten years or so, and there's nothing new about it. A lot of dogs die, but in a couple of years you've got as many as you need again. Well, this time the government boys claimed the Eskimo camps would all die of starvation without their dogs to hunt with, so they used that as an excuse to send the Mounties to round up the Cumberland Sound people and bring them into Pang to live.

To live on what? There was far too many people for the country around Pang to feed.

When I heard what was going on, it was too much for me. I quit the Company, went back to Pang, and set up as what you might call a free trader. So far as I know I'm the only independent trader left in the eastern Arctic, and the Company isn't too pleased about me. Neither is the government. Because what I set myself to do was help the people hang on until, and if, they wanted to turn into white men. A lot of them still wanted to live in the camps. I wanted them to have time to make up their own minds. Meanwhile, I did whatever I could to help them live the way they wanted to.

My store isn't meant to take a profit out of here for some outfit down south. I make just enough to live on and keep my family, and that's it. And I try to find ways for the natives to be independent. Of course that means they have to make some money too. That's the trap. But, here now, pass that bottle, will you....

Most of Peyton's energies had been directed into making Pangnirtung a premier producer of sealskin clothing. He had taken samples of the work done by Pang people to Montreal ateliers, who gave him orders for embroidered sealskin boots, gloves, and parkas.

Once he was convinced a market for sealskin sports clothing existed, Peyton set about increasing the take at Pang. He taught himself ballistics, the chemistry of explosives, and other erudite skills. Then he began supplying hunters with flat-trajectory ammunition specifically designed for seal hunting (he loaded the ammunition himself), at less than half what the Company charged for standard loads. Within two years the take of seals at Pang had doubled. It could have been increased still more, but at a meeting of the camp elders it was agreed that a thousand seals a year was probably the maximum number that could be killed without reducing the seal population.

"It wasn't me called a halt," Peyton explained. "It was the people themselves. I told them we could easy sell two thousand skins a year, but they just smiled and said *nowk*—no. One old fellow, who was like a foster father to me, and went to church too, told me it was because *Sila* wouldn't like it. *Sila*, you know, is supposed to be sort of the goddess of the sea and the mother of all the animals."

Getting the skins processed was the next challenge. Using traditional methods, the women of Cumberland Sound couldn't begin to deal with the quantity of skins now available. Unfortunately, then as now, commercial sealskin tanning was virtually a Norwegian monopoly. Almost all Canadian seal skins, whether from the Arctic or from the enormous slaughter of harp seals in Newfoundland waters, went to Norway for processing.

Peyton set out to break this monopoly. He badgered DNA to establish an experimental tannery at Pangnirtung which could eventually serve Eskimo communities across the north, but he got nowhere with the bureaucrats.

"Them fat-asses in Ottawa told me it was too complicated for Eskimos to handle! Too complicated! Eskimos been tanning seal skins since the world began, if not before! You ever hear of such goddamn foolishness?"

Peyton went back to Montreal where he found a small tannery that claimed it could do the job. Five hundred hides were shipped to this company...which ruined them, and very nearly ruined Peyton into the bargain, for he had bankrolled the experiment. Commercial production of Canadian seal skins remained, and remains, firmly in Norwegian hands.

I had to look around for something else to help us out and it looked like Eskimo art was a coming thing so we tried to start an art co-op. The powers that be said no to that one too. They claimed they was worried the market might get flooded. I believe they want to fix it so's only the well-off buy Eskimo art. They want to limit production and keep the prices up. Well, by the Lord, people here at Pang might have something to say about that!

Expo 67's coming up next year. Biggest blowout Canada's ever had, with people coming to Montreal from all over the world. A lot of them are going to want to take something Canadian home with them, and what better than something Eskimo?

If Ottawa won't let us sell art to the rich, I figure we can sell stuff ordinary folk can afford. Not souvenir junk, you understand. Honest-to-God Eskimo stuff. I talked to all the camp bosses and asked for ideas. They came up with making beach stones into pendants with little drawings etched onto them of animals, birds, people, and the like. They told me it was something the old people did long ago—not a new thing like them big soapstone carvings are.

The idea caught on like a house afire. Not every native is an artist but they're all experts when it comes to using their hands. Pretty soon pendants was piling up by the boxful. They got better and better. Some even had pictures inlaid in walrus ivory. Some folks started making brooches. Everyone, even the kids, got into the act, scouring the beaches for miles around looking for just the right little stones. And all hands was having fun.

Dealers down south liked the samples I sent down and orders have been coming back in fine style. It's good stuff—see for yourself.

Peyton showed me a drawerful of charming little pieces as good in design and execution as work being done at Dorset and other designated Eskimo craft centres. I bought some as presents for friends—at a retail price of two dollars each!

Pangnirtung pendants and brooches may have pleased makers and buyers, but they did not please those who controlled Eskimo art sales. I met one such expert before my trip concluded. I showed her the pendants I had bought.

"Yes," she said with disdain, "I know about them. A very unfortunate development. Those things could cheapen the market so everyone would suffer. Ross Peyton ought to know better."

Peyton may not have known better then, but he would discover that the new order in the north could exert pressure every bit as powerful as the old orders had been capable of. I am not privy to the details, but have been told that few, if any, of the pendants and brooches from Pang made it to market.

We had arrived in Pang at a bad moment. Peyton had just heard that Ottawa had ordained a final end to the traditional camp system. The remaining camps around the fourteen-hundred-mile perimeter of the sound were to be "centralized" as quickly as possible. Forty prefab Eskimo houses were to be erected at Pang in 1966, and more the following year.

That'll sink our sealing plan. Can you imagine six hundred people jammed in here? Hunters will be tramping each other to death! I asked the DNA administrator at Frobisher what the hell he thought they were all going to do for a living. "Don't you worry, Ross," he says to me. "The men'll be driving bulldozers for the mining companies that're coming into the country. The women will be able to buy out your little shop overnight. And the kids will all be able to go to school."

He didn't say anything about the fact those new houses aren't free. The Eskimos have to pay rent for them, you know. And they have to pay electric bills, and those are heavy up here where we have to use diesel generators. They have to buy fuel oil for space heaters too, and that stuff costs near as much as rum. There's no talk about all of that. Just pipe dreams about bulldozers! It's enough to make a man want to tear somebody in half!

This I'll tell you. So long as I'm here—and they can't very well run me out, though there's plenty would like to—Pang people aren't going to have to go on the pogey same as they do in Frobe to keep body and soul together. No, my son, if they stop us on the seals we'll surely find something else to do.

On my way back to Peyton's house that evening, after a walk around the settlement enjoying the warm red light shed by the almost-but-not-quite setting sun, I encountered an Eskimo boy of perhaps thirteen. I could see from the clothing he wore that he was one of the lucky ones who had been sent away to the south for an education.

"*Chimo* [hello]," I said.

"Hello yourself," he replied in English. Then, "You give me some money, mister?"

I did not tell Ross Peyton about this little encounter. But that night as I lay in my sleeping bag, words he had spoken earlier came back to haunt me.

"...We'll find something else to do."

CHAPTER TWELVE

The Icie
Mountains

THE ICIE MOUNTAINS IS MY NAME FOR THE OTHERWISE nameless range that encrusts eastern Baffin Island with a welter of peaks and glaciers, then marches north to Lancaster Sound, crosses eastern Devon Island, and becomes the spines of Axel Heiberg and Ellesmere islands. Eleven hundred miles long, the range continues for another three hundred miles to the pole itself as the submarine Lomonosov Ridge.

Some of the peaks of the Icie Mountains tower as high out of the sea at their feet as do many famous peaks in the Rockies above their surrounding valley floors. The fiords gouged between them are among the deepest and most spectacular extant. Admiralty Inlet, on north Baffin, is the longest, largest fiord in the world.

It is not their mass alone which makes the Icie Mountains so impressive. They carry on their shoulders a splendid assemblage of glaciers. Baffin boasts two immense plateaux of ice, a thousand feet thick in places, rimmed by the teeth of surrounding mountains. They are remembrances of times past—that may come again.

At first glance the world of the Icie Mountains appears somewhat lifeless but the tundra vegetation flourishing in its sheltered valleys nurtures many animals, including caribou, foxes, wolves, arctic hares, and ptarmigan. Some of the great cliffs walling the fiords provide high-rise homes for sea bird colonies numbering in the millions. The sea thundering at the foot of the cliffs is singularly rich in life. Seals, walrus, narwhals, and those few great whales that have survived the decimation of their kind feed in the rich waters of the southbound Canadian Current. Cod and other marine fishes abound, and char link salt waters with fresh.

DCL's entry into this world of wonders was preceded by an auspicious omen. As we were being ferried out to the plane at Pang, the boat carrying us was intercepted by a pod of narwhals. These were the first to visit the fiord that summer, and the young man running the outboard went wild with excitement. Having no rifle with him, he tried to ram one of the grey-white ghosts. Warned by their sonar, they instantly sounded.

A meeting with narwhals is always a rare event and I was delighted. As well as by the weather, which was superb: bell-clear, almost windless, and a balmy fifty degrees Fahrenheit. It was, in fact, so fine a day that Doug proposed a modification to our plans.

Our next destination was Clyde River, halfway up the east Baffin coast. We had intended to avoid the worst of the intervening mountains of the Cumberland peninsula by flying up Kingnait Fiord then crossing a relatively low saddle to Padlei Fiord, which runs east into Baffin Bay. Now Doug suggested a more exciting alternative.

"Anybody wanna see what a real big glacier looks like close up? Map says that big white sucker called the Penny Ice Cap is pretty near nine thousand feet high. But we could skim over it."

The walls of Pangnirtung Fiord reverberated to the roar of our take-off. The Otter laboured, gaining height as quickly as she could. At a mile high and still climbing we rose clear of the fiord's narrow constraint and headed northwestward, paralleling the foot of the ice cap.

For thirty miles we flew beside and below that monstrous presence seeking a chink in its armour. At last we came to a glacial river, milky with its burden of powdered rock, spewing down braided channels from the flank of the ice. Its valley seemed to offer an avenue of approach but we soon found our passage gated by an ice barrier so riven and faulted by meltwaters, and so discoloured by the burden of debris it carried within itself, that it appeared more like a solid wall of rock.

DCL surmounted this barrier, and we found ourselves flying above a river of ice a mile wide flowing inexorably out of the heart of the Penny Ice Cap.

DCL followed the sinuous course of this frozen river, striped and striated by veins of sand and gravel gouged from the containing mountains, for twenty miles, steadily ascending until at last we emerged over the cap's bald and gleaming dome. Thereafter we flew another fifty miles above the surprisingly smooth and visually unremarkable surface of a frozen ocean in the clouds.

Our route down from the glacier followed a descending ice tongue that ended abruptly in a fiord leading into Baffin Bay through Canso Channel. Icebergs breaking off from the tip of the tongue sailed slowly towards green Atlantic waters.

We now set a northwesterly course along the coast, crossing a sequence of gigantic fissures, some of them as much as eighty miles long and walled by cliffs two thousand feet high. It seemed as if the earth itself had split asunder.

Mountains and glaciers kept edging us closer and closer to the coast until we reached the mouth of Nudlung Fiord, where Roy pointed out a tiny white pimple on the crest of massive Cape Hooper. This resolved itself into the stadium-sized dome of a radar station, but in a setting such as this even man's mightiest constructs seemed paltry.

The waters of Baffin Bay to starboard were now hidden beneath closely packed floes out of which jutted innumerable icebergs. The coast was so solidly embargoed that no ships, not even icebreakers, had been able to reach it this season. Usually the polar pack riding south on the Canadian Current eases its grip by late September and the blockade is briefly lifted before oncoming winter reimposes it. However, in some seasons the window fails to open; then those who live upon this coast find themselves isolated for another year...or two.

Orthodox history tells us that Martin Frobisher and his men were the first Europeans to visit east Baffin Island. In truth they were late-comers. At the turn of the first millennium a man named Thorgisl Orrabeinsfostri sailed and rowed along most of the forbidding coast we were now flying over.

Historians generally regard Thorgisl's voyage as a failed settlement venture from Iceland to Greenland that met disaster on the east coast of Greenland. As I believe I have demonstrated in my book, *Westviking*, they are in error.

In 997, thirteen years after planting a colony in southwest Greenland, Erik the Red invited Icelander Thorgisl Orrabeinsfostri to join him in his new settlement. Thorgisl set out for Greenland in a *knorr*—the standard ocean-going vessel of the Norse of that day and age. She carried Thorgisl's family and slaves together with another family headed by a man named Iostan.

The heavily laden vessel sailed west from Iceland in thick weather. Navigating mainly by dead reckoning she missed Cape Farewell, Greenland's southern extremity. By September the voyagers had made their way northward well into Baffin Bay.

What follows is my abbreviated paraphrase of the *Floamanna Saga*, a thirteenth-century Norse account of Thorgisl's story.

Late one day they wrecked their ship on a shoal in a certain fiord under the glaciers. The ship broke up but all the people were saved. They gathered up as much of the ship's wreckage as they could and built a hut, dividing it in half between the two families.

Around mid-winter Thorgisl's wife, Thorey, gave birth to a child named Thorfinn.

The second night of Christmas there came a loud knock upon the door. One of Iostan's men said, "Good tidings must be come!" and ran outside. He failed to return and in the morning Iostan and his men went looking for him and found him dead. The next evening another of Iostan's men went mad and died. Six of them died before Iostan caught the sickness himself and died. Then, one after another, so died all those in Iostan's party.

Thorgisl and his men spent their time building a boat from the wreckage of the ship. Winter passed but the party could not get free of the fiord because pack ice blocked the entrance. So they spent the summer season hunting and gathering food for winter, but when the following spring came, they still could not get out of the fiord.

One fine day Thorgisl decided to climb high up on the glacier from where he might be able to see if the pack was slackening. Thorey, now confined to bed, pleaded with him not to go, but "he would have his own way, as always." His older son, Thorleif, together with the other two freemen in his party, Col and Starkad, went with him up the glacier. They climbed all day until bad weather forced them to turn back. On reaching the camp they saw that the boat they had built was gone. They went into the hut and found the place ransacked, their chests missing, and the slaves vanished.

Then they went deeper into the hut, which was very dark, and heard a gurgling sound from Thorey's bed. Thorey was dead, but her son was sucking at her body. When Thorgisl examined her, he found a little wound under her arm, as if she had been pierced by a fine knife. All of the berth where she lay was soaked in blood. This was the greatest grief Thorgisl had ever suffered.

That night Thorgisl watched over the boy, knowing the child would starve to death unless something drastic was done. So he took a knife and pierced his own nipple until the blood flowed. Then he let the child suck at it until water, then milk emerged. Thorfinn nursed thereafter on his father's milk.

It is told that the slaves who had stolen the boat had taken all the provisions, as well as the very doors off the house and even the bed hangings. All the tools were gone.

Thorgisl and those with him now set out to build another vessel. Since they had no tools, they built a skin boat. In this Thorgisl, his two sons and the two freemen set off, following the example of the slaves, making their way out of the fiord and turning south along a shore lead which had opened at last.

When winter came on they hauled their boat ashore. One morning Thorgisl saw a great carcass drifting in an opening in the pack. Two giant women in skin clothing [doubtless native hunters who had killed a walrus or narwhal] were tying up big packages of meat. Thorgisl ran at one of them and struck with his sword as she was heaving the load on her back, and slashed off her arm close to the shoulder.

So they got the carcass for themselves and had enough food from it for the rest of the winter, but had nearly run out by the time spring came. Then they set off again, sometimes dragging their boat over land-fast ice and sometimes over moving pack ice. That summer they got as far south as the Seal Islands, and there they wintered.

At the beginning of the next summer they set off again. They dragged their boat over ice until stopped by certain cliffs, whereupon they set up their tent and stayed there, but were almost out of food.

One morning Col came out of the tent and found their boat gone! He dared not tell Thorgisl, considering his leader's worries were great enough. Finally Thorgisl came out and, looking around, saw the boat was gone. "Now," he cried, "I don't see how we can survive, so the best thing we can do with the boy Thorfinn is to kill him."

Thorleif pleaded that there was no reason to take such drastic action, but

Thorgisl insisted it be done. Col and Thorleif took the boy off, but could not bring themselves to kill him and so brought him back, and Thorgisl thanked them. "You have stopped me from committing a great crime. I would ever after have been considered a worthless man. But I am not myself."

One day they came out of the tent and saw two natives with their missing boat. The natives made off without it. Now they continued working their way out of the fiords in which they were trapped. Finally they got into open water [Davis Strait]. They were exhausted and terribly thirsty. Then Starkad said, "I have heard that thirsty men have mixed salt water and urine." So they took the bilge scoop, urinated in it and mixed it with sea water. But Thorgisl took the bilge scoop and threw the stuff overboard. At that moment they saw drift ice, rowed to it, got water from it, and went on their way.

Thorgisl's little band rowed and sailed east in the open water of Davis Strait until they reached the west coast of Greenland. After spending this fifth winter with a Norse family outlawed from Erik the Red's settlement, they continued south to a much-belated reunion with Erik.

Their stay in Greenland was short. Thorgisl had had enough of this new world so he and his companions took passage on a ship bound for Iceland. Just before reaching home, the vessel was caught in a terrible storm and the boy Thorfinn, who had lived through so much, was drowned.

Thorgisl nearly went out of his mind with grief. Even after they had made land safely he would not be parted from the body of his son. He had to be tricked into leaving it, whereupon Col took it to the graveyard and buried it. Thorgisl threatened to kill him for that, but later came to his senses and they were reconciled.

Then Thorgisl said it was no wonder that women loved the children they had nursed at their own breasts better than they could love anyone else.

CHAPTER THIRTEEN

Sweetie Pie

CLYDE RIVER (CLYDE, AS IT IS GENERALLY CALLED) crouched in a cove on the north side of the inlet of the same name. Diminished almost to the vanishing point by the fiord's majestic cliffs, by the massy loom of the Barnes Ice Cap to the west, and by the lofty headland of Cape Christian hanging over it, Clyde gave the impression of a mouse effacing itself in the presence of a herd of elephants.

Splashing down in the cove, we dropped anchor and waited for someone to come and ferry us ashore.

Nobody came.

Several boats and canoes lay drawn up on the beach and people were coming and going about their business, but apart from an occasional glance we were ignored.

"What the fuck's wrong with them?" Doug asked plaintively. "Deaf *and* blind?"

"Maybe they think we're another lot from DNA," Pete suggested.

Since our shouts for assistance went unheeded, we had no choice but to haul up the anchor and paddle DCL to shore using our one real paddle and a snow shovel. This made for an ignominious arrival.

I asked a burly fellow busy rolling oil drums up the beach where I could find the area administrator.

"*Atchoo*," he sneezed without looking at me.

I recognized this as "don't know" in Inuktitut.

"Police?"

"*Atchoo.*"

This unrewarding exchange was interrupted by the arrival of a slightly built young white man who actually smiled at me.

"Hi. Name's Philip Cove. Welcome to Clyde."

"Thanks. But if this is a welcome, what happens if they don't like you?"

He laughed. "Don't take it personally. The Eskimos hereabouts are the most independent characters in the eastern Arctic. They've seen so many planes and ships since the Yanks started building their radar station on top of Cape Christian, they likely wouldn't look up if a moon rocket landed. As for the whites, well, there's only five of us: the Mountie, two teachers, the Bay manager, and me. The teachers are down south for the summer, and the Mountie and the Bay guy aren't on speaking terms so they mostly stay home sulking. Come on up to my place and have a drink...if you've brought any."

We followed him to his recently built, handsomely furnished, pre-cut-log bungalow.

"Not my place really. Belongs to the administrator, if and when Clyde gets one. I'm just here on four months' contract to DNA. Supposed to evaluate the economic prospects for the area and come up with plans for, I quote, 'viable implementation.'

"Actually, I've just finished my B.Sc. in geology at University of Calgary and what I don't know about economics would fill a bunch of books. But I needed a summer job, and DNA hired me."

Cove may not have been a trained economist, but he was a sharp-eyed observer. Aided by a bilingual camp boss named Kudluk, who had effectively adopted him, Cove had garnered a great deal of knowledge about the Clyde people in particular, and the inhabitants of the vast stretch of fiord-riven coast between Cape Dyer and Pond Inlet in general. Moreover, he was happy to share what he had learned.

The Eskimos on this coast have a funny history. You've likely noticed as the arctic pack drifts south it sets against the coast and that means they're cut off from sea traffic most of the time. In the old days traders and missionaries often couldn't get in at all so this coast pretty much got left alone until the war brought in the military to build radio stations for planes being ferried to England. And after the war, DEW Line sites to keep track of what the Russkies were doing.

That meant icebreakers and airstrips, and the coast got opened up a bit. Three so-called settlements—a U.S. airbase and two DEW Line stations—got started at Broughton, Padloping Island [both well to the south], and here at Clyde.

The natives never used to live in settlements. They lived in groups of up to half a dozen families—what old northern hands call camps. They were scattered all along six hundred miles of coast. They moved inland to more open country near the head of the fiords in summer for fishing, caribou hunting, and berry picking. Come fall they went back out to the coast for seal, walrus, narwhal, and polar bear.

That's how the most of them still live. There's close to six hundred Eskimos between here and Cape Dyer, and less than a hundred live in the settlements. The rest are out in the camps, not because they have to be, but because they want to.

It's the way they like it. They've got what the books call a subsistence economy. Most of what they need they catch and use themselves. Being so isolated they never got mixed up much in the fur trade, so they don't bother much with that. When a man gets a seal, chances are it'll all be used by his family, or some other family, and no trader will ever see hide or hair of it.

HBC men figure Clyde's a dead-end posting because there's so little business. About all the natives bring the trader is the occasional bear hide, and a few fox skins if they happen to have some spare time and feel like a little trapping. Last year they only traded 105 foxes at Clyde and the post manager got so depressed the Company had to ship him out.

These people don't seem to want most of what we've got and, so far, we haven't been able to make them want it. If all of us whites pulled out tomorrow the natives would hardly know we'd gone. Oh, I guess they'd miss their tea and tobacco and flour, and hunting would be harder without guns and ammo, but they'd get by.

They just aren't into the cash economy. Not yet. But, of course, sooner or later that's the way they've got to go. My job this summer is to see how the local resources can be converted into cash. I can tell you I don't see many ways to do that. We've started a little handicraft industry, mostly making Ookpiks—owl dolls—out of stray bits of seal skin and feathers, and embroidered kamikpac—sealskin boots—to sell to the Americans at Cape Christian base. But you couldn't support more than a couple of families on the cash from that.

The fur trade? Nope. This ain't great fur country at the best of times. Maybe something could be done harvesting sea mammals like walrus, but where's the market? And anyway, if you started killing the sea animals on a commercial scale you'd soon end up the way the whalers did—killing off their own business.

Communications is the biggest obstacle to changing things. Almost everything has to come in by sealift but you never know when the ships are going to make it, or if they are. Air transport is pretty well out, except for emergencies. Can you imagine what it'd cost to put all-weather landing strips in a country like this? There are a few, but they belong to the military and they're mostly in the wrong places for the native people anyway. It's tough to run a business here when you never can tell if you can ship your product out or not.

To tell you the truth, I don't really see any other way for people here to make a living except off the land. More or less the same way they've always done. Sure, they can have better boats and hunting gear, and medical attention available, and other stuff, but their real jobs would be doing what they've always done, and really like doing.

I'm likely going to say just about that in my report. Which means I'll never get another job with DNA. But what the hell, I'm going to be an oil geologist anyhow.

We've got about twelve Eskimo housing units here now. The plan is to put up twenty more, if the ship gets in this year. In a couple of years the plan is to have all the camp people living permanently at Clyde or Broughton. There'll be maybe two hundred and fifty to three hundred people here then, depending on how many kids get born meantime.

It's not up to me to say if that's a good idea or not. It's how it's going to be. Makes administration a whole lot easier, and maintaining an infrastructure— electricity, sewage, that sort of thing—possible. But the main reason for it, so the story goes, is education. All the kids will get to go to school. They'll go up to what passes for Grade 6 here in Clyde, then go outside for as long as it takes. The principal teacher here told me: "Maybe it's tough on the old folk, but it's the only way their kids are going to survive in the real world." You could ask Kudluk what he thinks about it.

We walked through the little community to Kudluk's summer camp which, for generations, had been pitched on the shores of the bay near where Clyde now stood. Kudluk's home was a ten-by-twelve-foot wall tent of stained canvas with a rusted length of stove pipe poking out through its roof. Seven large and friendly dogs were staked in a semi-circle facing the doorway. Kudluk, a robust man of about fifty with deep-set black eyes and a surprisingly long, straight nose, emerged to greet us and invite us inside where his comely young wife was hurriedly blowing up the embers in a sheet-iron camp stove, bringing a kettle to the boil.

We drank quantities of sweet, black tea while Cove brought the conversation around to the impending centralization. Kudluk's English was adequate but he preferred his own tongue so Pete translated.

"Inuit lived around here in my father's father's time," Kudluk related. "They liked it here. *We* have liked it too. We, the men and women who live here now. We do not want to change the way we live but the *kablunait* say we must. They say all Inuit must give up the camp life and come and live in Clyde because our children need to go to school. We older people don't want to have to live in these cold wooden *kablunait* houses all winter, but the *kablunait* say we must. For the sake of our children.

"Well, you know, we love our children very much, so what can we do? For our children we will have to do it. *Ayorama*—it can't be helped. It will be very hard."

"So," I said as Cove and I walked back toward the administrator's house, "it's clear what Kudluk thinks, but what do the youngsters have to say about it?"

"You can find out right now. See that pretty girl coming along dressed like she was in Montreal or Calgary? Her name's Elizabet. Ask her what *she* thinks."

Elizabet was fifteen, and flaunting it. She wore flame-coloured lipstick, a scarlet and blue, satin-textured sports jacket, and pink slacks. From the beach where he was pumping gas into DCL's tanks, I heard Roy whistle his appreciation. Elizabet was carrying a large, braided basket with a fitted cover. I started the conversation by asking if she had just been shopping at the Bay.

"No," she said, a ready smile exposing gleaming teeth. "I've got Sweetie Pie in here," and she proudly lifted the lid.

A fuzzy white kitten blinked milky blue eyes at me then stood up as if the better to display the garish purple ribbon around its neck.

"Good God! This must be the only cat on Baffin Island!" I exclaimed.

"If not in the whole eastern Arctic," Cove added. "A cat's got about as much chance of surviving the dogs up here as a fart in a windstorm. You know that, don't you, Elizabet?"

"Oh sure. But I don't go out to the camps and live in a smelly old tent with all them dogs around. There's no dogs running around in Clyde. If there is, the Mountie shoots them. I stay with my aunt that works for the teachers. Lives in a new house the government give her. It's pretty small but it's got electricity and a shower."

"You don't like camp life?" I asked.

"Ugh! It's so dirty. I throw up with the stink of old seal skins. If *you* like raw fish, *you* can eat it! I can't wait 'til the plane takes me back to school in Ottawa. My three friends and me share an apartment there. It's got everything, even colour TV, and Sweetie Pie's safe down there."

"What do you plan on doing after you finish school?"

"*Atchoo.* Maybe go south for good."

"And do what?"

"*Atchoo*... but for sure I don't want to go back to any camp up here no more."

"And there you have it," Cove commented as Elizabet closed the lid on Sweetie Pie and walked nonchalantly away. "None of the girls I've met who are going to school down south want to come back here to live. Some don't even want to visit. What would Elizabet *do* if she came back? There's no job for her, and she sure won't make a hunter a good wife because, after five or six years away, she just isn't on the ball when it comes to playing a wife's role up here.

"It's not much different for the boys. After five years south some of them can hardly even speak Inuktitut. They are pretty useless as hunters, but don't want to admit that and don't want to learn. They think that's old stuff! But there's almost no other kind of work for them.

"The thing is, not many of the Eskimos I hear about who went south seem happy there. So what's the future going to be? Darned if I know but it looks like either they stay south and are miserable, or they come back and are miserable here."

Doug had gone off to the radio station. When he rejoined us, a frown was shading his usually placid countenance.

"Weather guys say all kinds of shit's going to dump on Clyde tonight. We could be socked in for a week. Better get out while we can."

I glanced apprehensively at the sky, which was already hazing over. Pete nodded affirmation. Docilely we followed the captain to his ship.

DCL climbed past Cape Christian with its disfiguring pustule of a radar station and turned northwest toward the next settlement—Pond

Inlet, 260 miles distant. To seaward of us an armada of icebergs lay locked in a matrix of solid arctic pack, embargoing the coast more effectively than a fleet of battleships could have done. It was a blockade which this year would not be broken until mid-September, and then only through the determined efforts of one of Canada's most powerful icebreakers.

A wall of fog was rolling in from the far-distant open water in Baffin Bay. It was going to be a close thing whether we reached Pond before the bad weather did. Doug kept nudging the throttle forward until it was well past our usual cruising speed. DCL seemed to shake a bit more than normal, but otherwise gave no indication she was engaged in a race.

We had been airborne less than half an hour when Doug switched on the intercom.

"We got outta *there* just in time. Clyde's socked in already. Hope Pond stays open 'cause we ain't got nowhere else to lay our little heads."

The cloud ceiling was descending inexorably, forcing us closer and closer to the towering coastal ramparts. It was a great, if transient, relief to fly out over the mountain-free mouth of felicitously named but fiercely formidable Sam Ford Fiord.

Sam's fiord slices eighty miles inland to the foot of the Barnes Ice Cap, walled for much of its length by ebony cliffs a thousand feet high. Beyond this horrendous slash in the hide of Mother Earth the Baffin coast juts eastward to form the massive Cape Adair Peninsula. Doug would have preferred to outflank Cape Adair by following the coast, but fog was already engulfing its sea cliffs. There was nothing for it but to shape a course across the base of the bulge.

Soon we were in the midst of the Bruce Mountains, a tangle of white-headed peaks, octopus-armed glaciers, and crumbling moraines. The overcast pressing down upon us forced us to fly ever closer to the "deck," at one point thundering through ice canyons well below the crests of their containing glaciers. I cannot speak for my companions but *my* relief when we at last emerged over Dexterity Fiord was nearly as monumental as our surroundings.

Dexterity's several sinuous arms (two of which are fifty miles in length) were mostly ice-choked but there were a few open patches.

Doug would later tell me he had found these stretches of open water almost irresistible.

"Sure would have liked to set down for a while. Only I figured we might be stuck 'til hell froze over."

The Dexterity Fiord complex has been visited by few white men. Nineteenth-century whaling ships occasionally sought shelter in its outer reaches, but its inner fastnesses were seldom plumbed. In 1894 the Dundee whaler *Terra Nova* did steam some distance down one arm of the fiord and came upon a native settlement. A boat was launched and a party sent ashore. The whalers found themselves in a "village" whose only occupants were the skeletons of thirty or forty people surrounded by hunting and household gear, including an umiak and several kayaks.

There were no indications of violence. The mystery deepened when the visitors opened some caches and found quantities of decayed animal skins, fat, meat, and bones. Starvation had not been the killer.

When the boat's crew reported what they had found, their captain made a laconic note in the log then turned *Terra Nova* about and headed back to the open sea. He suspected the natives had died of plague. He may not have been far wrong, though it could have been measles, smallpox, influenza, or any one of several scourges brought to Baffin Island by European and American whalers; these diseases were all fiercely lethal to native peoples.

Ninety-five years after *Terra Nova* made her macabre discovery, and twenty-three years after I flew over the place in DCL, Claire and I entered Dexterity Fiord aboard a small cruise vessel. The waters were still uncharted so the skipper proceeded warily, radar, depth sounders, satellite-positioning gadgets, and other electronic marvels pinging and flashing excitedly from the bridge consoles.

A party of ring seals accompanied our cautious progress as I watched from the bows. They were remarkably trusting, considering that their kind have been prime prey for arctic peoples since time immemorial. They reared high, the better to peer up at the huge interloper.

The nearly vertical cliffs that hemmed us in were even more awesome as seen from sea level than from the air. Occasional ice tongues from unseen glaciers pierced the towering walls. There was no sign of terrestrial life except for greenish discolorations on the brute rock surfaces where lichens clung.

Having penetrated some thirty miles into this gloomy domain of fissured rock and ice, we rounded a bend and suddenly discovered ourselves in an arctic Shangri-la. Before us lay a mile-long curve of sandy beach backed by rolling tundra prairie through which a small river traced a shimmering course into the fiord. The whole was framed by ice-rimmed mountains at a sufficient distance that they did not dominate this hidden Eden.

Several hundred snow geese which had been feeding on grasses and sedges just beyond the beach launched themselves toward us and passed overhead so close I could see their glittering black eyes. Distant movement on the tundra resolved itself into a herd of placidly grazing caribou who seemed quite unperturbed by our arrival on their scene.

The anchor chain paid out and we boarded rubber boats and headed for shore. Archaeologist Maxwell Moreau and I were in the lead boat. We had not gone far before he grabbed my arm with one hand while pointing with the other.

"See those hummocks on the ridge beside the beach? I'll bet a bottle of the best that's an old Thule occupation site! Yes, by the Lord, you can see the whalebone rafters!"

We counted eight large, mossy mounds, from each of which massive bones protruded as if from the graves of ancient monsters. Moreau was so excited he could not wait for the boat to nose up on land, but jumped over the side into the frigid water and splashed ashore at a run. When I joined him he was ecstatic.

"Look at it! Pure Thule. Four or five hundred years old and just the way they left it. Never been scavenged for bone by Eskimo carvers, or for souvenirs by bloody tourists!"

Indeed, apart from the fact that the sod coverings of the roofs had long since collapsed, these semi-subterranean stone houses were virtually intact. We could, and did, crawl into some through stone-lined entrance tunnels to lie upon the mossy sleeping ledges and try to imagine what life might have been like here in Thule times. Soot deposits from soapstone cooking lamps still discoloured the walls of a cooking niche. Protruding from the thin layer of slow-growing moss upon the floor of one house was an ivory harpoon head of the kind Thule people had used for killing walrus and small whales.

Judging from the size of a nearby midden heap, Max concluded people might have been living at this site since the twelfth century, which is when the first Thule migrants from the west are believed to have reached Baffin Island.

"And," he added as he peered into an old cache pile, "descendants of those first settlers may have been living here, in these very houses, until a century ago. You can see this must have been a good place to live for a very long time."

Indeed, the Thule houses were not totally abandoned even yet. While poking around in them I encountered several stubby little lemmings. They did not seem resentful of my intrusion. Who knows? Perhaps they were happy to see the return of the big, bifurcated animals who had built these lemming palaces in the first place.

Claire joined me and we walked to the mouth of the little river, half a mile away. Here, on an ancient raised beach now three hundred yards from the water's edge, we noticed several ill-defined depressions. Moreau identified these as Dorset house sites. Flint flakes abounded near them and we found several of the tiny artifacts called microliths, which Dorset people used as weapon points, knives, and scrapers. Max hazarded a guess that the site might have been occupied by Dorset, and even pre-Dorset, people for two or three thousand years before these first settlers were displaced by incoming Thule.

Thule people had not been the most recent human inhabitants.

An Inuit encampment sprawled across a portion of the beach close to the present shore of the fiord. Someday it, too, may qualify as an archaeological site but when we saw it, it was an arctic garbage dump. The gravelly ground was strewn with bones and bits of skin and sinew from caribou, seals, foxes, and dogs. Pieces of defunct snowmobiles, ten-gallon gasoline drums, old rubber boots, countless tin cans, strips and chunks of multi-hued plastic, and scraps of manufactured clothing littered a site where circular skin *topays* might have stood in *Terra Nova*'s day. If so, they had been replaced in our time by canvas wall tents with plywood floors and sheet-iron stoves.

The most abundant artifacts were hundreds and hundreds of Pampers, which lay where they had been blown into drifts and windrows. Organic decay comes slowly in the cold and arid Arctic, so those Pampers will doubtless continue to signal the arrival of modernity in the hidden fastnesses of Dexterity Fiord for a long time to come.

There was other evidence that the last occupants had been fully abreast of the times. It included a used tube of crab (louse) killer; a fancy pink polyester brassiere, slightly torn; and a large, empty scotch bottle.

"Must have been quite a party," Claire murmured as we headed back to our boat.

CHAPTER FOURTEEN

Jonasee and Paulasee

DCL'S ONGOING FLIGHT TOWARD POND INLET WAS made ever more difficult by the baleful Baffin Bay fog that forced us away from the coast and into a morass of peaks and snowfields northwest of Coutts Inlet. These features showed on our aeronautical charts only as dotted lines overlaid with the legend: RELIEF DATA INCOMPLETE. Fortunately Doug was not navigating by the map. He was flying, as he admitted later, "by guess and by God!"

At 6:00 p.m. the Otter skirted the shoulder of a nameless glacier behind Mount Herodier and finally broke out above ice- and fog-free waters.

Thirty or forty single-storey buildings were strung out along a pre-cipitous slope on a southern shore below a huge sign made of white-washed boulders spelling out the words POND INLET. We had reached the metropolis of Canada's Far North.

We taxied to a floating dock where a glum young white man curtly informed me I had to see the administrator. "Right now! And better not keep him waiting."

I expected trouble, but administrator Gordon Rogers and his wife, Grace, turned out to be as welcoming and hospitable as northerners usually are. They served us dinner (literally with candlelight and wine) in the new house DNA had just built for them and apologized for the coolness of our initial reception.

"Since word of Murray Watts's plans for the Mary River iron mine got out," Mrs. Rogers explained, "we've been plagued with droppers-in.

Journalists, mining promoters, radio reporters, even an Otter full of Japanese steel makers. Gordon has to be especially careful what he says. He's a civil servant, you know, and Ottawa has long ears."

"Yes," I agreed, "*and* long claws. But what's happening at Mary River? You can tell me. I'll be discreet."

Rogers looked dubious. "You? Discreet? Well, never mind. Watts himself is on his way here from Resolute in his Cessna. Should be arriving any time. He'll be happy to tell you all about his mine."

A legend in the north (and in stock exchanges), Watts was an old-time prospector, but very modern promoter, whose companies were currently "developing" a vast iron ore deposit at Mary River on Milne Inlet in the Eclipse Sound complex southwest of Pond.

Half an hour later his little Cessna splashed down and moored alongside DCL. It would remain, the pilot said, only long enough to refuel before heading south. However, when I shamelessly told Watts I was gathering material for a documentary about northern development, he made time for an interview.

A smallish man with a large presence and the gift of the gab, he looked as if he would have felt equally at home staking a mine or sitting at a desk in a Bay Street office.

So you've heard about Mary River. Everyone will before long. This is the biggest, most significant iron ore deposit in the world, except maybe for one in South America. And the richest. We've already proved reserves of 127 million tons that're 65 to 68 per cent pure iron. The stuff doesn't need pre-treatment. You can feed it straight into the smelter. And Mary River is only the tip of the [he chuckled] ironberg. The ore body runs all the way south down Baffin Island pretty near to Hudson Strait. Enough to keep the Baffin Island Ore and Iron Mines Company in business for a hundred years.

We've been given a great deal of encouragement by Northern Affairs and particularly by the minister, Mr. Arthur Laing, to use Eskimos as labourers, skilled workers, and even technicians....The number of people employed in construction we would estimate at two thousand. The number permanently employed, five or six hundred, which would mean a population at Milne Inlet of two thousand to twenty-five hundred people. When we double the initial production to 2.5 million tonnes we'll double the population. That will easily take care of employment of the whole Eskimo population in the eastern Arctic. Though, of course, some skilled workers will have to be brought up from the South.

Capital costs will be high, naturally, which is the reason this development must have government financial help until we can make out on our own. This is a breakthrough proposition. You see, once Baffin Island Ore and Iron Mines gets operating, the way will open up to develop many other deposits that have already been found up here, including lead, zinc, copper, and even some precious metals.

Of course it is a short shipping season. Only about two and a half months, which means you have to get a lot of ore out in a short time. The answer is giant ore carriers, ships of from 150,000 tons up to 500,000 tons. That way we'll be able to stockpile for eight months and get it all out during the open-water season. We also count on federal government icebreakers. One of them, the d'Iberville, is down in Milne Inlet right now testing ice conditions.

I tell you, Mr. Mowat, in ten years this part of the world will be right at the centre of things. Lancaster Sound could be as busy a ship channel as any in the world, with oil, liquid gas, iron, and base metals going west through the Northwest Passage to the Pacific, and manufactured goods coming back into the Atlantic. Keep your eyes on it!

The Cessna pilot had an anxious eye on us. He was in a hurry to be on his way for it had begun to drizzle; the fog was closing in, and daylight was fading fast. Watts was clearly reluctant to leave an open microphone, but eventually the Cessna taxied out and took off.

Rogers had a somewhat different view of northern development.

Resource extraction is certainly on all our minds, these days. I don't believe it's all bound to happen, though, or that every Eskimo wants to become a miner. We've got other possibilities. There's a great potential for tourism. We've got a great fisheries potential. Greenland sharks, for instance. They're plentiful, and we're looking into markets for their meat and skin, as well as for the livers, which are full of vitamin A.

We've also got one of the few concentrations of narwhals in the world. Apart from the sale of its tusk for ivory carving and such like, the Hudson's Bay Company has started buying the skins, which make a very fine leather.

There's room for efficient and expanded utilization of all the wildlife resources. Sport and trophy hunting for caribou, musk ox, polar bears, wolves, seals, walrus. Even some kinds of whales could become moneymakers again the way they used to be. But education is going to be very important so these enterprises can be cost-

effective and sustaining. A non-educated Eskimo may make the better hunter, but an educated Eskimo will make more money. Whatever we get—mines or millionaires wanting to shoot polar bears—giving the Eskimo a good education will make the difference in how well he does.

Rogers's bailiwick embraced a territory extending six hundred miles east to west and about five hundred north to south, including the three settlements at Pond Inlet, Grise Fiord, and Arctic Bay.

Grise Fiord is a mere slit in the mountainous coast of Ellesmere Island. In 1966 it was inhabited by two DNA employees, two RCMP constables, and ninety-three Inuit. Of these not one was a native of Ellesmere Island itself. In fact this vast extension of the Icie Mountains, stretching north from Jones Sound into the polar basin, had been uninhabited throughout historic times until 1922 when RCMP outposts were established at Grise and Alexandra fiords as a demonstration of Canadian sovereignty in the face of Norwegian claims to the high Arctic islands. However these toeholds proved so difficult to maintain that they were soon abandoned.

In 1951 the Hudson's Bay Company planted a trading post at Grise in order to harvest Ellesmere's untouched fur resources. With Ottawa's blessing the Company inveigled two unrelated groups of Inuit—one from Pond Inlet and the other from distant Port Harrison on the east coast of Hudson Bay—into allowing themselves to be transported to Grise which then became one of the most isolated human communities in the world.

The new outpost was intended to serve the HBC's commercial interests while establishing a Canadian presence in a region where U.S. military activity was proliferating, often without Ottawa's knowledge or blessing. The experiment proved disastrous for the natives. Hemmed in by mountains and glaciers, they were unable to find enough animals to feed themselves, or to pay for what they needed from the trader. Becoming more and more dependant on welfare for sheer survival, they pleaded with their white guardians to return them to their old homes; but their pleas fell on deaf ears.

Rogers did not wish to talk to me about Grise Fiord, although others at Pond Inlet were more forthcoming.

"Place is a hell-hole," I was told by a man who had flown relief supplies to it. "More like a Russian gulag. Why do you think they keep *two* Mounties up there? You ought to look into it."

I would have done so, except that Lamb Airways would not cooperate. When asked why he would not fly me to Grise, Doug simply shrugged his shoulders. He knew that I knew that all northern air charter outfits relied heavily on DNA contracts. I did not press the matter.

The second of Rogers's three communities was Arctic Bay, 160 miles west of Pond on the shore of Admiralty Inlet. In 1966 Admiralty Inlet's 250 inhabitants were a famously self-sufficient people. Two thirds of them were still living in camps scattered across some thousands of square miles. The single tiny settlement, at Arctic Bay, had only one white resident, the HBC post manager.

"They're old-style people at Arctic," Rogers told me. "They like to go their own way and they can be mulish if pushed too hard. I predict they'll be the last Eskimos in this part of the world to come over to the side of progress."

He could hardly have been more wrong.

Bad weather kept us from visiting Arctic Bay in 1966, but when I did get there two decades later, it was to find a shabby, native adjunct to a mining operation, cursed with all the ailments that afflict such communities. Glass from broken pop and liquor bottles; tin cans; plastic debris and waste paper littered the rocky ground. The sprawl of unpainted and dilapidated houses was crammed with and surrounded by cheap consumer goods, much of which had never had any real function here and were already broken and discarded. Every male over ten seemed to have an all-terrain vehicle and to be spending most of his time astride it. Countless snowmobiles in various stages of disrepair were strewn about awaiting the attention of some non-existent junk dealer. Amongst them were several rusty pick-up trucks which could only be driven on the twenty miles of dusty gravel road linking the settlement with the mining site at Nanisivik.

Nanisivik was a base metal mine owned by Texas Gulf. It was the only producing mine among the many potential El Dorados whose praises had been sung by Murray Watts. It had proved to be worth exploiting only because it held a lode of extremely rich ore which was relatively accessible and so could be mined in what amounted to a high-grading operation.

With the opening of Nanisivik the Inuit of Admiralty Inlet were encouraged, not to say suborned, into settling at Arctic Bay to provide a cheap source of local labout. Their contribution was invaluable to the profitability of the mine, but by 1989 the lode of high-grade ore had been nearly exhausted and the word was out that Nanisivik was soon to be "rendered inactive"—which meant abandoned.

At the time of my visit the few Inuit who still had jobs worked mostly underground or at menial surface tasks. The majority were unemployed; they and their families existing chiefly on welfare and relief. The once self-reliant out-camps had become no more than memories. Drunkenness was endemic and solvent sniffing an increasingly popular pasttime, especially among the children.

The only significant relationships these people still maintained with their land was "recreational hunting," which entailed the use of high-powered outboards and snowmobiles to procure what amounted to token quantities of country food.

Pond Inlet in 1966 seemed a potentially viable attempt at implementing the Northern Vision. Pleasantly situated along a curving shoreline, it faced a panoramic view of icy peaks on Bylot Island just across Eclipse Sound down whose broad reach a stately procession of icebergs paraded. Pond's mostly new buildings were still neat and tidy-looking. The three hundred or so native inhabitants seemed robust, reasonably contented, and in no way lacking in self-esteem. Rogers gave most of the credit for this happy state of affairs to his predecessor.

"Bill Barry was administrator here when the centralization policy was first being implemented, and he didn't believe in pushing Eskimos too fast. When the first housing units arrived, he not only allowed, he *encouraged*, people to put some of them out at the camps rather than mass them all here in the community.

"As a matter of fact, he made it an unwritten rule that no one *could* live in the settlement unless he had a full-time job here. The result was that everyone continued to be pretty well self-supporting, either from cash earned at work or from what they took off the land, or a combination of both.

"I've relaxed that rule, but do strongly recommend that anyone coming to live in the settlement bear in mind that he's got to have a job or else go hunting seriously. Welfare just is not given out here unless it's a case of real need."

One of the most pervasive and enduring tragedies of Inuit life in modern times has been the ravages wrought by tuberculosis. The so-called White Killer rampaged across the north almost unimpeded until after World War II when Ottawa finally took effective cognizance of it.

Doctors accompanying government ships then began searching out its victims. The most severely afflicted were shipped south to sanitaria.

Many of those in whom the disease was too far advanced to be curable died in the south, often without contact with their distant families, and sometimes without even the solace of the presence of any other Inuit. In consequence, natives throughout the north greatly feared evacuation to a southern hospital, considering it tantamount to a death sentence.

By the 1960s diagnosis and treatment had so far improved that patients, especially younger ones, stood a good chance of recovery. One such was Jonasee, a young Pond Inlet man.

I eighteen now. When I six I get TB and sent down south to the San. Went in government ship to Quebec, then in train to Mountain San in Hamilton. At first was pretty scary being so far away from family, but was away four years so I forget a lot about them.

They treat me good in the San. That's where I pick up English. They had a school there. When I was cured I got sent back to Pond and out to my family's camp.

I cry all the way home. Not want to go back to the camp because not same there. I could not speak much Inuktitut any more and couldn't understand a lot the old people said. Was ten and couldn't work dogs, or hunt like other boys in camp. Some people laugh at me. Others try to help and after a while I'm feeling glad to be home again.

When I eleven I kill my first seal and that make me feel pretty good but I want to go more to school. So my parents left the camp and went in to Pond to live so I could go to school that started up there.

A few years after that a doctor on the ship found out I had TB again. This time have to go down to Toronto. Was there a year. Very hot place down there, specially summertime. This time I glad to go north again, but now was in Grade 8 and there's no Grade 8 in Pond.

On the way back to Pond, in the ship, social worker ask if I want to go to school in Churchill in Manitoba. I agree with her, so was only home a month and they fly me to Churchill. Was two years there, with about one month back in Pond each summer.

Yesterday I got something special in mail. Grade 9 diploma! So I go back to Churchill, maybe next week if plane comes. Stay there 'til get Senior Matriculation, if I can.

Churchill's pretty good. Dances and movies and lots of things to do. Some kids get homesick, but not me 'cause I already been away from home so much. Just about anywhere is home now.

My parents run hostel here in Pond for camp kids coming to school. My brother and sister go to school here, but last spring three doctors came on government ship C.D. Howe with special X-ray machines, and find thirteen more people here got TB. One is my young sister. Now she in Toronto. Was big shock to everybody that all that TB was still here. Kind of shattering.

Asked how he felt about the traditional ways of Eskimo life, Jonasee replied:

Never heard too much about that because old people couldn't talk English, so never got to know real Eskimo stuff. Sure, I go hunting sometime. With snowmobile. But mostly go for fun. Guess I'd pretty near starve if I had to live off the land.

Sure don't want to go back to camp life. If I can I'll go to vocational school at Churchill. Learn carpentry, metalwork, mechanics. The girls get home economics. I don't think them girls could come back and marry a hunter in the camps, but they could marry a man working at a job in the mines, like I hope to get.

One afternoon Rogers took me in his outboard-powered canoe to visit a camp twenty miles east of the settlement. The waters of Eclipse Sound were so still and cold they looked like congealing oil. Tattered grey cloud hung motionless upon the peaks and glaciers of Bylot Island to the north and upon the ice caps to the south. Shreds of mist draped Mount Herodier, looming over the place we were headed for.

The camp consisted of one hut made of old packing crates, three DNA "issue" houses of the cracker-box variety, two tents, and a semi-subterranean old-style house built with walls of stone and sod. This last, the reincarnation of an ancient Thule dwelling, was currently occupied by a gaunt old fellow named Angatiuk, notable for his scraggly white beard and piercing black eyes almost hidden in a tangle of wrinkles.

Rogers guessed Angatiuk was about sixty-five. As camp boss he welcomed us into his rather dank and rankly smelling sod house. We drank tea with him and his equally elderly wife while he showed us some crude but powerful carvings he had done in narwhal ivory.

One portrayed a hunter in a kayak throwing a bird spear; another, a polar bear brought to bay by a dog. A third was an inscrutable female figure. I asked who she might be. Angatiuk spoke no English, but Rogers identified the carving as a representation of Sredna, the powerful spirit who rules the undersea world.

"The old chap is supposed to be a Christian," Rogers explained later. "Church of England. But he wasn't always one, and the old beliefs die hard...*if* they die."

Full of tea, we went down to the nearby shore where several people were cutting up a narwhal killed the previous day. A semicircle of dogs waiting hopefully for scraps made way for us without complaint.

"Camp people seldom tied their dogs," Rogers noted. "They claimed it made them mean. The dogs lived in and about the camp and would send packing any hungry bears that got too close. Snowmobiles won't do that for you." This last with a glance at a brand-new snow machine still in its crate.

A squat middle-aged man with a rifle slung on his back shyly offered us some narwhal muktuk. I reciprocated by extending my tobacco pouch. He filled a capacious pipe before shuffling along the beach to take up a lonely stance on a point jutting into the sound. His name was Paulasee.

"He's had bad luck," Rogers told me. "This summer the medics on the *C.D. Howe* found his whole family—his wife and both his daughters—have TB. So they've all been sent south and now Paulasee's afraid he'll never see any of them again. We've all told him different but I don't think he believes us. He's in a bad state, really. Sits around fooling with his rifle. I worry about him. He wouldn't be the first chap up here to do himself in because his family got sent away."

It began to rain as we headed back toward Pond. Fulmars wheeled through the grey murk like disembodied spirits. A ring seal surfaced close ahead, peering myopically at us before slipping back into Sredna's realm.

On the chance the seal might reappear, Rogers stopped the engine. In the ensuing silence we heard the distant, hollow reverberation of a rifle-shot echoing from the direction of Mount Herodier.

"Likely someone taking a crack at a narwhal," Rogers said, but his voice lacked conviction.

I suspect he too was thinking of Paulasee, sitting on the shore in the spectral gloom, cradling his gun.

Lost Leviathan

M Y FIRST ENCOUNTER WITH POND INLET PEOPLE took place at Churchill in 1947. I was sheltering from a late-summer blizzard in the bar of the Hudson Hotel when a worker from the grain elevator stomped in, demanding everyone's attention.

"You guys oughta get down to the pier! They's a goddamn whale there big as a friggin' boxcar!"

Twenty minutes later the pier was fringed with people, myself among them, parka hood pulled up against the freezing spindrift. Next to me three young Inuit men in white men's clothing hunched their shoulders. They had been flown south from Pond Inlet two months earlier to be trained as truck drivers for a high-arctic radar site, and they were seriously homesick. When I had first met them earlier in the day, they had been morose and withdrawn; now they could hardly contain their excitement.

"Eeee! Yisss! *Arvek!* The Great One! Look you!"

The frigid waters heaved, and there it was: a glistening blue-black monster as massive as an upturned ship looming through the storm murk not a hundred yards from the concrete cliff on which we stood. I heard a muffled *whooooooffff* as steamy jets spouted twenty feet into the air and blew back upon us, bringing a touch of warmth and a rank, fishy smell.

The Inuit were beside themselves.

"Breathe well!" they shouted. "Be strong! Go north!"

The whale spouted three times then sounded, seeming to roll down into the depths like a living wheel. The snow thickened and we saw nothing more of Arvek.

The Pond Inlet men joined me back in the bar. What we had witnessed, they told me, was the greatest being in their world. In their forefathers' times, Arvek had been everywhere saltwater flowed: "In all the bays, all the channels. So many, nobody could count them!" Then, they told me, big ships began arriving on the Baffin coast—sailing ships first, followed by steam vessels. A decimation of the great whales ensued. Now so few remained that Pond Inlet people counted themselves lucky to see a single one during the course of several years.

I count myself lucky to have had that long-ago glimpse of the leviathan at Churchill. *Balaena mysticetus*, Greenland whale, bearded whale, Grand Bay whale, arctic right whale, polar whale, bowhead whale, as it has been variously called in different times and places, is now one of the rarest animals in the world of waters.

A giant among giants, it had a lifespan of a hundred or more years; could attain a length of seventy feet and a weight of at least a hundred tons—although in later times (after we had laid our doom upon its kind) few survived long enough to reach fifty feet and sixty tons. Shaped something like a gigantic tadpole, a full-grown Arvek was wrapped in a blanket of blubber as much as two feet thick which could be rendered into as much as seven thousand gallons of oil. It carried in its mouth an enormous "head" of the horny substance called baleen (whalebone) with which it sieved thousands of gallons of ocean for its sustenance, consisting for the most part of shrimp-like creatures an inch or so in length.

The prodigious quantity and high quality of oil and baleen to be derived from Arvek made it the most valuable of all whales—and therefore the most rapaciously pursued.

Its commercial worth was discovered rather late because Arvek lived in arctic and subarctic latitudes where it remained inviolate until 1607, when a sailor named Henry Hudson came upon it while trying to find a polar passage from Europe to Cathay.

Unable to penetrate the pack, Hudson coasted along the edge of the ice. On his return to Europe he described a "great store of whales of enormous size" that were slow enough to be overtaken by rowed boats; seemed unable or unwilling to defend themselves; and, because they were so fat, did not sink when dead. All of which meant they could be killed relatively easily, then towed ashore where their blubber could be peeled off and converted into oil.

Then, as now, oil was money. By 1612 a massive oil rush was underway in the arctic and subarctic waters lying between Greenland and Novaya Zemlya, fifteen hundred miles eastward.

English whalers dominated the new killing grounds at first but before long were being challenged by the Dutch. The rivals fought pitched battles for control of Spitzbergen's fiords as sites for "factories." However, this human conflict was as nothing to the war both nations waged against Arvek.

By 1622 the Dutch alone were annually sending as many as three hundred ships and from fifteen to nineteen thousand men to "fish" leviathan in and around Spitzbergen's icy waters. They built a sprawling town called Smeerenberg (Blubbertown) on one of the more southerly fiords, into which their fleet annually towed as many as fifteen hundred whales to be stripped of baleen and blubber—after which the bloating corpses were turned adrift to dot the surrounding seas with islands of death.

The whaling fleet burgeoned and Arvek began to disappear. By the end of the eighteenth century it had been virtually extirpated east of Spitzbergen. By 1790 as many as two hundred thousand had been butchered. By 1800 only scattered pods of adolescents—called "nursery" whales—remained in the waters east of Greenland. Their turn soon came.

In 1810 the grotesquely named Hull whaler *Cherub*, Captain Jackson commanding, came upon several pods of these formerly despised nursery whales, and a massacre ensued. Soon every corner of *Cherub*'s holds and deck space was so crammed with blubber that no room remained for the "produce" from thirteen additional young whales whose corpses were moored alongside. There was nothing for it but to cut these adrift and abandon them, though not without "very great distress at the losses occasioned thereby to the Owners of the ship."

Having devastated Arvek in the Greenland Sea, the whalers pushed west around Cape Farewell into Davis Strait. The Dutch began dropping out of the game, leaving it to British ships to carry the massacre north into Baffin and Melville bays, then west to the coast of Baffin Island. The log of the Hull whaler *Cumbrian* in 1823 contains this account of what was being done to the whales near Lancaster Sound and Pond Inlet.

"We turned south and along the floe-edge lay the bodies of hundreds of flenched [flensed, or stripped of blubber] whales and the air for miles around was tainted with the foetor which arose from such masses of putridity. Toward evening the numbers we came across were even increasing, and the effluvia which assailed our nostrils became almost intolerable."

Cumbrian's men killed "as many whales as the ship could safely carry, twenty-three in number, yielding about 240 tons of oil." Between them the three dozen English and Scots whaling ships in company with *Cumbrian* that season killed and flensed 749 1/2 whales—the "half" being a suckling young one killed with its mother.

Some whales died particularly hard, as Albert Markham discovered while on the Dundee whaler *Arctic*. In 1866 *Arctic* had been the first whaler to enter Prince Regent Sound to the west of Pond Inlet. There she had found "virgin ground" enabling her crew to kill forty Greenland whales in less than two weeks. In 1873 *Arctic* returned to Prince Regent Sound and Markham steered one of her boats on a "rally." I have abbreviated the original text from *A Whaling Cruise to Baffin's Bay* by Albert Hastings Markham, London, 1875.

Yesterday forenoon whales were seen from the crow's nest, about five miles off and all boats were ordered away in chase. It was nearly 2 o'clock when I saw a heavy blow some distance ahead accompanied by a small one, which my harpooner pronounced to be a "monstrous big fish with its sucker."

Away we went in chase, another boat in company. The whale rose close to Harker Hunter in the other boat who, pulling quietly up, got his harpoon in. But though so easily struck, she was not so easily killed. We succeeded in getting close up and gave her another harpoon. She immediately flew off at a terrific rate, towing the two boats at at least six knots an hour.

It was five o'clock before any other boat came to our assistance, when five more harpoons were buried in the monster's flesh, and several lances plunged in, but the brute would not die. Three rockets were fired into the unfortunate animal that clung to life with such tenacity. Eventually the ship came up and took the lines on board yet, singular to relate, the fish actually towed the ship and seven boats at the rate of three miles an hour. The water in which we were towed was coloured with blood; but her furious struggles gradually weakened and at nine o'clock we succeeded in giving her the coup de grace with a lance, and she expired amidst the cheers of all hands. We had been six hours fastened to this fish during which she had towed us upwards of fifteen miles.

Killing a whale was by no means the end of the exercise. The carcass had to be hauled alongside the ship and flensed in the water. The blubber was then hauled aboard, cut into chunks, and stowed in tanks to be carried back to Dundee for rendering into oil. Whaling of this kind did not make for a tidy ship, as Markham notes: "The state of the ship is now indescribable. The only *clear*, not *clean* part of the ship is along each gangway. The Captain says: 'If we get another fish or two we shall be in a fearsome mess.'"

The mess *did* become more fearsome until everything was coated with oil, blood, and slime, and the stench became so powerful it could, as one old whaler put it, almost have been shovelled into the tanks along with the decaying blubber. Whalers did not complain about this. It was the stink of money.

On her triumphant return to Dundee, *Arctic* unloaded the blubber and baleen from twenty-eight Greenland whales—thirteen females and fifteen males. The oil alone was worth £19,000, or about $1.8 million in today's Canadian dollars, and the baleen was valued at as much again. *Arctic* also brought home the tusks and blubber of nineteen narwhals and the pelts of twelve polar bears as additional trophies of a successful arctic cruise.

Hers was almost the last such "bumper voyage." Although the Dundee fleet tallied two hundred whales in 1874, thereafter the catch drastically declined. During the next decade so few whales were killed in eastern arctic waters that British whalers had also to become sealers. Between 1890 and 1900 they slaughtered two and a half million harp and hood seals on the ice pans in Newfoundland and Labrador waters. These were in addition to countless multitudes butchered by

Norwegians and Russians off the east coast of Greenland and in the Barents Sea. This commercial slaughter is still continuing, especially by the Norwegians and the Canadians. The seals are now "harvested" mainly for their reproductive organs, which are in demand by many Pacific Rim countries for use in aphrodisiacs.

American whalers who followed the British into Davis Strait and adjacent waters (including the Canadian Sea) proved to be at least as effective killers as their trans-Atlantic cousins. By the latter part of the nineteenth century, Arvek had become a rarity in northern waters accessible from the Atlantic. But all was not lost for the whaling industry because at mid-century Yankee whalers discovered Arvek's last refuge, far to the northwest in the Bering, Chukchi, and Beaufort seas.

In 1849 the first Yankee whaler to go through Bering Strait reported such enormous numbers of bowheads that the bulk of the American whaling fleet flocked post-haste to these "unfished" waters. Here Yankee ingenuity and greed initiated a carnage that might have awed even the Dutch butchers at Smeerenberg. They killed every whale they could overtake, regardless of size, sex, or age. Indeed some ships' crews made a specialty of killing calves.

In 1852 a Yankee captain described the activities of his countrymen:

"The great fleet moved north toward the Pole and there the ships of all [our] whaling ports now are, lending their united efforts to the destruction of the [bowhead] whale, capturing even its young....The whales have diminished since I was first here two years ago...how can it be otherwise? Look at the immense fleets fishing from Cape Thaddeus to the Bering Strait! By day and night the whale is chased and harassed....There could not have been less than three thousand killed last season, yet the average quantity of oil is only about half as great as it was two years ago. The fact speaks for itself and shows that it will not long be profitable to send ships to the Arctic."

In 1855 whalebone sold for the modern equivalent of Canadian $60 per pound, but ten years later was worth double that. An orgy of destruction followed during which the American fleet killed thousands of bowheads *solely* for their "bone." By 1910 the Bering-Chukchi-Beaufort Sea tribe of Arvek had been reduced to a remnant.

The horrendous Norwegian turn-of-the-century invention of a

cannon firing an explosive harpoon from the bow of a fast steam-powered killer ship initiated a new and worldwide whaling holocaust whose victims were mainly from the rorqual family (principally blue, fin, humpback, sei, and minke whales), all of which were too swift to be taken by sailing vessels or whaleboats.

As the twentieth century progressed, Arvek became an almost mythical creature. Occasionally an arctic traveller would report having seen one pursuing its solitary way through the channels between the Canadian Arctic islands, or in the Beaufort or Chukchi Seas. By the end of World War II, during which men were too busy killing each other to pursue whales, it even seemed possible that their numbers might be slowly recovering. It was at this juncture that native people, especially in Alaska, began killing Arvek—not for sustenance, as their ancestors had done, but as an assertion of their native rights and, in civilized style, for sport.

Alaskan and Canadian Inuit currently engage in this kind of killing using modern equipment and weaponry, including fast powerboats, spotter aircraft, exploding shells, and large-calibre rifles designed as anti-tank weapons. The assault is directed at the two or three hundred Arvek which constitute the last remnant of the species.

Dr. Floyd Durham, an American biologist who has spent years studying bowheads, reports that the "sinking loss" of those being harpooned or shot in Alaskan waters is close to 80 per cent. During one season's hunt he saw thirty bowheads "struck" by native hunters, *of which only one was recovered.* On one occasion Durham witnessed the killing of a female bowhead accompanied by a suckling calf. Because the dead female was far too heavy for the natives to haul out on the ice, they turned the carcass adrift after cutting off perhaps 10 per cent of the blubber and muktuk. The orphaned calf was left to die of starvation.

Between the years 1996 and 2000 Inuit in Canada's new self-governing Inuit territory of Nunavut killed at least three Greenland whales, to demonstrate their right to treat the living resources of their country as they saw fit. Only a few hundred pounds of meat and blubber were taken from the carcasses, which were then abandoned.

Such wanton acts of slaughter in the name of enshrining native rights may well be the thin edge of a wedge which, if driven home, could lead to the general resumption of commercial whaling by several nations, especially Norway and Japan, which are vocally and financially generous in their support of "aboriginal whale hunts."

When I began my arctic journey of 1966 I hoped to at least catch a glimpse of Arvek. I saw only the whitened bones of those who had perished long ago. I have since made lengthy sea voyages in Davis Strait, Baffin Bay, the Labrador Sea, Denmark Strait, and the Greenland Sea— all of which were once lush pastures for the Greenland whale.

I saw nothing of Leviathan.

Only Arvek's ghost lingered there.

CHAPTER SIXTEEN

Ruins, Old
and New

I HAD HOPED TO TRAVEL WIDELY IN THE VICINITY OF Lancaster Sound, that great east–west channel connecting Baffin Bay with the Beaufort Sea and the Pacific Ocean. But hopes in the Arctic become actualities only when weather permits, and the weather gods were uncooperative. Rain changed to sleet as a full nor'easter slammed into the sound, putting a stop to distant travel by sea or air.

Pond's residents reacted in Inuit fashion. Foul weather is a time to enjoy life. An impromptu dance was staged in the new school. Jonasee invited me to attend, then amused himself inciting mostly elderly women to claim me as a partner. The complicated round and square dances inherited from long-departed English and Scots whalers were far beyond my competence, and I made even more of a public fool of myself than is my usual wont.

I was enjoying Pond, but the rest of my crew were not. The plywood walls of the transients' quarters where we were bunked vibrated like sounding boards to the monotonous obligato of rain and sleet pounding on a metal roof. Roy and Doug were getting antsy. They had now flown almost half the distance contracted for, without mishap, and were perhaps apprehensive that our luck might run out.

For reasons of his own, Pete, who had spent several years during the fifties as manager of the HBC post at Pond, also seemed anxious to be out of there. Heavily outnumbered, I agreed to press on, if and when the weather moderated.

Doug woke me early one morning to say he had been on the radio to Resolute on Cornwallis Island, 350 miles west of Pond, and had been assured conditions there and at Arctic Bay were improving. Doug reckoned if we could reach Arctic Bay we would stand a good chance of being able to push on to Resolute.

Grumpily I dressed, swilled a mug of cold coffee, and slopped down to the dock to take a turn at the handle of the wobble pump as Roy topped up DCL's tanks. Then the sleet turned to pelting rain, forcing us to take shelter in the plane's cold interior.

The cabin was by no means as spacious as it had been when our journey began. Because mail service to most northern communities was poor to nonexistent, every aircraft that happened by became an unofficial postie. We had already carried many nameless bundles and bedraggled envelopes laboriously addressed in Eskimo syllabic script, but at Pond we became a major carrier.

Someone had asked Pete to take a few char to fish-hungry relatives at Resolute. The "few" turned out to be about 150 pounds of sun-and-wind-cured (and powerfully odoriferous) char fillets. Someone else had put aboard several five-gallon plastic pails of narwhal muktuk also consigned to Resolute.

We had also acquired a mysterious eight-foot-long, seal-hide-wrapped bundle of something so heavy two people could hardly lift it. I didn't discover what this was until several days later when, after I nearly broke my ankle on it, Pete admitted it contained a number of narwhal tusks. This trove of ivory (which was worth, if not its weight in gold, at least in silver) accompanied us for the duration of our journey. The reason for its presence aboard was never disclosed.

We spent two hours squatting in the Otter's cabin moored to the dock, while rain pelted furiously against the fuselage and Doug worked the radio looking for better weather. Shortly before noon, he raised the Hudson's Bay manager at Arctic Bay who reported in a chirpy British accent that he had a ceiling of about five hundred feet under which he thought we might be able to slide or, "if it gets too thick you can go boating on the water...."

Our plan, if such it could be called, was to slip across Eclipse Sound under the overcast then find some fog-free valley in the rugged Borden Peninsula through which we could reach Admiralty Inlet and Arctic Bay.

We had flown only a few miles, skimming three hundred feet above wind-whipped waters with mountains rearing into an impenetrable smother of black clouds on our port side, when Doug signalled me to put on headphones.

"Bottom just fell in at Arctic. No way we can get in there now even if we could find it. Resolute's out. And Pond's closing down. Best thing we can do is nip down Tay Sound and make a run for Igloolik."

Igloolik was in the northwest corner of Foxe Basin, 250 miles to the south. To head for it would mean abandoning Lancaster Sound and the high Arctic, but there was now no other choice.

The Otter banked so steeply a wingtip seemed about to slice the surface, then we were flying into Tay Sound close enough to deck level to panic a pod of narwhals. We felt rather than saw cliffs looming on both sides of the narrow gut. At its foot we found ourselves faced by a horrifying barrier of rust-red crags, presumably an exposure of the fabulous iron ore Murray Watts had talked about.

Doug opened the throttle and hauled back on the control column. DCL pointed her heavy nose skyward at the maximum rate of climb. The engine thundered. And our cargo, including the pails of muktuk, slid toward the tail of the plane.

I hung on to my seat in mortal fear that DCL would stall and fall back into the scree so close below. I should have had more faith. She climbed rocket-like for perhaps two interminable minutes before Doug eased the column forward. The climb continued at a more tolerable angle through grey murk which seemed almost palpable. Gradually it thinned, and we broke out at last to find a *second* layer of overcast ceiling off the sky a thousand feet above us.

The Otter levelled out as I leaned forward to glance at the instrument panel. Altitude 6,640 feet. Course 192—a little west of south. This was goodbye to Lancaster Sound, but we were not to be allowed to put Resolute out of mind. One of the buckets of muktuk had overturned and the slippery contents had come sluicing around our feet to soak our sleeping bags and sundry other items, becoming a redolent presence we would have to live with for the duration of our journey.

Flying between two proximate layers of dense cloud was not unlike being trapped between two thick slices of black bread. Fortunately the slices stayed far enough apart to let us through, and shortly before 4:00 p.m. the cloud began to dissipate. Bits of blue sky appeared, then sunlight, and we caught glimpses of land and water far below.

We were now approaching Fury and Hecla Strait, the northwestern exit from Foxe Basin and the Canadian Sea. The basin was still sealed by thick winter ice which solidly surrounded Igloolik Island. Clearly no ship had yet been able to reach Igloolik, and it appeared none was likely to do so in the near future. However, the ice in the harbour had melted sufficiently to create a pool of open water large enough to accommodate DCL. We splashed gratefully down into it.

Our reception turned out to be as chill as the surrounding ice. It appeared that at some point in our journey a "cautionary" had been radioed to the administrators of all northern communities, warning of my possible arrival and suggesting I be treated "with reserve." Some chose to ignore the injunction. Others took it seriously. Igloolik's administrator reacted to our arrival as if we were carriers of bubonic plague.

It had been a long day and we were tired and hungry, yet only with difficulty were we able to obtain grudging permission to shelter in a ten-by-twelve-foot transit shack containing one chair, a broken table, and a double bunk *sans* mattresses. The HBC store was closed, and not even Pete was able to prevail upon an intransigent manager to open up and sell us some necessaries. The one thing available to us was gas—a supply of which, so the administrator presumably hoped, might encourage us to take ourselves elsewhere.

We made do with what we had. Supper consisted of hors d'oeuvres of sliced muktuk and char briefly marinated in rum, followed by canned hash fortified with more muktuk and char.

The muktuk originally destined for Resolute now began to earn its passage. Narwhals are unknown at Igloolik and because of the ice no white whales had been killed there that summer so muktuk of any sort had not been available for almost a year. When word got around that we had a supply of that prime delicacy, our popularity knew no bounds—within the Eskimo community.

Igloolik's whites continued to keep their distance, with the exception of a silver-bearded priest who introduced himself as Father Franz Van de Velde, OMI (Oblates of Mary Immaculate).

A man with the glittering eye of the Ancient Mariner, he seemed unaware that I was *persona non grata*. Or maybe he felt I might still be rescued from Satan's clutches. In any event, he constituted himself my guide to Igloolik and took me on a tour of "his" village, as he somewhat wistfully called the place.

The tour centred upon an almost stone-by-stone examination of St. Stephen's, the largest and most unusual church in the Canadian Arctic. Approximately the size of a hockey arena, it had low walls of crudely quarried chunks of granite and a barrel roof that gave it a vague resemblance to an enormous megalithic mound.

This strange edifice, the first Roman Catholic cathedral in Canada's Arctic, had been constructed over a ten-year period by a handful of Inuit converts (the majority of Igloolik's population were Anglican) under the direction of an Oblate from France called Father Fournier. Formidable excavations in a nearby outcrop testified to the enormous amount of time and labour that had been devoted to the task.

Although possessed of great faith and perseverance, Father Fournier seems not to have quite known where he was. The stone-built, mostly mud-mortared, uninsulated structure turned out to be unheatable in winter and at any other season was so damp its inner surface either ran with water or was sheathed in ice. Despite walls dangerously cracked by frost, it nevertheless still dominated Igloolik (though for how much longer was problematic) as a symbol of Western man's unshakeable faith in himself and his ways, even in the face of the cold realities of the northern world.

Fury and Hecla Strait has, since dim antiquity, been a major water route for human beings moving between the eastern and central arctic coastal regions. Igloolik Island is remarkable for the remains of habitations built by those aboriginal travellers upon its ancient raised beaches during at least four thousand years.

Having with some difficulty shaken off Father Van de Velde, I walked the ancient beaches. They appeared to have recently suffered an artillery barrage, being pocked and marred by countless shallow holes. Archaeologists were responsible for some of these but most had been dug by local people looking for tools and artifacts from ancient times to sell as souvenirs to American service men at a DEW Line site south of Igloolik.

As I poked about, I was joined by a jaeger, a gull-like bird with the attributes of a hawk, which hovered close by ready to stoop on any lemming I might disturb. Neither of us was rewarded with anything of much interest, but I found some entertainment in looking back at the settlement of Igloolik and wondering what archaeologists of the future would make of *its* ruins. The remains of its church will at least reward them with something more substantial than the debris from the flimsy plywood and metal structures spawned by the Northern Vision.

If the settlement offered few material attractions, there were human ones. In the midnight dusk I came upon three attractive teenage girls flying kites in front of the sepulchral church. When I asked what they were up to, one replied with a laugh: "Send letter to stars up there. Maybe they send back stuff from Eaton's catalogue."

Shades of the Cargo Cult, I thought to myself as I walked thoughtfully away.

Then there was the Reverend Noah Nashook, pastor of the Anglican Church. A shy little man only recently ordained, he was glad of a gift of muktuk and reciprocated by inviting me into his modest house for a mug of tea. He told me he was in serious trouble with his bishop because of his inability to resist a scheme proposed by Father Van de Velde.

According to Noah, the Oblate priest had demanded that the two faiths hold a joint service in the virtually derelict stone church. Noah thought the priest might be trying to muster all the spiritual force locally available in an attempt to restore Father Fournier's crumbling dream.

"'Father,' he tell me, 'God want this.' I say I not sure. He keeping say, 'Yes, is God's will,' so after I say okay."

The service was duly held, and for the first time cavernous St. Stephen's was almost filled. The frost-riven walls did not collapse, as Noah had been half afraid they might, but when news of the event reached the Anglican bishop of the Arctic at his headquarters in distant Toronto all hell broke loose.

"Bishop make pretty hard on me, you know. I think I lose my job now. What you think?"

When I refused to hazard a guess he added phlegmatically, "*Ayorama.* Can't be help. I go back my father's camp at Sisorarsuak then."

Noah Nashook kept his job. Father Van de Velde returned to Belgium, and the great stone mausoleum of St. Stephen's continues its inexorable decay, soon to become one more ruin among many.

In the year 1966, six hundred and eighty Inuit were associated with Igloolik. Forty of them formed a community at Foxe Main, the huge radar surveillance base at Hall Beach forty miles to the south. Most of the remainder still lived in thirteen camps scattered over the tundra plains of northern Melville Peninsula and parts of southern Baffin Island.

"Igloolik people strong for the land," Noah assured me. "Lots of walrus, ring seal, square flipper seal, sometimes harp seal. Caribou most times. Char and trout. Ducks and geese. Plenty to eat and make clothes. People don't like stay in Igloolik. Better, you know, live like old people lived. Stay mostly in camps and only come in here maybe two, three times a year to church and trade. Now, government men want everybody stay in here. Say they build wooden houses with electric, water, oil stoves, for everybody live in right here."

"Will the people come?"

"Maybe. Most think better if kids go to school here instead of policemen fly kids south. Then kids stay in hostels down there and don't see except few weeks in summer."

At the time of our visit about sixty natives were in the settlement waiting for the supply ship. Two were men I had met in the spring at Spence Bay. Josiah Kadlutsiak and Jack Makonik sought me out with a gift of caribou meat from Jack's people's camp at Parry Bay. They also brought me one of Igloolik's specialties—a walking stick made from the stretched, dried penis of a walrus.

"Very good," Josiah told me proudly. "Can bend; don't break. Soldiers at base pay fifty dollars. Fellow at Frobisher want all we can get for tourists. We don't get many this year. Maybe somebody tell old man walrus go play somewhere else."

"Sredna, maybe?" I suggested.

He grinned, but did not deny the possibility.

I had heard that Father Van de Velde possessed a remarkable

collection of penis bones—the rod-like structures found in the penises of most marine and some terrestrial mammals. According to report, the largest item in his collection was the penis bone of a whale, over five feet in length.

I asked Jack if the story was true.

He exchanged glances with Josiah, then both men smiled.

"He got all them things when he at Pelly Bay. Biggest one, and smallest one too," Josiah admitted.

Jack laughed. "I *see* that small one one time. Come from lemming. Easy lost, so Father, he keep under magnify glass on table."

CHAPTER SEVENTEEN

God's Country

OUR NEXT OBJECTIVE WAS PELLY BAY, TWO HUNDRED
miles west of Igloolik. The weather cooperated with a bright
and cloudless day of the sort that can make arctic flying an
almost transcendental experience.

The course took us across rough and rocky Melville Peninsula and
icebound Committee Bay. Then came a traverse of the stark Simpson
Peninsula upon the spine of which stood another of the ubiquitous
radar domes. We gave it a wide berth because, so Doug explained,
"Those bastards don't like civilian planes. Wouldn't put it past them for
some asshole to take a potshot at us."

He had to be joking, or so I thought; but just then we spotted something that glittered compellingly against the chocolate-coloured bog
below. Doug banked so we could all have a good look at the crumpled
wreckage of a four-engined freighter. What remained of wing and fuselage looked not unlike a huge horizontal cross half-buried in the
muskeg and pointing directly toward Pelly Bay, now only a few miles
distant.

"Welcome to God's Country," Doug said soberly as we began our
descent.

Pelly Bay could not have borne much of a resemblance to God's
Country in the eyes of its first European visitors—a party of
Englishmen who arrived in the region in 1829 searching for the North
Magnetic Pole.

Commanded by ex-naval Captain John Ross, this expedition was a private and impoverished one. Its transport was an elderly side-wheel steamer bravely named *Victory* which had spent most of her already long life as a sedate coastal packet running between Liverpool and the Isle of Man.

It would have been hard to find a less likely vessel for a voyage of arctic exploration. Nevertheless, Ross and his crew of twenty-two steamed off for Lancaster Sound with high hopes of pinpointing the position of the elusive magnetic pole. The voyage became a prolonged purgatory when *Victory*'s paddle-wheel propulsion proved no match for the North Atlantic—or for ice. Her crew had to rely on her auxiliary sail as they nursed her around Cape Farewell, through the pack of Baffin Bay into Lancaster Sound, then southward into Prince Regent Sound.

They were lucky, and unlucky, in that this summer was exceptionally warm. Both Prince Regent Sound and its southward extension, the Gulf of Boothia, were relatively ice-free, allowing the little vessel to work her way as far south as Felix Harbour on the eastern coast of Boothia Peninsula. Here she wintered less than a hundred miles north of Pelly Bay.

Several parties man-hauling sleds explored to the south and west during that winter. In January one of them encountered a group of Netchilingmiut—Seal People—whose world this was. Unlike so many Europeans both before and after, Ross and his men admired the natives and treated them with respect. Had they not done so they would, in all likelihood, have failed to survive.

Living conditions aboard *Victory* during the eight months of winter were abominable, but there was no loss of life and all hands were sustained by the belief that summer would release them and their vessel. It was not to be. When warm weather belatedly returned, it was not warm enough and *Victory* remained frozen in, doomed to spend a second winter in her cramped little harbour.

Ross and his men fraternized with the Netchilingmiut, from whom they obtained country food, especially seal and caribou meat, which almost certainly saved them from the terrible scourge of scurvy. From the natives they learned how to live and travel in the land to such effect that they actually succeeded in "finding" the position of the perambulating magnetic pole, which in those times was wobbling about under

Boothia Peninsula. What the Netchilingmiut may have thought about this accomplishment is anybody's guess. One can imagine them shaking their heads pityingly as the *kablunait* expended time, energy, and substance in pursuit of a chimaera as insubstantial as the wind itself.

When the succeeding summer again failed to set *Victory* free, Ross reluctantly decided to abandon her and try to reach Lancaster Sound, more than three hundred miles away, in the ship's open boats. On May 29, 1832, he wrote in his journal:

"The colours were hoisted and nailed to the mast. We drank a parting glass to our poor ship and, having seen every man out, I took my own adieu of the *Victory*...the solitary, abandoned, helpless home of our past years, fixed in immovable ice 'til time should perform on her his usual work."

Dragging their boats over the intractable ice, Ross and his men travelled painfully northward. When shore leads availed, they launched the boats and continued by water, beset by gales, drifting pack, and shortages of almost everything. Some weeks they made good only a dozen miles, and those with bitter labour. When summer ended and new ice began to form, they knew they were not going to make it.

They put ashore on Fury Beach, seventy miles short of Lancaster Sound, and prepared to spend their third arctic winter in a hut hurriedly built from materials abandoned on this desolate shore years earlier when another British ship, the *Fury*, had been wrecked there.

Two men died that winter but, defying the odds, the rest survived and in the early summer of 1833 again took to their boats. On August 26 off Cape York in Lancaster Sound, they saw a distant whaling ship and rowed desperately toward it.

"Unluckily a breeze sprang up just then, and she made all sail to the southeastward and we were soon left astern. About ten o'clock we saw another sail who appeared to be lying-to; we thinking she had seen us. This, however, proved not to be the case as she soon bore away under all sail....It was the most anxious moment we had yet experienced [but]... at eleven o'clock we saw her heave-to and lower a boat which rowed toward our own...."

Safe at last aboard the Hull whaler *Isabella*, Ross noted: "Never was seen a more miserable-looking people than ourselves....No beggar could have outdone us...unshaven since I know not when, dirty, dressed in the rags of wild beasts and starved to the very bones."

Victory's deep penetration of the Gulf of Boothia was a feat not to be repeated until late in the twentieth century when a modern icebreaker finally succeeded in reaching Pelly Bay.

In 1966 Pelly Bay was still very much a backwater in the flood tide overwhelming the New North. Icebound throughout most of every year, its Netchilingmiut inhabitants had little commerce with the outside world except by dogsled or when visited by occasional float- or ski-equipped planes.

DCL came in low over a string of wall tents fronting a smaller version of Igloolik's church. This one sported a squat tower topped by a wooden cross. Three other stone-built structures clustered close to it and, scattered around what was clearly the centre of the community, were a few shacks. Well away from the church stood a group of shiny new wood-and-metal buildings with DNA's signature writ large upon them.

Although the bay itself was choked with ice, a shore lead about a hundred feet in width had been opened by the ebb and flow of the tide. DCL sideslipped to a touchdown in this narrow waterway.

Until the mid-1930s there had been no white man at Pelly Bay. Not even the usually ubiquitous HBC had been able to establish itself there. In consequence the people of the region had remained effectively free of the influence of traders, missionaries, or government.

Then, in 1935, Father Pierre Henri, OMI, newly arrived in Canada from Brittany, set out from a tiny Oblate mission at Repulse Bay to make a "spiritual reconnaissance" of Pelly Bay. Travelling on the dogsled of a local man, the priest vanished into the winter darkness. Nothing more was heard of him until two years later when he re-appeared at Repulse to announce that the Netchilingmiut were ripe for conversion and he had been chosen by God to be their shepherd.

Despite having to rely on dog transport for his supplies, all of which had to come either from Repulse Bay in the south or from equally distant Gjoa Haven in the west, Father Henri began building his "foundation" on the southeast coast of Pelly Bay.

There was to be no question of its permanence. As Father Fournier had done at Igloolik, Henri and his successor, Father Van de Velde, built with rocks, upon rock. Lack of quarrying experience or tools did not deter them. There was an inexhaustible supply of granite, clay, and mud; labour was supplied by natives who, once they had been converted to the Faith, could be dragooned into the task of raising God's house.

Like it or not, Pelly Bay was going to become the heart of God's Country in the Arctic. Between them, Fathers Henri and Van de Velde laboured for twenty years to make it so. They erected a church, a presbytery, a hall, and a workshop, all made of granite boulders mortared with clay and, initially, roofed with seal and walrus hides. In their cul-de-sac at the bottom of the Gulf of Boothia, they created a little theocracy and ran it with an iron hand. As time passed, stories began reaching Igloolik, Repulse, Gjoa Haven, and even farther afield, of the absolute power the priests at Pelly Bay exercised over the native community. The old camp system was dismantled and the people concentrated around the mission which had obtained a trader's licence from the federal government. This enabled it to restrict trade to basic goods such as rifles and ammunition, axes, knives, and traps. Profits from the furs and skins taken by the Netchilingmiut went toward the maintenance of the mission and of the Oblate order. Governance of the people was rigidly autocratic. Strangers coming to Pelly Bay had to conform to the dictates of the priest or find themselves ostracized and forced to leave.

This was the way things stood until the early 1960s when DNA finally took cognizance of Pelly Bay. Then the Vision began to exert its sway even over this remote backwater, and soon the fabric of the tiny church state began to disintegrate. The decay was symbolized by the fate of the stone church. The annual cycle of freezing and thawing crumbled the mud and clay mortar until, by the time of my visit, almost half the main structure had collapsed. It was evident that the rest must soon follow.

Ironically, the Oblates' campaign to keep change away from Pelly Bay ended in undermining the very principle the priests had so strenuously espoused. In the early sixties word spread that the best-preserved example of pre-colonial Eskimo culture was to be found at Pelly Bay. Thereupon, anthropologists, ethnologists, sociologists, and others of that ilk began flying in to the little settlement in such numbers as to validate the quip "The standard Eskimo family now consists of seven Eskimos and a visiting scientist." Even the wealthy and prestigious Ford Foundation funded a three-year scientific study of the Pelly Bay Netchilingmiut.

Then in 1964 DNA flew in five DC-6 loads of building materials and supplies. The four-engined freighter landed on the bay ice. Thereafter nothing at Pelly Bay was the same.

A new priest arrived to understudy and then replace Father Van de Velde who was moved to Igloolik. Father Gossart was a fox-faced young man from Quebec who, when I met him, appeared confused as to whether modern technology was a good thing for the Inuit or not. I talked to him in his newly built, well-insulated office, the materials for which had been flown in. It was equipped with a typewriter and short-wave radio.

"There is only around 140 people in our community," he told me, "and they live mostly close around. It's probably one of the last settlements where they still live mostly their old way. The people are very self-reliant and real healthy too."

I asked my standard question: "Do you think they'll be able to continue making their living from the land?"

"I hope so, myself. It should be so. There will be lots of improvements when we get all the new housing in. They are flying ten houses in this winter. Now we must organize to sell our products outside. Perhaps we will send frozen char out in the empty planes.

"These people can do one thing that is unique, I think. They can still make old-fashioned Eskimo tools, weapons, even kayaks. Museums want these things very much. This spring I think we shipped out twenty seal harpoon sets. They also make bows and arrows. There is not many places where people still know how to do that. One man has made a kayak for the museum in Ottawa, and a museum in Boston wants ten deer spears. Anybody can buy those things from us. Our bone and ivory harpoons hang on people's walls in the south. It may be the people can stay here because they keep these old skills. There are many museums in the world. It would be a good business, I believe."

Father Gossart was so anxious to demonstrate his concern for maintaining Eskimo culture that he arranged a drum dance in my honour.

This was surprising because the Oblate order had long maintained that drum dances encouraged pagan beliefs and had banned or severely discouraged such activities in most arctic communities.

Instead of being held in a tent as in olden times, this dance was staged in Father Gossart's kitchen under the watchful eyes of a large and garish plastic statue of the Virgin. The two drummers were middle-aged men dressed in castoff white man's clothing emblazoned with the logos of southern baseball teams. The audience consisted of my party, Father Gossart, and his Eskimo servant.

The drummers seemed uncertain as to what was expected of them. They stared glumly at the floor until the priest spoke sharply in Inuktitut. Then, reluctantly it seemed, they offered a lugubrious version of what looked like a Hollywood-style Indian war dance. Even the priest's servant appeared embarrassed by the performance.

As Pete climbed into his sleeping bag that night, he was philosophical about the incident.

"It's not as bad as it looked. I talked to the drummers later. They told me they were scared to do the real thing in front of Gossart and the Holy Virgin but they *do* know how. With Van de Velde gone, the old shaman stuff is actually coming back a bit. It's the women pushing it. They've been carrying the stuff in their heads.

"Did you notice those big *inuksuak* on the hill behind the settlement? They were built just this spring by a bunch of the younger men. Gossart thinks they're Eskimo art that'll bring in the tourists! He hasn't a clue they really represent the old times. I don't know if the young guys believe in *inuksuak* spirits. Maybe it's just a way of thumbing their noses at the church. But Father Van de Velde would certainly blow his top if he knew what they've been up to.

"The drummers told me there was a real drum dance and tent-shaking party at Kellet River not far from here a month ago. A bunch of the people were camped down there, fishing char. They claim they saw the spirit of an old lady pop out of her mouth and fly right out the tent like the shamans used to do it in olden times. They said she lay there on the floor like she was dead, all the time making the tent shake like it was going to fly right across the bay. That I would *love* to have seen!"

Me too. I at least managed to meet the "shaker." Iktuk was her name.

She was a powerfully built woman, strong-featured with a distinctly aquiline nose and a full head of bushy grey hair. Her authoritative, even domineering manner was reinforced by spidery and somehow intimidating patterns tattooed in faded blue on her wide chin and across both cheekbones. When I was introduced to her she looked me up and down for a long moment, then muttered something that set two women seated nearby whistling with laughter.

"What'd she say?" I asked a bit apprehensively.

"She said—" Pete had trouble keeping a straight face "—'White men's dogs get uglier every year.' But don't take it too hard. She says worse things about most whites."

I asked Iktuk for an interview and was curtly refused. "Says she has nothing to say to *kablunait*," Pete translated. "Just go away from our land and don't waste time going. Tough old cookie, ain't she?"

Before leaving Pelly Bay I examined the church compound. A dozen dogs had been staked out behind the presbytery and the ground around was covered with their dung. There was not, however, sufficient of it to conceal the shards of scores of shattered wine bottles which, presumably, had once contained communion wine.

Turning my back on the malodorous ruins, I climbed to a cemetery on the ridge. The graves were simple rock cairns of the kind used by Inuit since time immemorial. The only notable difference was that the occupants of these modern tombs had been accompanied into the hereafter, not by an assortment of grave goods, but by small and mostly fallen wooden crosses.

There was one exception.

From a dark aperture in the wall of a grave unmarked by a cross a set of false teeth elegantly carved from what must have been walrus ivory grinned at me enigmatically.

Space Station in Foxe Basin

BOUND NORTHWESTWARD FROM PELLY BAY WE WERE soon over the glacier-scoured Harrison Islands, an archipelago of lithic monsters thrusting their armoured heads out of the marbled ice of the Gulf of Boothia. Then came Boothia Peninsula itself, which, with Somerset Island to the north, constitutes a de facto boundary between the eastern and the central Arctic.

Far ahead we could glimpse the ice-free waters of St. Roche basin and, on its nearer shore, could see our destination, a sprinkle of diminutive buildings surrounded by a rocky desert resembling a waste of well-worn linoleum. This was Spence Bay.

Roy, who had liked most of the places we had so far visited, was not impressed with this one.

"Godawful-lookin' country, Farley! How come we're stoppin' here?"

On a bitterly cold April day some four months earlier I had boarded a ski-equipped DC-3 bound for Spence Bay from Yellowknife on the shores of Great Slave Lake. The plane and its owner/pilot, Bob Engles, had been chartered to fly the circuit court of the Northwest Territories eight hundred miles northeastward to hold a murder trial at Spence. I was aboard as a guest of the court. It was this earlier trip which had led to the one we were now on.

Engles's DC-3 had once been the personal plaything of a Texas oil baron who had fitted it out with red plush seats, a cherry-coloured carpet, and purple velvet curtains—a decor which might have been appropriate to a Mediterranean brothel but was somewhat at odds with the Arctic ambience.

The passengers included defence and prosecuting attorneys, a court reporter, several RCMP officers, and territorial judge Jack Sissons. There was also a thirteen-year-old Inuit girl returning home to Cambridge Bay from school in Yellowknife to bury her father, who had died a week earlier of alcohol poisoning. According to the coroner's report, "the death of his wife and his son from tuberculosis, and the absence of his daughter at residential school had rendered him suicidal."

It was typical of seventy-four-year-old Jack Sissons that he should make room on an official plane for a stranded native girl. Since becoming chief justice of the Northwest Territorial Court in 1955, this rural Albertan had made it his business to encourage new attitudes—judicial and otherwise—in dealings with the natives. He insisted that their special circumstances, needs, culture, and limited comprehension of the laws promulgated by southern Canadians be taken into consideration. As court reporter Everett Tingley put it, "The judge pays real close attention to what the natives have to say. He *listens* to them; and every decision he makes takes into account the way *they* see things and the way they've always lived."

Soon after Sissons arrived, the Inuit began calling this balding little man with the cherubic face *Ekotojee*—He-Who-Listens.

The new territorial judge did more than listen. He made it a precept that justice should be brought *to the people in their own country*, rather than having them flown far south to face trial in the alien environs of Yellowknife or, worse, in Edmonton.

The journey we were making was very much a case in point. Instead of having accused and witnesses who were involved in a murder that had taken place on Boothia Peninsula brought south to him, Sissons was taking the court north to them.

April is still winter in the far north, and it was snowing when we left Yellowknife. In consequence we saw little of the world around us until nearly four hours later when the DC-3 broke through heavy overcast to land at Cambridge Bay, the administrative centre of the central Arctic.

Seen from the sybaritic luxury of Engles's plane, the bleak cluster of low buildings almost buried in drifts seemed to answer well enough to the traditional southern concept of the north as a "white hell." We had no opportunity to investigate the place for ourselves, lingering only long enough to unload the orphaned girl and pick up an RCMP constable who was to be a witness at the trial.

Our course was now due east for Gjoa Haven. The overcast had thinned, enabling us to see where we were going, but we could make little of it. Buried under snow and ice, land and water were virtually indistinguishable. We passed from the frozen wastes of Queen Maude Gulf to snow-covered King William Island without even knowing we had made the transition.

When we touched down on the harbour ice at Gjoa the temperature was twenty-six below zero Fahrenheit and a stiff breeze was sending wraiths of ice crystals scurrying across the frozen bay. The DC-3 became the instant centre of a little universe as most of Gjoa's population clustered around her, puffs of frozen breath eddying from parka-clad figures assembled for a glimpse of illustrious visitors and to bid Godspeed to the community's two teachers—a husband and wife team—who had been selected for jury duty at the forthcoming trial.

We reached Spence Bay late in the afternoon. The plane did not remain there long. Judge Sissons, the police, and most of the others disembarked, leaving the sheriff, prosecutor, defence attorney, and me to continue on in search of more jurors. The engines surged, skis clattered across the rough bay ice, and we took off into the gathering dusk.

Pelly Bay was to have been our next stop, but the weather was fast deteriorating. Engles read the omens and decided to seek refuge at the DEW Line airstrip at Hall Beach, where he could make an instrument landing. By the time we reached Foxe Main, as the station was called, it was already shrouded in ground drift heralding the onset of a blizzard. We landed just in time.

Foxe Main consisted of a number of aluminum-clad structures laid out in the shape of a large hollow square surrounding four gigantic antennae, the whole being situated on a windswept ridge. Viewed through a haze of blowing snow, it could have been mistaken for a lunar outpost.

The other-worldly feeling intensified when we went inside to find an environment not unlike that of a submarine. Accommodation modules were filled with tiny cubicles whose few windows were heavily curtained as if to exclude even visual contact with the outside world. Water and ventilation pipes and electric cables cluttered ceilings and walls. Heat and humidity were semitropical, producing a sour fug which added to the claustrophobic atmosphere. The U.S. lieutenant who was our escort phlegmatically assured us that "you get used to it."

"Yeah," Pete muttered, "if you don't mind being an alien on your own bloody planet!"

Foxe Main housed fifty-five U.S. and Canadian servicemen (no women) and employed five Eskimos, who lived at the native settlement of Hall Beach five miles away. Although the site was jointly commanded by a Canadian squadron leader and a U.S. major, final authority was, of course, vested in the American.

Judge Sissons had dealt with this reality a year earlier during a flight in an Otter bound from Tuktoyaktuk to Coppermine. The plane had not long been airborne when a late-winter storm closed in behind and ahead of it. One by one, all possible airstrips were socked in until nothing remained open but a DEW Line field. For "security reasons" such places were strictly out of bounds to civilian aircraft, but Sissons's Otter had no choice. It made an emergency landing at the site.

Sissons was climbing out of the cabin when a jeep braked to a stop beside the Otter and the American station chief, a colonel, leapt out to order the judge back aboard the aircraft.

"You can't land here, goddamn it! This is a restricted area! You gotta leave—right now!"

The diminutive Sissons cocked an eye at the storm scud already obscuring the runway, then at the irate officer.

"Sir, I am the judge of the Northwest Territorial Court. I am charged with bringing justice to every corner of this, Her Majesty's realm. I am here on Her Majesty's soil as a matter of right. But you, sir, are an American citizen. You are here as a matter of licence. If either of us must leave, sir, it must be you."

Although some diplomatic exchanges between Ottawa and Washington resulted from the incident, Sissons's judgement was upheld. Which is why we had been able to land at Foxe Main.

The inmates were not a happy lot. Their faces were pale and oily like those of people forced to sit up all night in a crowded airport. "Fish bellies" was how our sheriff described their unnatural pallor. Tension pervaded the place. Too many men cooped up in too confined a space for too long.

They welcomed distraction. Our unexpected arrival ignited an explosive party that raged through the cubicles and corridors until well after dawn. A few fights and a plethora of broken glass resulted, but the uproar was not, as a disoriented U.S. lieutenant loudly asserted, instigated by "you fucking Canadian Commie-lovers!"

Our Crown prosecutor was of the opinion that the denizens of Foxe Main were stir-crazy. Considering that they were an integral part of the alarm system that could trigger a nuclear exchange between East and West, this was not a reassuring assessment.

The storm passed by during the night, enabling us to depart at 9:00 a.m. Engles set course for Cape Dorset, on the far side of Foxe Basin, where three prospective jurors awaited us. By 11:40 we were in sight of the high hills behind Dorset. Unfortunately the settlement itself and the bay upon whose ice we had hoped to land were cloaked in black sea fog swirling in from a lead of open water outside the cape.

We had come a long way, and Engles was not one to be easily rebuffed. Circling wide, he descended in an attempt to slip in under the skirts of the fog bank. Dim glimpses of islands raced past my window. The murk darkened and suddenly the DC-3 began climbing steeply at full throttle. I breathed again.

It was decided we should now try for Coral Harbour, two hundred miles back to the west, where it might be possible to round up a brace or two of jurors. However, before we were halfway across Foxe Channel, Coral reported *its* strip shut down by drifting snow.

Engles shrugged philosophically and set course for Repulse Bay, two hundred miles to the northwest. Then, when Repulse also reported ground drift too thick to let us land, we headed for Igloolik, now almost four hundred miles to the northward. It seemed to be the one remaining place within range where we could touch down and gas up. Except, of course, for Foxe Main, but that was to be considered only as a last resort.

By now the day was almost done. Fuel was running low and exhaustion setting in. We rumbled on above a faceless wilderness until, miraculously, Igloolik Island appeared. Its ice strip lay invitingly open to our view. We roared in under a lowering overcast and landed, but did not linger. No avgas was to be had here and the DC-3's tanks were almost empty. Hurriedly we took aboard three Eskimo jury candidates and then, there being nothing else for it, headed for Foxe Main.

We went to bed with the whine of a rising gale to lull us to sleep and next morning a full blizzard was raging. Nevertheless Engles taxied our DC-3 out onto the section of runway designated for ski-equipped aircraft...and there we sat, buffeted by ferocious gusts of wind. Visibility remained close to zero though at one point we glimpsed a dog team passing under one wing, its Inuit driver waving a heavily mittened hand in ironic salute. It was 11:00 a.m. before we were away at last, flying "on the beam," with nothing but swirling snow visible around us.

Shortly after noon the skis chattered to a halt on the ice at Spence. We had flown close to 2,200 miles since leaving Yellowknife and there were few settlements in the central Arctic or Foxe Basin we had not visited, though we had experienced little or nothing of the reality behind any of them.

Except, of course, for Foxe Main. But what had *it* to do with reality?

CHAPTER NINETEEN

A Company
Man

W E STEPPED ASHORE AT SPENCE BAY FROM OUR
trusty red Otter to be met by Ernie Lyall. A lean little man
in his late fifties, lantern-jawed and blue-eyed (though
dark of skin), Ernie was currently employed by DNA after having been,
as he proudly put it, "in service with the Company" for most of his adult
life. He had welcomed me to Spence Bay on my April visit. He seemed
happy to do so again; perhaps because he had found in me a willing listener, and Ernie was a storyteller.

*My folks belonged down on the Labrador. My daddy's daddy was a Scotsman come
out to work for the Moravian missionaries as a carpenter. He married a native lady
and settled at Nain.*

*I was born there in 1910, but next year the family moved away down north
to Port Burwell on Killinek Island at Hudson Strait where the Moravians was
building a mission. My daddy was carpenter and storekeeper for the missionary.*

*We lived at Burwell 'til I was twelve. It was a great place. Lots of seal, walrus,
white bears, whatever you wanted. The Eskimos was scattered out on the country
them times, but two or three families worked for the mission so I grew up talking
Eskimo good as English. I never felt much different from them people.*

*There was nineteen kids born in our family so we was never lonely. The biggest
thing in our lives was the seal fishery. Every autumn the natives and us shot
hundreds of harp seals. Mostly the skins was made into waterproof sealskin boots,
'cause the mission was the main supplier of skin boots for the whole of Labrador,
Newfoundland, and even the Old Country.*

Somehow my old man got the idea I was swinging too close to the natives, so he sent me to the Moravian boarding school at Makkovik. Then, when I was fourteen, out I went to St. John's to Bishop Field College. That was hard on a kid like me. Other kids called me a native and I spent as much time fighting as studying. When I was sixteen I cut loose and joined the Hudson's Bay Company. Signed up for five years as an apprentice for next to nothing. I didn't give a hoot about that though 'cause I was heading back north where I belonged.

In 1937 I was what you'd call a senior clerk at Arctic Bay when the Company decided to set up a post on the east side of Boothia Peninsula, and I was told to go along there aboard of the Nascopie, the Company's steamer.

We was to take everything with us, including a bunch of natives from Cape Dorset. So we loaded everything on the ship, including all the dogs, and all the stuff we needed to build a new post. It was going to be run by Lorenz Learmonth, a real old hand who was manager at Gjoa Haven at that time. He was to board the Company schooner Aklavik coming from the western Arctic and try to get through Bellot Strait in her if they could, and meet the Nascopie coming from Montreal. I was to be Learmonth's clerk.

The Gulf of Boothia was pretty near jammed full of ice, so it was decided to put the new post at the east end of Bellot Strait, and call it Fort Ross after old Sir John Ross who explored around there in the 1830s.

Bellot Strait is only about a mile wide and usually choked solid with ice. But if a ship could get through there she could make the Northwest Passage either way. Which is what explorers had been trying to do for a hundred years.

When the Nascopie poked her way into the mouth of the strait, by golly, it was wide open! Just a few floes was running through it on the tides. And right then we saw the masts of the Aklavik coming from the west. She came right on through. So I was there, you know, the first time a working ship come through the Northwest Passage.

Fort Ross turned out to be a very good place for me because this is where I hitched up with Nipasha. She was a daughter of Kavavouk, the camp boss of the Eskimo bunch the Nascopie brought from Cape Dorset. A hundred-per-cent Company man, he was more like a real father to me than a father-in-law. Nipasha was still pretty young then, but old enough in the Eskimo way of thinking.

Nipasha and me had a kid, and that was all right until 1940 when the Company wanted me to go back to Arctic Bay. It was a promotion but they wouldn't let me take Nipasha and the kid along. Far as I was concerned she was my wife, but the Company had a rule against its employees marrying native girls. You could sleep with them, but not marry them or anything like that.

The Company was the biggest part of my life, but I didn't want to leave Nipasha. Kavavouk, he said I should stay and if the Company fired me, I and my family could live with his crowd. Well, that's what I up and did.

I lived with the Eskimos about ten years. Kavavouk and me would travel by sled to distant camps and deal for their fox skins. Then we traded the skins into Fort Ross, so we got along fine with the Company men there, and did very good for ourselves.

In 1949 the Company asked me to come back to help open a new post they was going to build at Spence Bay. There was no talk about leaving Nipasha behind this time, so I was glad to go. To tell the truth, I never wanted to be out of the Company. I always was a Company man.

I liked working for the Company because, you see, the Company looked after the natives. For one thing, it wouldn't let them just hang around a trading post wasting their time. It'd give them an outfit and send them off to the trapping grounds. If they found the trapping wasn't too good when they got there, the Company might even ship them to some other place where there was good trapping. That's what we done with the people from Cape Dorset.

It's very bad for people to hang around a settlement the way they do here at Spence Bay now, because there's no seals here and they can't get their own kind of food. In the old days, and the way the Company tried to keep it, they'd mostly live off the land. So long as they got some tools, and shells, and tea, tobacco, and a bit of sugar from the post, they was well satisfied.

Fort Ross was closed in 1946 on account of there'd been so many bad ice years when the Nascopie couldn't make it down Prince Regent Inlet. Whoever it was decided to put Fort Ross on the east side of Boothia in the first place should'a' knowed better. All they had to do was read old John Ross's book about how he lost his ship there.

I've read that book and I guess I've visited just about every place Ross was at. You can still see where they harboured the Victory—and lost her—and every place they camped when they was exploring, and after, when they was trying to get out of the country alive.

Most places still looks like they was there day before yesterday. Bits of half-burned barrel staves still on the stone fireplaces; tin cans not rusted out even yet; and bones of what they could kill to eat and, sometimes, of the men who didn't make it. Many's a time I've camped on their old camps, and it give me some funny feelings.

Back in 1939, after we got Fort Ross built, Lorenz Learmonth sent me seventy miles north along the coast of Somerset Island to Fury Beach where Ross's people spent the winter when they was trying to get out to Lancaster Sound in their longboats.

Fury Beach is a mile and a half long and from one end to the other there's old barrels, barrel hoops, anchors, tin cans, chains, piles of coal, old ropes, tools, iron bars, everything you could just about imagine. Most of it come from the Fury, a British exploring ship was wrecked there in 1825. We found one of her big bronze cannon, and three of her iron ones Ross's men had set up on a ledge in the hills behind to signal any ship that might happen by. But, of course, no ships could get into Regent Inlet any more than the Victory could get out.

Me and a chap named Patsy Klengenberg, who was part of the Aklavik's crew and come from the western Arctic, found the graves of two of Ross's fellows. You couldn't dig into the frozen ground to make a proper grave, of course, so they had built them graves on top of the ground with stones and such. We opened the end of one and you could see the frozen feet of one fellow sticking out of a rough-made coffin and the black socks still on his feet. I picked up a brass button and I wanted to get into the rest of the coffin and see what relics I could find but Patsy was scared out of his wits, so all I did was take the button.

The natives that started coming into Fort Ross had lots of stories about the Ross expedition. They would tell us how their grandfathers saw the Victory when she was froze into winter harbour and, of course, it was the first ship they'd ever seen. They was quite leery about going close to it until two white men come out and met them, and showed they was friendly, and invited them aboard.

I forget how many Eskimos was in the first party but one of them was named Toolalarik. Once they got aboard, the white men invited them into a cabin to sit down and have dinner. Well, you know, when an Eskimo goes into an igloo the first thing he does is take off his skin clothing, especially if it's deerskin, and shake the snow out of it so it won't thaw and get wet.

So there was all these people jammed in there, and Toolalarik was trying to get his parka off, and the knife he had in his belt got shoved into the calf of his leg. It made quite a wound and later it got infected and gangrene started. There was a doctor on Ross's ship and he finally had to amputate Toolalarik's leg. Then the ship's carpenter set to and made him a wooden leg, and when he got healed they fitted it on with rawhide lashings and it worked very good.

Poerlak, the fellow told me the story, said that when Toolalarik got old and died the people buried him, but took the wooden leg off and threw it into a pond because, you know, it wasn't really part of him though he'd wore it most of his life.

Poerlak said the leg was still in that pond and people could still see it there. Well, we didn't believe the yarn but we told him if he'd bring us that old fellow's wooden leg, we'd pay him something for it. We thought that was the end of it, but darned if he didn't go off and fetch the leg. Now it's in the Company museum in Winnipeg. They know it's the real thing because it's got the doctor's name carved into it.

But I've yarned enough about them old times. You likely want to talk about what happened here at Spence last winter. Since you was here for the trial, Farley, you already knows a good bit about it, but maybe I can help with some of the rest of it.

CHAPTER   TWENTY

The Exiles

ON FRIDAY EVENING, APRIL 15, 1966, THE FLUORESCENT lights in a classroom of the newly built school at Spence Bay glared down upon a strange assembly. A gentle-faced older white man clad in the forbidding majesty of a judge's gown sat at the teacher's desk. Facing him with an earnestness that was almost a parody on the earnestness of the children who normally occupied the room, sixty-five mostly native men and women squeezed into school desks, overflowed folding chairs, lined the walls, or squatted on the floor.

Prominent in the foreground were several RCMP officers in crimson ceremonial jackets; four black-gowned lawyers; a group of immaculately dressed expert witnesses; and a clutch of employees of Northern Affairs, among them Ernie Lyall.

Massed toward the rear of the room, unsmiling and unspeaking, were more of the people whose land this was. Clad in parkas, plaid shirts, and gay cotton frocks, they were dressed as if for a dance—but their demeanour was as sombre as if they were attending a death watch. They had been *told*—not invited—to gather here to witness the way southern justice would deal with two young men of their race who had transgressed against the white man's law.

The Court of the Northwest Territories came to order.

Shooyuk E5-883 and Aiyaoot E5-22, both of Levesque Harbour, do jointly stand charged in that, on or about the 15th day of July, 1965, at or near Levesque Harbour, they did unlawfully commit capital murder of Soosie E5-20....

Shooyuk E5-883 and Aiyaoot E5-22 stood as the court clerk read the details of the charges against them. Their faces showed nothing, even when Ernie Lyall translated the charges into their own language. The grave ritual in which they were central figures was incomprehensible to them. They stood immobile, with downcast eyes.

The prosecution began its case at 9:00 the following morning. By 11:00 p.m. a verdict had been rendered and sentence passed.

Late in the summer of 1913 the Hudson's Bay Company established what was then its most northerly post, at Cape Dorset on the southwestern tip of Baffin Island. Thereafter the Inuit of that region, a singularly competent and effective people, were no longer absolute masters of their own destinies.

In the spring of 1926 one of them, a man named Sangalee, fathered a daughter. She was a fine, large baby who, according to custom, should have been named after an ancestor. However, Christianity had followed the Company to Cape Dorset, and the Anglican missionary christened the child Susannah. The people could not properly pronounce the name. They called her Soosie.

Soosie's early childhood was lived during the halcyon days of the white fox boom. Trading posts spread across the arctic islands and along the mainland coast from Hudson Bay to the Bering Sea. The way of life of all but the most inaccessible Eskimos changed from an emphasis on meat hunting to fox trapping.

Then in the early 1930s the price paid for a good white fox pelt plummeted from as much as a hundred dollars to five or less, which, in terms of the value an Inuit actually received for a skin, meant as little as fifty cents. Many trading posts shut down.

Hard times and famine ensued throughout the Arctic.

During 1931 and 1932 nearly three-quarters of the children born to Cape Dorset people died of malnutrition or its attendant diseases during their first year. Soosie was one of the survivors.

At this juncture the Company made a proposal to the Canadian government. Ownership of the immense high Arctic archipelago now known as the Queen Elizabeth Islands had been disputed by Norway, the United States, and other powers. The Company suggested that Canada's claims of sovereignty could be strengthened by settling these vast, currently uninhabited lands, with "Eskimos who have been made indigent by the current economic problems." The Company undertook to do the "settling." The government accepted the offer, subject to the proviso that, should the settlers become dissatisfied with their new homes, the Company would repatriate them.

In the autumn of 1933 the post managers at Cape Dorset, Pangnirtung, and Pond Inlet began recruiting colonists. This was no easy task since the people were closely bound by tradition and familiarity to the places where their ancestors had lived and died. The Cape Dorset manager found no recruits until he enlisted the help of Kavavouk, a camp boss who had become prosperous as a Company man and who would later become Ernie Lyall's father-in-law.

Kavavouk assured the Cape Dorset people they would be going to a country where game and fur abounded, and would be provided with equipment and food until they were well established. He also reaffirmed the post manager's assurance of a passage home if they should be dissatisfied with their new country.

A desperately hard winter gave added weight to Kavavouk's arguments and finally his cousin Sangalee (Soosie's father), together with several other heads of families, agreed to make the move.

When the Company's supply ship *Nascopie* steamed out of Cape Dorset Bay on August 14, 1934, twenty-two men, women, and children stood at the rails watching the hills of home fade in the distance. Among them was eight-year-old Soosie.

At Pangnirtung the settlers were joined by three families and, at Pond Inlet, by three more. Then *Nascopie* steamed on toward the forbidding coast of Devon Island. On August 23, she dropped anchor under Devon's high and icy mountains.

The colonists were landed at Dundas Harbour on the shore of a steep-walled fiord almost surrounded by an ice cap which rose to six thousand feet. This land might have been habitable by Titans—it was not so for mortal men.

Although no native people had ever lived here, the place *had* been briefly occupied by white men. In 1924 the government had established a two-man RCMP post at Dundas Harbour in an early attempt at showing the Canadian flag. For a short time that flag had whipped and frayed in the fierce winds funnelling off the ice cap, but the fiord had so imprisoned the policemen that they could neither patrol nor hunt sufficient meat to feed their dogs. The post was soon abandoned.

Dundas Harbour was totally alien to the life experiences of the Dorset settlers, who were used to a land of rolling hills and tundra plains. Here were no caribou and few foxes. Before two months had elapsed, they were longing to return to their own country. The Company employee who was their nominal guardian explained that nothing could be done until the ship returned the following summer. So they, together with the Pond and Pangnirtung families, endured privation that winter, surviving on handouts from their guardian, who was comfortably ensconced in the snug house built by the police.

When, late in the summer of 1935, *Nascopie* finally reappeared, the "colonists" were determined to board her. But she anchored well offshore and, having landed a quantity of supplies from a lighter, quickly steamed away. The people were told that *next* year, if they were still determined to leave, the ship would take them home.

The second winter at Dundas Harbour was worse than the first. In a desperate attempt to obtain seals, one hunter, Kitsualik, ventured too far out on the ice and was carried away on the running pack. It took him a week to regain the land, by which time he had lost all his dogs and was himself close to death. Several children died that winter and the rest of the colonists survived on relief rations doled out by the Company agent.

Separated only by the narrow gut of Bellot Strait, Boothia Peninsula and Somerset Island together form a gigantic finger thrusting northward from the arctic mainland. In the early 1930s this region was exclusively occupied by the Netchilingmiut—Seal People. No trader had yet succeeded in planting a post among them. The Company had tried to do so but had been rebuffed by shallow, ice-filled seas, and by the Netchilingmiut themselves, whose preference for their own way of life was so strong that intruders bringing winds of change were made to feel unwelcome.

In the mid-1930s the Company determined to make a new assault on this last Inuit redoubt. A post was to be established, and the intransi-

gence of the Netchilingmiut was to be dealt with, by planting "domesticated Eskimos" in their midst.

The people selected for this role were the Baffin Island families who
had been transported to Dundas Harbour.

In the autumn of 1935 the Company apprised government officials
that Dundas Harbour had proved to be unsuitable and requested permission to move the people to a better place. Although the newly chosen site had no bearing whatsoever on Canada's desire to proclaim her
sovereignty over the Arctic Archipelago, permission was granted for
this new removal.

On a late August morning in 1936 the sonorous blast of *Nascopie*'s whistle again echoed from the high cliffs surrounding Dundas Harbour. By
the time the ship dropped anchor, the entire population, dogs and all,
had gathered at the shore, desperate to embark. One of Soosie's surviving sisters recalled the feeling on that day.

"Everyone think now they going home. Bad times over now. Pretty
soon we see all people we leave behind at Cape Dorset."

But when *Nascopie* cleared the fiord she headed *westward*, bound not
for Cape Dorset but for uninhabited Elizabeth Harbour on the southern coast of Boothia, not far from where John Ross had endured two
terrible winters. In her holds she carried materials with which to build
and stock a trading post. The Baffin Island Inuit aboard did not yet
know they had been chosen to help make that post successful.

The ship penetrated only a short distance into Prince Regent Inlet
before being stopped by impenetrable ice. She turned back and two
days later anchored at Arctic Bay in north Baffin Island, where young
Ernie Lyall was chief clerk at the Company post. A decision was made
to offload the "settlers" and their materials and supplies here, and to
pick them up the following summer for a second attempt on Boothia.

The Pangnirtung people absolutely refused to leave the ship until it
took them home. The Pond Inlet families, whose home lay only 150
miles distant from Arctic Bay, agreed to go ashore, but kept their own
counsel about what they would do after landing.

Most of the Cape Dorset people were for following the lead of the
Pangnirtung families. But Kavavouk, the Company man, insisted they

must go ashore. There was an RCMP detachment aboard ship which, said Kavavouk, would force them off if they did not go voluntarily. Company employees explained that, in any case, it was now too late for *Nascopie* to return them to Dorset this year. However, if the people were still of the same mind when *next* summer came, they *would* be taken home.

Again the Dorset families found themselves in alien country. Hesitant to impinge on the hunting grounds of the Arctic Bay Inuit, the Dorset refugees huddled close to the trading post and for the third successive year survived essentially on dole. The Pond Inlet people quietly slipped away home.

During that long winter the Company changed its plans. Lorenz Learmonth, post manager at Gjoa Haven, had long been anxious to open the heart of the Netchilingmiut country to trade. During the winter of 1936 he persuaded the Company to mount a dual assault. The auxiliary schooner, *Aklavik*, would attempt to reach Boothia from Tuktoyaktuk in the west while *Nascopie* made a similar attempt from the east. If either succeeded, a post would be established at Bellot Strait. If *both* made it, the age-old dream of a commercially useful northwest passage would also have been realized. In either case the Netchilingmiut would, as a Company historian put it, "have been brought into contact with the modern world."

Ice conditions during the summer of 1937 were exceptionally favourable. The little *Aklavik* wormed her way through the pack to Gjoa Haven, then to and through Bellot Strait, where she found *Nascopie*, laden with the bulk of the wherewithal with which to establish the new post of Fort Ross.

This wherewithal included the Dorset families, who had re-boarded the ship at Arctic Bay in the belief that, when *Nascopie* finished her northern supply rounds, she would drop them off at Cape Dorset on her way south. Instead of which, on the last day of August they found themselves huddled disconsolately on a rocky foreshore below the site of the future Fort Ross, watching the smudge of smoke from *Nascopie*'s funnel vanish on the autumnal skyline.

A man named Napachee-Kadlak vividly remembered how his people felt.

"Now all know never go home. Some women they cry and don't eat nothing. Nobody like this place. Netchilingmiut don't like to see strangers. We don't know this country. We don't know what to do."

Lorenz Learmonth knew what to do. The Dorset people would be of no use to the Company if they succumbed to apathy and hung around the post. His solution was to send them to the uninhabited northern tip of Somerset Island where, it was thought, necessity would force them to pick up the threads of life again, while at the same time they would open up a virgin source of fur.

The young man chosen to manage the northern outpost, which was grandiloquently named Port Leopold, was Ernie Lyall.

Lyall and his charges had a hard time of it. Sea-ice conditions at Port Leopold were as bad as they had been at Dundas Harbour. There were almost no caribou and, indeed, the country roundabout was so inhospitable the Netchilingmiut had never attempted to make use of it. After two semi-starvation winters, the Company finally permitted Lyall to bring "his" Eskimos south again. But some of them refused to go to Fort Ross. They chose instead to camp on the north shore of Creswell Bay, a reasonably hospitable place some sixty miles north of Fort Ross.

From here they made a final plea to be returned to Cape Dorset. They were refused. In fact, that same summer *Nascopie* brought out two *additional* Cape Dorset families who had been persuaded to emigrate by glowing accounts given to them of the prosperity being enjoyed by the original migrants.

When *Nascopie* landed the newcomers at Fort Ross, she also disembarked an unseen and deadly passenger. Before the end of October, fourteen of the Fort Ross Eskimos had died of influenza—and six more were dead at Creswell Bay.

Weak from the disease (which had afflicted almost every man, woman, and child) and lashed by violent blizzards which had made the east coast of Somerset Island infamous among the Netchilingmiut, the Creswell Bay survivors began the first winter in this, *their sixth place of exile.*

A rampart of cliffs paralleling the north shore of Creswell Bay promised some shelter from the gales. Kitsualik and another man built snow houses halfway between the cliffs and the shore, but Jamesee,

Johanee, and a young man named Josee built theirs close under a rock wall which towered a hundred feet above them.

Soosie, now fourteen, had become a strikingly handsome young woman who stood nearly a head taller than the rest of her people. Sharply intelligent, she was a paragon of domestic skills. Although betrothed to Josee, she was still living with her family. The young couple had intended to marry the previous autumn but the epidemic had killed both Josee's father and his uncle, thus making the young man the sole support of two widows and five children. So he was not ready to take on the responsibilities of yet another family.

December blizzards roared over Creswell Bay with such fury that it became almost impossible to hunt seals at their breathing holes on the wind-burnished ice of Prince Regent Inlet. Meat became scarce. Dogs began dying. People were growing gaunt.

During the first week of January the winds died down, but snow continued to fall heavily. Jamesee and Johanee moved their families into igloos on the offshore ice in order to be nearer the sealing grounds. Josee considered following suit but, because he had eight people to house, decided to leave his dependants where they were while he himself hunted from Jamesee's small igloo. Luck was with him. One day he managed to spear two big seals. Happily he hauled them home to his big snow house in the lee of the cliffs, and that night he and the women and children feasted.

That same night the north wind began to blow a living gale. Well fed and warm, the family was unperturbed by the skirl of the wind reverberating through the walls of the snow house. Slowly the sound grew muted and the people slept. They did not realize that the roar of the blizzard was being muffled by a torrent of drifting snow driving over the edge of the cliff and burying their snow house.

Some hours later when Josee tried to go outside he found the entrance tunnel so solidly blocked it took him an hour to cut his way out. When he eventually broke through it was to find himself in a world of appalling turmoil.

"Snow coming over cliff like a river," he later testified. "Nothing could I see. It was as if my head was under freezing water. The snow filled up the hole I dug even while I tried to look around. The igloo was buried. I thought we better get out of there."

Scrambling back into the igloo which, because it was now blanketed under many feet of snow, and lit and warmed by several seal-oil lamps, seemed especially snug, Josee told the women to dress themselves and the children in their warmest garments.

"We have to go!" he ordered urgently.

The women began to obey, then paused. If the storm was so bad, how and where would they find safe shelter? Burdened by children, they might not be able to reach Jamesee's or Johanee's small igloos, or even find them in the blinding drift. They decided it would be better to stay where they were until the storm ended. Even if they could not then dig their own way out, Jamesee and Johanee would surely find and free them.

Josee was unable to change their minds. He lingered for a while in an agony of indecision, then made his choice. He would go anyway. The oldest child, a boy of ten who already considered himself enough of a man to make his own decision, also struggled into his outer clothing and followed Josee out the tunnel. In due course these two reached Jamesee's igloo out on the ice.

The blizzard raged for another day and night. Then came a lull. Josee, Jamesee, and Johanee made their way to shore against a wind still powerful enough to sometimes bring them to their knees. The ground drift hid all landmarks and the snow was still rolling over the cliff edge like an avalanche. The three men searched hard but could find nothing to indicate where the buried igloo lay. Finally the rising wind, keening at hurricane pitch, forced them to retreat to the shelter of the igloos on the ice.

When the storm finally blew itself out and the grey light of a short winter day returned, the three men again went back to shore. By then the landscape appeared so changed as to be almost unrecognizable. An immense and faceless drift more than a mile long sloped from within a few feet of the crest of the cliff almost to the beach. The bewildered searchers had no way of ascertaining where, under that mass of hard-packed snow, two women and four children lay entombed.

Desperately they probed and dug. They stood together and shouted at the top of their voices—and got no answer. For nearly a week they tried to penetrate the anonymous white shroud until, exhausted and borne down by sorrow, they accepted defeat.

Early in February Josee walked to Fort Ross and reported the tragedy. The post manager radioed the police detachment at faraway Pond Inlet. The police replied that they would send a sled patrol when they could. Satisfied that he had done all that the white men might require of him, Josee returned to Creswell Bay where he and Soosie became man and wife.

On February 27, Constable J.W. Doyle and two Inuit men set out from Pond Inlet, three hundred air miles (but closer to twice that distance by dog team) from Creswell Bay. They travelled south through Baffin's mountains to Foxe Basin, then turned west and north to follow the precipitous coast of the Brodeur Peninsula. On May 5, after two months' travelling, the three were finally completing the dangerous crossing of Prince Regent Inlet's broken ice when they saw a dog team approaching. Its driver was Josee, who had driven a hundred miles out onto the ice in hopes of killing a polar bear.

Doyle's party followed Josee back to the Dorset camp, where the policeman found "all the people very hungry." He gave them what food he could spare, but his own rations were almost gone so, three days later, he and his two companions set out for Fort Ross with Josee as their guide.

The disaster at Creswell Bay had been a principal topic of discussion at the post for three months. The whites there, including Ernie Lyall, had concluded in their wisdom that Josee must at least have been negligent; it was even suggested that he might have deliberately abandoned his mother, aunt, and four children in order to free himself of domestic obligations so he could marry Soosie.

"Eskimos don't have much sense of responsibility," Lyall later said. "If things get too difficult, someone may just walk away and leave, and those remaining have to look after themselves. Even if Josee's story was more or less true, he should have stayed in the igloo with his family."

With Lyall acting as interpreter, Josee was searchingly questioned. He tried to placate his interrogators by telling them what they seemed to want to hear and, in so doing, reinforced the belief that he was somehow culpable.

At least some of his inquisitors must have been aware that an Inuk will say what is not so if he believes this will please a *kablunak*. Furthermore, they must have known that to repeatedly question an

Inuk on a given point is to tell him he is not believed. And an Inuk accused of lying is deeply shamed thereby.

On May 18, Doyle, accompanied by Lyall, Josee, and the post manager, returned to Creswell Bay. Josee had not been officially charged with any crime but it was obvious to his own people that he was under suspicion.

Doyle needed the bodies of the missing people as evidence if charges were to be laid, so all the men in the Dorset camp were dragooned into a work party to search for the buried igloo.

Josee was permitted to live in his own camp with his young wife, Soosie. Nothing is known of what passed between them. Josee exerted himself to find the bodies which might incriminate him, and, in fact, it was due to his efforts that they *were* eventually discovered.

The searchers dug a shaft *thirty-four feet deep* at a point Josee indicated. The snow was so hard-packed it had to be hewed with an axe. It took eight men three days to sink the shaft. Then they drove a lateral tunnel twenty feet farther and found the igloo.

It was empty. A hole in a side wall showed where the imprisoned people had tried to break free. They had dug like moles, filling in the tunnel behind them as they dug it out in front. The searchers tried to follow, but the work was so laborious that Doyle decided to give it up and wait for the summer sun to melt the great engulfing drift.

He spent the next few months at Fort Ross as the Company's guest. Josee spent that time at Creswell Bay in deepening darkness of the spirit. People tended to avoid him. It was not that *they* thought him guilty of a crime, but the white men clearly did.

Constable Doyle returned to Creswell Bay on August 4. By then the corpses had melted out of the drift. They told a ghastly story. Confined in chill darkness, the imprisoned people had burrowed blindly, not to the southward, where they might have made an escape, but *westward* along the foot of the line of cliffs. One by one they had succumbed, their bodies entombed by the hands of those still scrabbling onward.

When Doyle travelled back to Fort Ross, Josee went with him—but now he was under arrest on suspicion of murder.

The *Nascopie* arrived at Fort Ross on September 14 carrying a police detachment whose senior officer served as magistrate. Josee was arraigned before Inspector D.J. Martin and formally charged with criminal negligence resulting in the death of two women and four children. However, *Nascopie*'s captain was impatient to be gone so, instead of being tried at once, Josee was remanded until *Nascopie* should return, *a full year hence.*

There being no jail at Fort Ross, he was released as a prisoner in his own custody and told to go back to Creswell Bay. And wait. He set out, freighted with memories of what lay behind, fearful of the vengeance threatened by the white man's law. Diminished and dishonoured in his own eyes and sullied in those of his people, he must have concluded there was only one way out.

He opened a bottle of patent liniment, clearly marked with the warning skull and crossbones...and drained it. He did this less than a mile distant from the skin tent whose translucent walls glowed with the light of a lamp tended by Soosie, his pregnant wife.

CHAPTER TWENTY-ONE

Ayorama

MOST OF THE CRESWELL BAY PEOPLE ACCEPTED Josee's death with resignation. *Ayorama*—nothing to be done. But Soosie believed the *kablunait* had destroyed her husband and, after being delivered of a stillborn child, her resentment against those who had brought her and her people to such a pass hardened into hatred.

Sangalee tried to soothe his daughter, but she paid him no heed.

The past several years had aged Sangalee far beyond his time, and it seems his will to live had drained away. One savagely cold February night in 1942 he crawled out from under the robes where he had lain for several days in the grip of a fever. Dressed only in sealskin trousers he left the igloo so quietly that none heard or saw him go.

Sangalee had gone walking on the land.

Soosie and her mother were now alone, but in the early spring of 1942 Soosie married Napachee-Kadlak. A gentle though rather ineffective man, her new husband tried to persuade her to move to Levesque Bay, just eight miles from Fort Ross, where the remaining followers of Kavavouk, the Company camp boss, lived. Angrily she refused. Never again, she told him, would she live close to the white men. Her hopes for the future rested in maintaining an independent way of life, not in relying on a trading post.

"She tell us," Napachee-Kadlak remembered, "we got to be *Inuit* again. Live like the old people and stay away from the *kablunait*."

Napachee-Kadlak bent to her impassioned arguments, thereby

hallowing the fact that the Creswell Bay exiles had found a leader in Sangalee's daughter.

During the summer and early autumn of 1942, Soosie goaded and guided her people through a frenzy of activity. Never before had they caught and dried so many fish. Never before had they made such prolonged and successful journeys into the interior after caribou. Never had they killed more seals. By late September the Creswell Bay camp was more than adequately provisioned against the long night of winter.

To the south of them disaster struck. Ice conditions prevented *Nascopie* from reaching Fort Ross with supplies for the year ahead. Kavavouk's people at Levesque Harbour, who were heavily dependent on the Company post, were soon in dire need. By March of 1943, when an RCMP constable patrolled to Fort Ross from Arctic Bay, most of the Levesque Harbour people were sick, some with what was clearly tuberculosis, many more of an unidentified disease that had already killed several. One of the dead was Kavavouk himself. His fealty to the Company had not been enough to save him.

Soosie's band had no contact with Fort Ross that winter and were spared both disease and starvation. They hunted vigorously on the sea ice for seals and bears and, when ammunition ran out, reverted to the use of harpoons and spears. For the first time in many years the returning sun of spring was not obscured for them by mists of sorrow.

They continued to do well. Four children were born to the Creswell Bay camp in the summer of 1943, and all survived. One of these was a son born to Soosie. She named him Aiyaoot.

That summer *Nascopie* again failed to reach Fort Ross. In consequence that remote little trading post became newsworthy. Newspaper headlines in the south proclaimed that two white men and the wife of one of them were marooned in the Arctic without food and fuel. A major rescue effort was mounted by the federal government. As soon as the autumnal ice grew strong enough, a Canadian Army officer was parachuted down to direct the Inuit in preparing a landing strip on the bay ice. When this was completed, a C-47 transport plane landed, picked up the officer and the other three whites, and flew them south to safety.

It did not evacuate any of the sick or needy people from nearby Levesque Harbour.

Fortunately for these people, Ernie Lyall did not abandon Fort Ross. Years later, when I asked him why he had stayed behind, he found it hard to answer.

"Don't know exactly. Things didn't look good at all, you know. Nothing left at the post and nothing to be got from the country. Was hard to see that big, near-empty plane take off and head south, but my wife and kids belonged to the Levesque Harbour camp so that was their people here; so they were sort of my people too."

The whites had rescued their own. It was left to Lyall to try to rescue those who had been abandoned. Summer passed, and winter again brought famine. Accompanied by Takolik, Kavavouk's son and Lyall's brother-in-law, Lyall set out by dog team in bitter December weather to seek help from the nearest Company post, which was at Arctic Bay, nearly *three hundred miles distant by the route the two men would have to follow, and which neither had travelled before.* The travellers had almost no food for the dogs and little for themselves except a few pounds of sugar. Their survival depended on twenty rounds of ammunition.

It took a week to cross the treacherous broken pack in Prince Regent Inlet, but the ice was their salvation for on it they found and shot a polar bear. On reaching the Baffin coast, they lost themselves in the mountains for ten days. By the time they reached Arctic Bay they were, as Lyall remembered, "mostly bones and fur."

They completed the return journey to Levesque Harbour with relief supplies in mid-January, but by the end of February all the food their two small dog teams had been able to haul home was gone. Undaunted, Lyall made a *second* trip to Arctic Bay, returning in early April. There is little question but that, without his help, many or most of the people at Levesque Harbour would have perished.

Meanwhile the Creswell Bay camp had required no assistance. Napachee-Kadlak and Jamesee made one hunting trip onto the ice of Prince Regent Inlet during which they killed two bears and a huge square-flipper seal. Hunters closer to home were able to spear a number of ring seals. Together, the men provided ample meat and fat to feed thirty-five human beings and to keep five teams of dogs in good condition. It did not matter to them that the Company post at Fort Ross was closed.

In early September of 1944, a man from Levesque Harbour who had gone to the empty trading post in search of scrap metal for sled runners hastened back, wild with excitement. *Nascopie* had finally got through and now lay at anchor in the harbour!

Within a week the post was open again, but its future was shadowed.

A Netchilingmiut shaman had had a vision in which he saw the whole region swept clean of human beings by a mysterious and lethal visitation. The old man warned people to leave the northern extremities of the country. In consequence, the Netchilingmiut entirely abandoned the upper part of Boothia Peninsula. The immigrants from Cape Dorset remained where they were, for they had nowhere else to go.

With the end of World War II, the value of white fox pelts soared, and the five families at Levesque Harbour began actively trapping again. Soon the Company store was selling them such exotica as battery radios, aluminum cookware, cameras, and gaudy articles of clothing made from new synthetic fibres.

Every effort was made to bring the Creswell Bay band back into the fold too. Eventually the glittering array of trade goods now available at Fort Ross had their effect. Although Soosie seems to have done her best to prevent it, individuals and even families began drifting south to Levesque Harbour.

By the spring of 1947 only Soosie's family and one other remained at Creswell Bay. Now Napachee-Kadlak insisted that his family too must move south. Only with the greatest reluctance did Soosie acquiesce.

"Very hard make her go," Napachee-Kadlak remembered. "She say if we go only bad things happen."

Soosie's pessimism was soon vindicated. In August, while northbound on her annual supply run, *Nascopie* struck a rock and sank at, of all places, Cape Dorset. Her loss determined the Company to again close Fort Ross—this time for good. In 1948 Ernie Lyall locked up the buildings and took his family to Gjoa Haven by dogsled.

After these abandonments, Soosie tried to persuade her people to move back to Creswell Bay where they would still be able to live off the land. At first she had little success because people believed the Company would either build a new post somewhere within reach of Levesque Harbour or perhaps—at long last—repatriate the exiles to Cape Dorset.

Soosie proclaimed these to be false dreams, and her vehement rejection of all that white men stood for began making people uneasy. When six families finally agreed to do as she demanded, it may have been as much because of a desire to placate her as because they believed she was right.

Shortly after these six families had reestablished themselves at Creswell Bay, and soon after the birds had proclaimed the coming of spring, people at both camps began sickening from an unknown and terrible ailment. Some were asphyxiated when the muscles of their throats and chests constricted. Some sank into comas from which, if they roused at all, they found themselves with crippled and useless limbs.

Poliomyelitis had come upon them.

Soosie was several months pregnant when she was stricken. She lost the baby. Although the disease did not otherwise cripple her, it struck deep into mind and spirit. During the remainder of this year she was lost in a bottomless pit of depression.

The outside world knew nothing of the new tragedy until mid-January of 1949, when a party of Netchilingmiut from Gjoa Haven found Takolik wandering destitute on the ice of Rae Strait after his dogs had died of starvation. He was en route to Gjoa bearing a message from a white man who had unexpectedly appeared at abandoned Fort Ross.

Surely it was an ironic trick of fate that brought Lorenz Learmonth back to Fort Ross at this fatal juncture. No longer a fur trader, Learmonth was indulging an amateur's interest in archaeology, investigating the fate of the vanished Thule people. At Fort Ross he had found himself faced with the dissolution of a people in the present. He could do little for them except write a message reporting their dire plight and give it to Takolik to deliver to Gjoa Haven, which had a radio link with the outside world.

Early in February, a ski-equipped DC-3 landed on the ice of Levesque Bay, bringing relief supplies and a doctor. The doctor found that several babies, five older children, and three adults had died there and at Creswell Bay of polio. The remainder were so weakened by starvation or crippled by the disease that none was able to hunt. Both camps were close to their last extremity.

The rescue plane made several trips to Levesque Harbour and to Creswell Bay ferrying polio victims out to hospital and bringing in supplies. These were distributed by Ernie Lyall, who had been hired by DNA to take charge. There were no more deaths, and by the time the ice melted in the spring, the survivors of the terrible winter seemed able to cope for themselves.

At this juncture Lyall was hired by the HBC to help establish a new post at Spence Bay, some six days' sled travel south of abandoned Fort Ross. Before going south Lyall, acting on instructions from DNA, told the people in the two camps that they too must now move to Spence Bay.

This they did not do—perhaps because they simply could not face another dislocation to yet another place of exile.

When they failed to appear at Spence, the authorities all but forgot about them. Occasionally someone from Levesque Harbour would appear at Spence to buy ammunition, but Soosie's camp—as it was now called—remained in effect a little world of its own.

In 1953 a party of scientists visited it. One of them wrote of Soosie:

She was a formidable woman. Good looking, and the biggest Eskimo I ever saw. She had three or four kids and kept them in great form even though the whole bunch was having tough times when we arrived. They were out of ammunition and hadn't been able to get many seals. Soosie made me nervous. She had a way of looking past you, as if she could see things you didn't know were there.

The following year Takolik's family and two others moved to Spence Bay, but although Soosie's Creswell Bay camp had now joined the remaining people at Levesque, Soosie remained inflexibly opposed to moving any farther south. During the tragic events of 1948–49, her behaviour had sometimes been erratic and even frightening, but these moods were becoming less frequent. She seemed to be returning to her old, indomitable self—until the spring of 1958, when an epidemic of what may have been measles struck the camp, killing three children, one of whom was hers.

At this juncture the authorities again intervened. One summer day an Otter arrived, bringing an RCMP constable and Ernie Lyall, who had once again left the service of the Company to work for DNA. The people were told that all children of school age were to be taken to a school far to the south—and would not return to their parents until the following summer.

"This was the worst thing for us," Napachee-Kadlak recalled. "Worse thing than hunger or TB. We love our children. Now we not got them any more."

Midway into her seventh pregnancy, Soosie reacted to the removal of her school-age children by suffering a total breakdown. She was taken to Spence Bay, then evacuated to a psychiatric hospital in Alberta.

A month after the children had been removed, the people of the combined camp at Levesque Harbour underwent their first examination for tuberculosis. Several were found to be infected. The most serious cases were flown out for treatment. Some did not return for years. Two never did return, having died in ultimate exile in southern sanitaria.

At this point we pass through a door at the end of the long, dark corridor which is the fateful history of Soosie and her people, and emerge into the harsh glare of the classroom court at Spence Bay. An eminent psychiatrist from Montreal is testifying:

"Soosie's symptoms were those of anxiety neurosis....She was exceedingly disturbed....Recovery was slow, but after the birth of the child she was carrying she seemed to make some progress."

Several months later Soosie was returned to Levesque Harbour, but in 1964 she again retreated from her broken world—this time in a straitjacket. After enduring electric shock treatments for six months, she was pronounced cured and sent "home" to a remnant of humanity which had by now shrunk to three women, five men, and twelve children.

And then Soosie vanished out of time. In her place came a visitation driven before the winds of madness.

This woman who had struggled so unrelentingly, and for so long, to preserve her family and her people, now threatened to become their nemesis. Racing through the camp, tearing her hair out by the handfuls, screaming threats at all and sundry, she brought terror into the lives of a community already near the end of its tether.

Snatching her own infant daughter from the pouch in her anorak, she flung the naked child down onto the stony ground. She pursued other people's children, pelting them with rocks. She began destroying the hunting and fishing gear which was the band's very staff of life. Sanity was tottering at Levesque Harbour. Reality was drifting away.

Here are the words of Kadluk, father of Shooyuk, one of the two accused:

"She tell everybody now she have to kill them. She go around blowing her breath on everybody to make them crazy too. We had to keep her off. We couldn't help it, because she was after the people. Three men caught her and she fought them very hard. They tied her up but always she got loose. Three times she got loose...."

One brief and pitiful respite in Soosie's spiral into darkness occurred when Napachee-Kadlak received a tape recording of messages sent by relatives in faraway Cape Dorset. Hoping to calm his wife, he played the tape to her.

"It bring back memories of times we was children in Dorset and real happy then. Soosie was good then when she hear it. She was real happy then...."

It was only a final, dying gleam.

A few hours later she was running through the camp, screaming that God had told her to kill all the people so they would at last be free.

The two other women, five men, and twelve youngsters could not seek help elsewhere. The sea ice was breaking up and the many rivers raging with meltwater made overland travel impossible. Yet they dared not stay in Soosie's vicinity. Even in ordinary times she would have been a match for any of them. Now she was imbued with a madwoman's fearsome strength.

Kadluk described their terrible dilemma.

"One day she jump on Napachee-Kadlak and try to kill him and we just got her away. Then she go to the shore and kill some dogs. Then we know we got to go somewhere."

On July 12 they fled across the shifting ice to a barren islet half a mile offshore. They had with them only what gear they could carry on their backs and in their hands. Beset by dread, they waited on the bleak reef for a deliverance that did not come.

Hour by hour, in almost perpetual daylight, they kept watch over the abandoned camp through Kadluk's old brass telescope.

"We very scared she take knife and come out to kill the people. We very hungry because too scared if men go away hunting she come to women and children. Now we see her throwing our things in the water. She looking like she watching things where there is nothing. She takes everything and shakes it, shaking the devil out of it. She had all the tents down and smashing the poles. We watching her breaking up our gear. The devil is telling her what to do."

For three sleepless days and nights the people on the islet watched and waited. Then they dared wait no longer. They had no more food and Soosie was destroying the equipment at the camp without which food could not be procured.

On the morning of July 15, Napachee-Kadlak and Kadluk spoke to their sons, Aiyaoot and Shooyuk. These were young men, but strong. And there was a task before them which would require great strength, if not of the body then of the spirit.

"I tell them they have to go back," Napachee-Kadlak recalled. "She have to stop smashing everything. Somebody have to stop her. I tell them to get knives away from there, but if she does come after you, don't do anything to her. I love my wife and don't want her hurt. But, if she really come after them, they better shoot...."

Fearfully the two young men crossed the loose ice and approached the shore. When Soosie saw her son and Shooyuk, she came running toward them, screaming imprecations. Hoping to frighten her off, they fired to one side. Still she ran toward them, swaying and swerving and waving her arms wildly.

The rifles crashed again. And Soosie E5-20 was released from her long exile.

In August, when the police plane with Ernie Lyall aboard as interpreter arrived to take the children away to school, Napachee-Kadlak handed Lyall a sheet of wrapping paper covered with the syllabic script. The paper contained a detailed account of everything that had taken place at Levesque Harbour between July 5 and July 15.

The subsequent RCMP investigation took a long time to complete. Meantime, the people at Levesque Harbour, believing that their explanation of what had happened had been accepted, were trying to rebuild what was left of their tattered lives. In October Aiyaoot and Shooyuk travelled to Spence Bay to buy ammunition for the winter hunt. Upon arrival there, both were arrested and charged with murder.

In Yellowknife, Crown attorney David Searle studied the police report and concluded that no charge more serious than that of manslaughter should be laid. He could see no point in adding new agonies to those the Levesque Harbour people had already suffered. However, the Department of Justice in Ottawa disagreed. Searle was instructed to proceed with charges of first-degree murder.

In so deciding, the purveyors of justice sentenced the handful of survivors at Levesque Harbour, as well as the accused, to a new ordeal of seven months' duration.

It was an ordeal which also left its mark on others who found themselves involved.

An RCMP constable was marooned by weather at Levesque Harbour for eight bitter February days while investigating the case, and was fed and sheltered by the very people he was charged with bringing to justice. Ernie Lyall, who had lived with the people as one of them, found himself the agent through whom they convicted themselves of having trespassed against the white man's law. Even the Crown attorney felt compelled to apologize to the court not once, but twice, for what he had to do. An almost palpable shadow seemed to veil the face of justice in the Spence Bay schoolroom—until the Judge tore the veil asunder.

In his address to the jurors, he flatly ordered them to acquit Aiyaoot of all charges, and to give Shooyuk the benefits of their compassion and understanding. This they did and, although they found Shooyuk technically guilty of manslaughter, they strongly recommended mercy.

John Sissons—He-Who-Listens—imposed a mandatory two-year sentence on Shooyuk, then suspended it, telling the youth to go home to his people and "try to forget the things that have happened to you, and try to live a good and happy life."

The casualties of that exercise of justice were multiple. By the end of the trial Napachee-Kadlak, husband of Soosie and father of Soosie's son, Aiyaoot, had become a shambling travesty of a man, his mind fixed almost solely on the past.

A month after the trial came to an end, Kadluk, father of Shooyuk, and one of the chief witnesses for the prosecution, nearly succeeded in drowning himself in the swirling waters of Bellot Strait, not far from the remains of Fort Ross.

And one had only to look into the faces of Aiyaoot and Shooyuk to see that these two young men, who should have been a fount of vitality to a broken community, were as traumatized as shell-shocked victims of war.

Some hours after the trial ended, I found Kadluk standing by himself on a stretch of exposed granite near the edge of the settlement. Awkwardly I tried to tell him of how I felt about what my people had done to him and his.

He did not look at me. His gaze remained fixed on the black rock emerging from the snow at his feet. After a while he murmured, so softly I could hardly hear:

"*Ayorama....*"

CHAPTER   TWENTY-TWO

Top of the
World

D CL TOOK A LEISURELY DEPARTURE FROM SPENCE
Bay bound for Gjoa Haven on the low-lying shores of King
William Island a hundred miles to the southeast. Not much
more than an hour later we touched down in a snug little cove named
for the ship in which, between 1903 and 1906, Norwegian explorer Roald
Amundsen made the first recorded transit of the Northwest Passage.

Prior to Amundsen's visit the place had been little frequented by
the native Netchilingmiut for it lay in a region of few seals or caribou.
Nevertheless it offered a safe harbour in which the explorer could
winter his vessel. For that same reason it later became the site of a
trading post.

Through almost forty years traders had drawn Inuit to Gjoa from
hundreds of miles of surrounding territory but, at the time of our visit,
the place appeared about ready for abandonment. Even three brand-
new DNA housing units perched near the shore seemed poised for
flight.

A few children were playing on the sandy beach. Our noisy arrival
hardly interested them at all, nor was it of any concern to a colony of
terns busy feeding their well-grown young on an adjacent sandbar. As I
walked up the sloping beach I felt a little like the invisible man.

The Arctic embraces enormous physical space but, in terms of its
human community, can be surprisingly small. I had not walked fifty
yards before meeting a pretty young woman of about sixteen in a shape-
less and tattered cotton dress, long black hair flying every which way in

the gentle breeze, her feet bare, and, at her heels, a magnificently dirty little boy.

"Bow-wow!" barked the girl, stopping squarely in front of me.

I was bewildered, even a trifle apprehensive until she added, with a smile:

"That was your dog, eh? That dog Mutt. Remember me? Meet you in Yellowknife in spring when you visit our school. Mary Kitsualik."

Indeed I did remember meeting a girl called Mary, a trim, decorous, neatly dressed teenager who produced a copy of my book *The Dog Who Wouldn't Be*, which she had won as an academic prize, and asked me to autograph it. Could this be the same person?

She laughed at my perplexity. "Guess I don't look much a student now, eh? I come home just for two months, then back to Yellowknife to go to school rest of the year. In Yellowknife I'm sort of *kablunak*. When I'm home I'm *Inuk* all the time."

Mary was summering with her parents and her grandfather, Kitsualik, in one of the new DNA cabins. I visited them there and drank tea and smoked with seventy-year-old Kitsualik while Mary hovered close by, keeping his mug filled or lighting matches for his soapstone pipe.

"Kitsualik was one of the best hunters and travellers around," George Porter, Gjoa's oldest resident and one-time HBC post manager, told me later. "He was one of them Eskimos the Company brought away from Dorset to Boothia back in the thirties. Him and his family was at Creswell Bay the time all them people got smothered in their igloos. That was too much for him so he brought his family across to Gjoa and got to be one of the big men hereabouts. Don't know as I ever met a better."

George himself was a thin, almost emaciated seventy-one-year-old of mixed white and Eskimo parentage. Although a travelling man for much of his life, he had spent his latter years running the Company post at Gjoa, which he considered home. He was somewhat apprehensive that it might not remain such for much longer.

"Gjoa Haven's goin' out. They never was good hunting close by, and now with the people all gathered in here by the government fellows, they got nothing much they can get or do. Looks to me like we might all have to pack it in."

But not quite yet. A Porter reunion was in full swing. George's oldest son with his Inuit wife and their four children had just arrived after a long, complicated journey from Yellowknife, where the son worked for a transportation company. And one of George's daughters accompanied by her six children had flown in from Cambridge Bay. The Porters' three-room house, though now seriously overcrowded, was a jovial and effervescent place, and the lunch served to us newcomers—boiled char and fresh-baked bannock with plenty of raisins in it—seemed exceptionally good.

"Old-time style," George remarked happily as we ate. "Used to be, summertime, all the people would get together in Gjoa from the country places all around, where they'd camped during the winter. Eskimos called it the Meeting Time. Everybody visited and danced and talked all night long like one big family."

George liked to yarn, and he liked rum. That evening he told stories until the midnight sun had dipped to the horizon and climbed well up again.

I was born on Herschel Island, away over there in the western Arctic, the day after Christmas, 1895. My dad was captain of a whaler and my mother an Eskimo lady.

Herschel in them times was a very lively spot. Yankee whalers coming into the north Pacific for bowhead whales had drove the bowheads, what was left of them, right into the Beaufort Sea.

The Beaufort, you know, is part of the Arctic Ocean so it can be a hell of a bad place for ice. Some years ships can get into the Beaufort going around Alaska—sometimes not—so to be sure of a chance at bowheads some whalers would winter-over at Herschel. Which was just a big sandbar about a hundred miles west of the mouth of the Mackenzie. No trees or nothing, just a very good harbour.

The year I was born six or seven whaling ships was froze in there with the most of their men living ashore in shacks. There was a bunch of traders too, and a lot of Eskimos. Must have been close to two thousand people altogether. It was the biggest and liveliest place in the whole Arctic.

It was kind of a no man's land too. There was no such thing as government or law and order. Whalers come from all over the world. They was white, and yellow, and black, and most shades in between, and mostly not the kind you'd want in your parlour of a Sunday. They lived rough and they were rough. Some would move in with Eskimo families rather than live with their mates in the dirty wooden shacks they built, and it was share and share alike with the natives. The whalers brought hard tack and salt meat and other stuff from their ships, and the Eskimos had the fresh meat and fish.

The whalers had no women of their own so they took Eskimo women. Some, like my old dad, married theirs. Most never bothered and after they sailed away in the spring never come back again.

There was a high old time at Herschel all winter, 'cept when there was sickness—measles, smallpox, influenza, stuff like that. There was a lot of TB. Sickness could get very bad, but most times it was square dances and get-togethers and lots of rum and homebrew. That led to trouble and quite a few people got killed one way or t'other. After a time the Canadian government got wind of it and round about 1904 sent two Mounties up to Herschel. Things quieted down some after that, not just because of the Mounties but the whalers was running out of whales and one by one the ships quit coming.

Most of the whalers give up, but my dad stayed at it. In 1914 he took me whaling aboard his ship and we was one of the last. We went east to Banks Island and killed five bowheads. Then we went west all the way to Herald Island off Siberia, but never saw another whale. That was just about the end of the whaling game. The whales was nigh all dead by then.

Herschel kept a-going though, because the arctic coast was a great place for white fox and fox fur was getting to be worth near as much as gold. Trading vessels began pushing east around Alaska, and some used Herschel as a base 'cause ships from San Francisco or Vancouver could unload goods there for small schooners to take farther east.

All sorts of people showed up. When I was ten I met Roald Amundsen at Herschel on his way from Norway to San Francisco in the Gjoa, the first boat to make it through the Northwest Passage. My dad took me aboard of her, but I never thought I'd end up living in the harbour where she spent a couple of winters.

In 1913 along comes another explorer—Vilhjalmur Stefánsson—and he tried to sign me onto his ship, the Karluk. You see, I had sailed a lot in my dad's vessels and so I could do most jobs at sea. And, of course, I knew quite a bit about ice. But I never liked the Karluk's looks so I didn't go. That winter she got caught in the pack and drifted pretty near to Wrangel Island in Siberia before she sunk.

Knud Rasmussen, the Danish fellow who drove a dogsled right across the top of the world all the way from Greenland to Alaska, come by too and I helped him out a bit with dogs and guides.

When the whaling finished, my dad got into trading. He had a schooner of his own and I helped crew her. When the poor old fellow died I started skippering small schooners for other companies trading from Herschel east as far as King William Island.

In 1926 when I was working for the Can-Alaska Trading Company, I took a boat into Gjoa Haven and wintered there, the first to do that since Amundsen's time. I was what you would call a camp trader. The schooner was my home but I was gone most of the time, driving my dogs all over the place to wherever I could find an Eskimo camp with fox furs to trade. I went north to Somerset Island, and south to Perry River. On one trip to Perry I brought back a hundred white fox skins worth maybe five thousand dollars in San Francisco at that time.

Couple of years later Can-Alaska put me in charge of the motor schooner Emma, a twenty-five-tonner. There was just me and a couple of Eskimos to run her to Gjoa, about a thousand miles east along a coast where there was only a handful of trading outposts with maybe one white man in each. Five posts, I believe, about two hundred miles apart.

When you left Herschel, you never knew if you'd get as far as Gjoa that season. It all depended on what the pack ice was doing. There wasn't no charts so you could run her up on a rock most anywhere.

My first trip in the Emma it took us near two months to work east to Perry Island, a couple of hundred miles short of Gjoa. Winter caught us there, and Emma froze in so we spent that winter trading out of her. When summer come, we took her on to Gjoa and built a post ashore. I left a fellow there and hustled back to Herschel with a full cargo of the very finest fur.

I could afford to take a holiday that winter. Went south on the last vessel out of Herschel all the way to San Francisco…mainly to get my teeth fixed. They was rotten from top deck to bottom deck. What with the travel time and things like that, I was gone the best part of a year. Travel was God almighty slow, but you had lots of time to enjoy the scenery, especially when the ship was hung up in the ice and the big floes was trying to put you under.

In 1932 I took the Emma east again from Herschel, and we got nipped by the ice and she sunk in Queen Maud Gulf. She went down so quick we never saved enough off of her to talk about, but the three Eskimos and me got ashore all right on the mainland near Simpsons River.

Well, then we had some real hard times. We had to wait where we was until everything froze up solid enough so the sea ice was fit to walk on. The only place we could get to was Gjoa. It took us twenty-six days with nothing to eat except a little bit of lean caribou meat. I don't say as I would have made it on my own. It was the Eskimos got us through.

The Hudson's Bay Company had started a post at Gjoa by then, run by Paddy Gibson. Their schooner, the Aklavik, with Scotty Gall skipper, was hauled out there for the winter.

Things didn't look good for us. Our post was down and out because of the Emma being sunk. The Company and Can-Alaska was deadly enemies, you understand. But in a case like this white men had to act like Eskimos and look after each other. Scotty and Paddy gave us a good part of their grub, though they could have traded everything they had for fur. Foxes was so plentiful that year, all the Eskimos got rich.

Scotty brought me back to Herschel next summer on the Aklavik, and Can-Alaska wasn't too pleased with me for I come back empty-handed and without the Emma. Just around then the Hudson's Bay Company bought out Can-Alaska so they hired me to run their boat between Herschel and Gjoa. That's when I married a girl from here and settled down to make Gjoa my home.

Not that I spent much time at home. Summers I'd mostly be sailing and that was never what you'd call dull. The old engine was always breaking down and we'd have to repair it with bits of whalebone and stuff like that. Sometimes the pack ice would shift us backward fifty or a hundred miles. Other times it'd put the squeeze on us and we wouldn't know was we going to sink or not. But there was lots of good times too. Sometimes we'd be wind-bound, maybe for as much as a week, so then we'd go back into the country hunting caribou or musk ox, or go visit the native camps. They was the best sort of people. Every trip along the coast was like visiting good friends and neighbours.

Winters I did a lot of sled travel, trading to the native camps. I've made sled trips from Gjoa west to Bathurst Inlet; south up the Back River to Pelly Lake; east to Igloolik; and north to Arctic Bay. I surely know what the backside of a husky looks like.

It was in 1940, I believe, when Sergeant Henry Larson, skipper of the RCMP boat St. Roch, *asked me to come on her when she started east from Herschel Island to try and get through the Northwest Passage west to east, and do it in just one season. Amundsen had done it going the other way, of course, but it'd taken* him pretty near three years. Well, I liked the sound of it so I signed on as special constable and interpreter. But mainly I was the pilot, though you'll find no mention of that in Henry's book about the trip.

Now the St. Roch was a big, strong boat built special for work in the Arctic, but like any other boat she could only get around when the ice would let her.

From Herschel it was plain sailing as far as Cambridge Bay, and I'm sure if we'd kept at it we could have pushed on to Gjoa, and likely through Bellot Strait into Prince Regent Inlet then on to Halifax that same summer. There was a plug of pack ice south of Cambridge Bay, but that was nothing unusual. All it needed was a bit of a west wind to move it out, then it would have been clear sailing.

Larson asked me what I thought we ought to do. I told him: Wait a bit. Give her a week or two to see would a west wind come. It was only the end of August so we had plenty time.

I don't know was it him or the big shots in Ottawa made the decision, but Henry got on the radio and then he turned the St. Roch around and off we went back the way we'd come to try and go north through Prince of Wales Strait into Parry Sound, then east through Lancaster Sound into Baffin Bay.

Well, you know, that really was the long way round. And, of course, nobody had ever managed to take a boat through that northern route. Big ice always stopped them.

It sure stopped us. Prince of Wales Strait was jammed solid with big old ice ten feet thick. By then it was too late to go south again so we put into Walker Bay on northwest Victoria Island, and that's where the St. Roch froze in for the winter, only a few days east of Herschel.

I didn't care too much about what the expedition did after that. Charlie Klengenberg's family was living in Minto Inlet, next to Walker Bay, and I was the best of pals with all of them so that's where I spent a good part of the winter.

Charlie was a Dane who shipped as cook on Yankee whalers. When he come up to Herschel around 1895, he jumped ship and set himself up as an independent trader. The next year he went east in an open whale boat with two natives, and it was him first visited the Eskimos around Coppermine Gulf—the ones Stefánsson later claimed he found, and thought they had some old Vikings as their ancestors.

Charlie did so good trading with them people, who'd never seen a white man before, that he bought a little schooner, married an Eskimo lady—she was my mother's cousin—and started a family. He didn't like having a lot of other white people around him so he settled east. When he died he left his wife and family at

Minto Inlet. His boys was the best go-getters in the north, and his girls the prettiest. Some of the girls married white men but all the boys married Eskimos. The old lady was tough and she was smart and she made them all live like Eskimos, and think like them.

They was a tribe of their own. Nobody could fish, hunt, trap, or travel like they done. The west side of Victoria Island was their paradise. It more or less belonged to them. White fox and muskox skins made them rich enough they could have lived like kings if they'd wanted but that wasn't their way.

Charlie's boy Patsy was my best friend. He told me once, "I been to San Francisco, Seattle, Vancouver, Nome. Been to all them places and if I wanted I could live there and be a Big Man; but I'd have to fight for it. I'd sooner stay down north where you don't have to fight your own people to make a living."

Come March 1941, Henry Larson sends word over to Minto Inlet he wants to make a sled patrol to Banks Island. So I borrowed dogs and gear from Patsy and took Henry there. We was forty-two days on that trip.

It was July before we could get the St. Roch out of Walker Bay. So then I piloted her back west to Tuktoyaktuk, near the mouth of the Mackenzie River, where we loaded supplies for the police detachment at Coppermine. From Coppermine we went on east to Gjoa, and that was far enough for me. I'd been away from my family a year and a half so I went ashore.

Larson took the boat on for Bellot Strait, but they'd wasted too much time freighting in the west and now it was too late in the year. So he got froze in at Pasley Bay on the west side of Boothia and had to spend another winter. Next year he did finally get through Bellot and make it south to Halifax and got a hero's welcome.

I've never said much about it, but the St. Roch could have made the passage that first season. And she would have, if she'd been my boat.

Most Canadians think Henry was the one that bust the passage by way of Bellot Strait, but that's not right either. Back in 1937 the Company schooner Aklavik, with Scotty Gall skipper, come into Gjoa from Herschel and Scotty told me he was supposed to go on east and meet the big Company steamer Nascopie coming from Montreal, and help set up Fort Ross on the eastern side of Boothia.

The only way he could do that, of course, was go through Bellot Strait. So that's what he done. After that he could just as easy have gone right on to Halifax or Montreal, but his wife was against it.

She was quite a woman, I can tell you: an Eskimo lady and a good mother, but a better engineer. She run the engine on the Aklavik *and she could make that old thing go, come hell or high water. She run it up to the day Scotty was in the wheelhouse and called for hard astern as* Aklavik *was coming in to dock. The engine never went astern and the boat run square into the dock with a hell of a bang. When Scotty jumped below into the engine room to find out what had happened, there was his missus lying dead. She'd had a heart attack.*

Anyway, Scotty's wife wanted to get back to Aklavik that time, where her kids was, so after they'd unloaded at Fort Ross they turned around and went on back through Bellot Strait.

I don't give a shoot what the history books has to say about it. Far as I'm concerned Scotty Gall and his missus and the old Aklavik is the ones ought to be up front there in the hall of fame. They done the Northwest Passage not just once. They done it twice—in the same season too!

CHAPTER TWENTY-THREE

Lots of Time

FLYING IN THE ARCTIC HAS CERTAIN ADVANTAGES, BUT
wings can also be a curse. One has to resist an almost irresistible
pressure to push ever onward. "Let's go!" becomes the watch-
word when "Let's stay" is what one would rather do.

There were valid reasons for keeping DCL on the go. Lamb Airways
needed its Otter for other charters. Pete had a deadline for his return to
Montreal. And there was a limit to how much money I could spend.
While we were at Gjoa Haven, Doug glumly announced we were "way
behind schedule" so I reluctantly agreed to hurry our journey westward. I insisted, however, that we *must* visit two special places—Bathurst
Inlet and Holman Island.

We left Gjoa on another fine summer day. An almost tropical sun
glared down on the still waters of the harbour. It was so balmy that several young huskies (husky dogs of any age normally avoid water like the
plague) were chasing each other about in a tidal pool.

George was on hand to wave farewell.

"You see any of them Klengenbergs at Holman, you tell 'em hello
from me!" he shouted as we clambered aboard. The starter whined. The
Wasp belched blue smoke and all too soon we were airborne.

Our objective that day was Bathurst Inlet, a tiny, old-style Hudson's Bay
Company outpost on the mainland coast some 350 miles southwestward of
Gjoa. We might have flown a more or less direct course to it but there was
no settlement along the way where we could refuel, so Doug opted to go the
long way round, by way of Cambridge Bay, where we could refill our tanks.

This route took us almost due west across the southern portion of King William Island, a tundra flood plain sodden with ponds and fretted by raised beaches. Ducks, geese, and shorebirds in uncounted numbers hazed its shores as they had doubtless done in 1848 when nearly a hundred survivors of John Franklin's expedition in search of the Northwest Passage perished of starvation and disease along this coast.

I was not sorry to put King William Island behind us as we began our crossing of Alexander Strait. So far we had seen no sign of the fearsome ice which had been the doom of Franklin's ships and people. Now we beheld an almost blinding swathe of white upon the northern horizon, and there it was—the impenetrable polar pack drifting inexorably southward from Melville Sound. This was the last "big ice" we were to encounter. I still see it in my mind's eye whenever I hear Franklin's name.

As we crossed the coast of Victoria Island tendrils of cumulus cloud streamed overhead giving notice of an end to the good weather.

Soon Cambridge Bay, yet another bastion of the New North, hove into view. Built in a hurry and still building, it sprawled across a sand and gravel moraine roughly levelled by bulldozers. Rows of suburban-style bungalows housed the whites at one end of town. Boxcar-style, prefabricated huts massed at the other housed the natives.

The afternoon was almost over before we touched down. Because Doug was anxious to refuel and be on our way, my companions busied themselves rolling gas barrels to the dock while I hurried to the HBC store to buy some grub for supper.

Casey Jones, the manager, was a talkative, engagingly friendly chap who warmly invited me and my crew to be his guests for the night so we could attend a beauty contest to choose the Queen of the Arctic Isles. The queen's prize was to be a polar bear rug which, Jones suggested, the queen might be willing to share with whomever tickled her fancy. When I passed this news on to Roy, he allowed that the prospect was interesting, but Doug dourly claimed he was allergic to bear skin.

"Cambridge used to be a real small post," Jones told me. "Couple of dozen families from the country round about used to come in to trade, was all. Now most have come in to stay. And there's a pile more from all along the coast between Gjoa and Coppermine on their way to hospital, or school, or some such thing. Like a goddamn transit camp. It's lively, though! Town's supposed to be dry. Yeah! Like an artesian well! I'd a sight rather be living over at Bathurst where there's nobody but the manager and a few country natives."

The weather was deteriorating. By the time DCL was gassed up and Roy had replaced a balky spark plug, the wind had risen alarmingly. Already there was a sprinkle of rain.

Jones strongly advised staying, but Doug was itching to be off. He was in such a rush that, as we taxied out, he stranded the Otter on a reef in the harbour. Roy had to hop into frigid water up to his waist to work a pontoon free, then engage in some fancy gymnastics to get back aboard.

The crossing to the mainland coast at Kent Peninsula took only a few minutes but rain forced us down to about five hundred feet and Doug considered turning back. However, when he contacted Cambridge radio, he was told the ceiling there was fast descending and heavy mist was already obscuring the harbour.

There now being little choice, we continued on our way, flying due west for the better part of an hour over wind-whipped Melville Sound to the mouth of Bathurst Inlet proper. The inlet is like a dagger thrust southward by the Arctic Ocean more than two hundred miles into the mainland tundra. This was prime muskox country; however we saw none of the shaggy beasts because our pilot wisely chose to stay over water where we were less likely to run into cliffs or mountains as visibility worsened.

We thundered on, staring anxiously ahead. At 8:20 p.m. we were greatly relieved to see the red roofs of a little cluster of buildings. The post, consisting of a store-cum-living quarters, two sheds, and an outhouse, seemed impossibly trivial in that vast expanse of rock and water. A full gale was now sweeping across the inlet and it would not have been surprising to see those puny human constructs blow away like a handful of cards.

DCL roared over this outpost of the White Man's Burden at mast level. Someone ran out of the house frantically waving us off. It was not that we were unwelcome but, as we could see for ourselves, waves which could easily have overwhelmed the Otter were breaking in a smother of foam and fury for half a mile offshore.

Ayorama. Nothing to be done. DCL waggled her wings in farewell, climbed briefly, then levelled off under the belly of the overcast.

Our failure to land here was the first major disappointment I had suffered. It was a severe one. Bathurst was one of the last of the old-time trading posts and the Inuit who traded to it were among the last to be truly living on the land. We did not know it then but in a few years this post too would be closed and its native people mostly gone. It is now the site of a high-cost, fly-in tourist lodge!

I had little time then to regret what we'd missed. The problem of what to do next fully occupied our attention. Cambridge was "out." We could have flown inland to find a lake or pond to roost on for the night, but Barren Grounds lakes during a gale are by no means ideal havens for planes on floats. Doug concluded we should try to reach the settlement of Coppermine two hundred miles farther west. We could do it, he said, *if* the weather got no worse and *if* the wind continued to boost us from astern. If not? Well, then we would run out of gas—in the dark.

Racing northwestward we swept over Wilberforce Falls, where the Hood River plunges into a seemingly bottomless chasm. On a still day, a plume of spray towers a thousand feet above the abyss. On *this* day the spray was being blown horizontal to the ground.

By 10:30 p.m. we were flying in semi-darkness, knowing that if and when we reached Coppermine we would be faced with a night landing on stormy waters. I felt this might be a good time to offer all hands a noggin of rum, but my companions were too intent on trying to spot the firefly flicker of Coppermine's handful of lights to accept this benison.

Roy saw them first. His shout was clearly audible even over the bellowing of the Wasp. Doug wasted no time on preliminaries. Ten minutes later we splashed down, hard, in what was certainly not a perfect landing. However, we were down *and* in one piece. Furthermore, as Roy told me with a smirk when he plumbed the tanks next morning, "with gas enough left over to fill your lighter."

We had thought our skin-of-the-teeth arrival might be the subject of some local interest. Not so. Apart from a couple of dogs skulking about, we saw no signs of life as we moored DCL to a floating dock. A few streetlights burned (dimly, for they drew their electricity from a temperamental diesel generator) and a few windows were illuminated, but no people were about. Somewhat nervously we made our way along a deserted street in the middle of which stood an empty truck. Had an epidemic struck the place? we wondered.

Then we became aware of a deep, discordant vibration that almost seemed to be coming out of the ground. We traced it to its source and found most of Coppermine's population packed into the settlement's largest building, a garage-cum-warehouse belonging to DNA. Vehicles and machinery had been unceremoniously pushed outside, and the townsfolk were inside having a ball.

A very large man relieving himself just outside the main door saw our hesitant approach and leapt at us, waving a beer bottle in his free hand.

"Jesus!" Roy cried, jumping back in alarm.

Pete stood his ground, to be inundated by a torrent of Inuktitut.

"We've hit it lucky," he told us when he had a chance to translate. "Boat came in yesterday from Tuktoyaktuk with the winter's beer supply on board. Seems last year she was a bit late and was carrying the beer as deck cargo when a hard frost came and busted half the bottles. *This* year nobody in Coppermine's taking any chances with an early freeze."

Two more Inuit, faces gleaming with sweat, fell out through the doorway blindly pummelling each other. They were followed by a tall white man who did not seem at all surprised to see four strangers.

"Hi," he said. "You guys are kinda late for the party but come in anyways and have a beer, if that's your fancy. Hotter'n hell in there but," with a glance at the two combatants who were throwing punches in all directions, "maybe a wee bit safer."

The greeter was Don Leary, principal of Coppermine's new school. He and other hospitable people now took us in hand. After a time the horrendous cacophony of several untuned guitars, percussion weapons, and accordions was replaced by the eerie twang of a caribou-skin drum being wielded by an aged but agile Inuk. Sometimes shuffling and at other times leaping, he sang a sibilant song while keeping time by rhythmically striking the rim of his hoop drum with a short baton.

His performance produced something of an illusion that the building had become a giant igloo, an illusion that seemed to affect all present for everyone became silently intent on the dancer. The transformation of a fractious hubbub into an almost mystical scene had been abrupt and sobering. Nor did the raucous party mood return. When the old man laid down the drum it was taken up by other elders to whom the audience gave the same rapt attention.

The first drummer was a man named Ikey Bolt. I spent much of the following day in his crowded, low-ceilinged little house listening to his stories.

Ikey was what a northern friend of mine would call "a pemmican man. Made out of dried deer meat held together with seal sinew and wolverine gut, mixed with fermented raisins to give him lots of hellery."

Seventy-two-year-old Ikey certainly looked as if his bony frame was indestructible enough to carry him to the century mark. He and his rotund wife, Edna, were the only surviving founders of the first "settlement" at Coppermine, though the place had not yet been named when, in 1918, they and Edna's father, the notorious Charlie Klengenberg, built the first house there.

By 1966 Coppermine had become one of the largest settlements in the Canadian Arctic, claiming almost six hundred inhabitants, most of whom had come in off the land during the preceding two or three years, drawn by the promise of a new way of life which would bring them the benefits and pleasures enjoyed by southern Canadians.

To house these hopefuls, DNA had erected sixty prefabs clustered in six compact rows in an area well away from the white part of the settlement. Most were of the almost windowless boxcar variety. Despite the fact that tens of thousands of square miles of unoccupied land stretched away to the east, west, and south they were jammed together cheek by jowl. Much larger houses, intended for white occupancy, had been built in the "town" itself. Each of these had the privacy and hygienic advantages of its own generous lot.

Ikey told us he had been born in the little Alaskan village of Point Hope, facing Siberia across the Chukchi Sea. At nineteen he was rejected by his girl and so, like many other spurned young men the world over, he went to sea. He signed on with a Yankee whaler which, half a year later, was shoved ashore near Barter Island by the ice of the Beaufort Sea and was crushed beyond redemption.

"All right," Ikey said to himself as he clambered ashore. "Whaling finish. Might as well go home."

This he proceeded to do, on foot. It was a seven-hundred-mile trek back to Point Hope and it took him four months. He hunted for his living and spent happy times with local Inuit families along the way.

When he got home to find that the girl he wanted had not changed her mind, he signed on as a deckhand aboard the schooner *Mary Sachs*, northbound under charter to Vilhjalmur Stefánsson's Canadian Arctic Expedition.

Ikey became the right hand of the man in charge of a base camp at Bernard Harbour. It was here that he met Charlie Klengenberg and was effectively adopted into that remarkable family.

"I live with them Klengenbergs long time. Charlie got many pretty daughters. One time his son Patsy, he say, 'Ikey, better you make up your mind for just one.' So I take Edna."

It was the right choice. Although not the most beautiful of Charlie's girls, Edna was a paragon of arctic wifely virtues. Not only could she cook and sew, she could do most things a man could do, including drive dogs, spear seals at the breathing holes, and trap foxes.

"Very damn good wife. Good trapper. Good shooter. We not stay home. Always travelling together. Even with kids. We do some trading. She trade better than any Hudson Bay man. Could be rich like Charlie, but Edna don't want. No, she say, hitch up dogs and let's travel! Lots of place we ain't seen yet."

A few years after his marriage, Ikey, Charlie, and another of Charlie's sons set off from Letty Harbour on the Parry Peninsula for a trading voyage to the eastward. This time Edna, who was eight months pregnant, stayed at home. The vessel was an old Mackenzie River scow with a sail but no engine. She was generally unseaworthy and quite hopeless in ice.

"No mind. Stay close to shore. If wind get bad, paddle to land and camp a while."

As they were nearing the east end of Coronation Gulf, a southerly gale caught them and blew them offshore. The waves rose and the barge began to come apart. Soon the three men were bailing for their lives. Fortunately the wind hauled westerly and blew the sinking scow ashore on the fearsome, cliff-bound coast of Kent Peninsula. Afraid she would break up completely, the men unloaded all the goods they could, and then, totally exhausted, crawled under a sail on shore and went to sleep.

When they woke, the scow was gone. The wind had switched back to southerly and blown her broken bones out into deep water, where she had sunk.

"We wonder how we go home now. Walk all around Melville Sound and Bathurst Inlet first? Hell of long way. Take a year, maybe. Charlie say, don't worry. We find something."

Find something they did. A few miles away they came upon the wreck of a steam whaler lost thirty years earlier at Cape Alexander near the eastern extremity of Kent Peninsula. All that remained of her was her boiler, some massive parts of her reciprocating engine, and a few wooden beams.

"Don't look much good to me, but Charlie say, okay, here is boat."

"'How we make boat of that stuff?' I ask. Charlie say, 'Don't know. Try anyhow.'"

Klengenberg concluded they might frame a vessel from the remaining timbers of the whaler; but what to sheathe her with? He looked at the boiler, which was constructed of curved iron plates riveted together, then told his crew:

"Go back to camp, get axes."

A dozen trade axes had been part of the cargo rescued from the scow. Using axe heads as cold chisels and wedges, the three men cut rivets off the whaler's boiler until they had freed a number of the curved iron plates. These they then flattened (more or less) by pounding them with the biggest boulders they could heft. Then they fastened the plates to the bottom and sides of a timber frame about twenty feet long, eight feet wide, and square at both ends. When the job was finished, the castaways found themselves in possession of something that looked more like a feeding trough for mastodons than a boat.

"Sure don't look pretty good. But maybe she float. We see."

Their creation, which had been constructed as close to the water as possible, now proved too heavy for three men to launch, even with the help of pries and rollers. So they spent two days digging a basin under and around their vessel and, when a high tide flooded the basin, she finally floated free.

"Not leak too bad neither. Two men bail all time could make it float. Made sail and mast from stuff save from scow, then go home."

It had taken the three men six weeks to construct their vessel—the "iron whale" Charlie called her—and it took them almost as long again to sail her back to Letty Harbour.

But, as Ikey said, "One thing we got lots of is time."

CHAPTER TWENTY-FOUR

We'll Be the Bosses

M EETING EDNA AND IKEY INCREASED MY DESIRE TO
visit Holman, home of the Klengenbergs, but Doug
demurred.

"It's two hundred miles north of here and way off our route. Have to cross two big stretches of open water to get there. It's late in the season. If the weather dumps on us we could be stuck there God knows how long."

Nevertheless, on the afternoon of our second day in Coppermine he agreed to "have a look."

We did not head directly for Holman. First, we did a weather reconnaissance, flying up the Coppermine River valley as far as Bloody Falls, a place from which, almost two hundred years earlier, a young employee of the Hudson's Bay Company named Samuel Hearne had become the first European to reach the mighty sweep of arctic coast stretching westward from the Canadian Sea to the Siberian Sea.

Between 1769 and 1772 Hearne explored a quarter of a million square miles of country at the top of the world. With no other company than that of reluctant Chipewyan Indians, he walked, winter and summer, some five thousand miles seeking a lode of copper reputed to lie somewhere north and west of Churchill. The difficulties he encountered defeated him twice over, but on his third attempt he reached the mouth of the river he named Coppermine.

Although it was nearly 4:00 p.m. Doug decided the weather was good enough for an attempt to reach Holman, so he pointed DCL northward and we began climbing to gain altitude for crossing Dolphin and Union Strait, which separates the mainland from Victoria Island's Wollaston Peninsula. The crossing was uneventful and by 5:00 p.m. we were again flying over land, but the sky ahead was darkening ominously.

It was then we discovered that the forty-five-gallon reserve drum of gas stowed in the back of the cabin was leaking. There followed a frantic snuffing-out of cigarettes and sliding open of windows. A gale immediately began howling through the cabin, blowing away the fumes but at the same time snatching Doug's aeronautical map off his lap and sucking it out an open window to flutter astern of us like a dying gull. Fortunately I had a spare map, though on a smaller scale. I hurriedly passed it forward. Doug glanced at it, then sat upon it.

The weather rapidly grew worse, "turning to gopher shit," as Roy succinctly put it. Doug had been seeking height for the crossing of Prince Albert Sound, which separated us from Holman, now less than fifty miles away, but the thickening overcast held us down to two thousand feet. I was gloomily observing the Sound below us being whipped into whitecaps, when we got a call from Holman. Conditions there had become too dicey for us to risk a landing.

There was nothing for it but to turn back. Roy's efforts to staunch the gas leak having failed, we were now enduring what was, in effect, open cockpit flying in bad weather.

By 6:30 we had regained the mainland coast, which was hazed by rain and mist. Again it was decision-making time. The weather had closed in on Coppermine. The alternative seemed to be a tiny place called Paulatuk some hundred and eighty miles to the westward. Too small even to be on my map, it had no radio, but Doug contacted a DEW Line station at Cape Parry, sixty miles from Paulatuk. When the station reported passable weather, DCL resolutely pointed her big red nose westward.

Flying close to the ground had one advantage. Because it was warmer there we were able to endure the open windows that sucked out the gas fumes. We grew hungry and I volunteered to feed the troops. Since I dared not fire up our Primus Stove, I filled Roy's electric coffee heater with a mixture of chopped Spam, mushroom soup, and canned tomatoes. It was hardly gourmet fare but, washed down with a little rum, it served.

Soon we were in very rough air, battling a fierce headwind. Low cloud and storm scud forced us ever lower over the Melville Hills, an immense accumulation of glacial drift resembling what a Dantean Hell might look like after it cooled. Our attention was happily distracted from this gloomy spectacle by the unexpected appearance of another living being.

A moose was plodding along below us. Just what this forest dweller was doing so far north of timber on the slag heap of the Melville Hills was anybody's guess. Doug dipped a wing in salute and the moose stopped, stared up at us for a moment, then plodded on. We wished it *bonne chance* in whatever quixotic endeavour it was engaged in.

By 8:00 p.m. we were about a hundred feet above the ground, which seemed to be rising even as the clouds descended. Doug was about ready to abandon the attempt to find Paulatuk and climb up into (and hope to get above) the cloud deck when we broke out of the murk. Some thirty miles ahead we could see the unmistakable hump of the Parry Peninsula and, off to the left, the waters of a great coastal lagoon glittering ruby-red in the last light of the setting sun. This was Paulatuk. DCL sank gratefully to rest upon the lagoon's placid surface. We had been airborne almost six hours, and enough fuel remained in the tanks to last about another twenty minutes.

Up to this point our east–west transit from Gjoa Haven across the top of the world had been both tedious and tense. Our failure to visit either Bathurst or Holman had in fact made it something of a bust.

Paulatuk was to make it all worthwhile.

Most of the settlements we had so far visited had been founded by Europeans to serve the interests of traders, missionaries, whalers, police, government officials, and the military. Paulatuk's origins were very different. The saltwater lagoon at the foot of Darnley Bay had been a haven for western Arctic natives through three or four millennia. Although the numbers of people living there had certainly ebbed and flowed, Paulatuk seems always to have had some human inhabitants, and upon occasion a good many of them, judging from the scores of ancient pit-houses, tent circles, and sod shanties scattered for miles along the lagoon's curving shoreline.

The surrounding country offered almost everything people needed.

Darnley Bay and its associated lagoons provided seals, white whales, even occasional bowheads, together with many other kinds of marine food ranging from fishes to mussels. The low and relatively fertile coastal plain lying between the sea and the Melville Hills was dotted with ponds which, in season, were alive with ducks, geese, and shore-birds. Caribou fed on the plain; musk ox grazed the slopes of the hills to the southward. The nearby Hornaday River hosted a heavy run of char and grayling, and a scattering of deep-water lakes a few miles inland abounded in whitefish and lake trout. Wood for building or for burning could be procured along the middle reaches of the Horton Valley, and seams of coal surfaced close by.

Inuit have often been categorized as a nomadic people. In point of fact, they were nomadic only within well-defined and familiar regions which provided them with the necessities of life. The people living at the foot of Darnley Bay had no need to roam great distances in order to procure what they required. They were a settled people making the best possible use of a large and varied domain.

At the time of our visit, the actual settlement consisted of a weath-ered Roman Catholic church; a small frame house occupied by the priest; several sod-roofed huts built of driftwood and turf; one new ply-wood cabin; and seven large and airy wall tents. There were no roads and not a mechanized vehicle of any kind was to be seen (or heard). Nor was there the usual clutch of towering oil tanks or acres of fuel drums. Even more surprising, there was no Hudson's Bay Company store or any similar symbol of commerce.

The cabins and tents straggled casually along the inner curve of the lagoon, well spaced, but not so far apart as to be unneighbourly. A score of handsome sled dogs wandered freely about performing their unofficial functions as sanitation patrol. They were fat, healthy, and amiable. Some of them came down to the shore to watch with inter-est as DCL taxied toward them. They contributed to a peaceable and very pleasant scene.

At other settlements we had usually been met (when met at all) by white men. There *was* only one white man in Paulatuk, an Oblate priest, a reclusive chap who kept his distance. We were welcomed by Paulatuk's *own* people, nearly a dozen of whom came to the shore to help us moor DCL stern-first on the sandy beach. They were most solic-itous about her safety and our comfort. The first words we heard from the middle-aged man who caught the line we tossed ashore were "Hello, you fellows! Bet you hungry! You wanna eat?"

Paulatuk's inhabitants were as insistently hospitable as any of the Inuit we had met to the eastward but differed from them in several respects. For one thing, almost all bore European names. For another, few could (as Pete confirmed) converse easily in Inuktitut, generally preferring English to their native tongue.

They were a good-looking, vigorous lot, many with light-coloured hair, a few with blue eyes, and several with sculptured noses on the Roman model. Although obviously not European, there was probably not one among them without European blood in his or her veins. Physically they belonged to a new, mixed race while remaining essen-tially Inuit in thought and spirit.

Despite its antiquity, Paulatuk's official existence dated only to 1935 when it was selected by the Oblate Order as the site for a mission. Until then the local people had called the place Ikarluak—Fishing Place. The surrounding region was Paulatuk—Coal Smoke Place.

The first missionary had found about a hundred people in resi-dence. Some were Anglicans but most were pagans or non-believers. Few showed any desire to embrace Roman Catholicism. The priest's presence was useful because he held a trading licence and so could pro-vide some of the few white man's goods that were required. Not that these independent-minded people (the priest categorized them to me as "intractable") liked traders much better than priests—they looked upon both as intruders. Indeed, an attempt in the 1920s by the HBC to establish a post at Ikarluak had been so firmly rebuffed that the Company had instead built at Letty Harbour on the Parry Peninsula, a good forty miles to the northward.

Paulatuk continued to thrive until the mid-1950s when the U.S. mili-tary began erecting its mighty DEW Line across the Canadian north. One of the sites chosen was at the tip of the Parry Peninsula. Big ships laden with equipment began arriving there, but the contractors found them-selves facing a shortage of manpower with which to unload the vessels, and to do the dog's work required on a massive construction project.

Attempts to attract workers from Paulatuk at first met with little success, though the carrot of high wages did initiate a minor drift to Pin Main, as the Cape Parry site came to be called. But when the Letty Harbour HBC post *and* the Paulatuk mission both moved to the cape, the drift gradually became a flow. By 1956 Paulatuk was, for probably the first time in thousands of years, virtually abandoned.

Although a large native presence at Pin Main had been desirable during construction, the military who occupied the completed station eventually decided that having natives living in such close propinquity was a nuisance and a health hazard. So in 1964 DNA began "closing out" the Cape Parry native settlement. The department did not have the intention of restoring Paulatuk to life. Its former residents were to be shipped to "growth" communities as far to the east as Cambridge Bay and as far west as Tuktoyaktuk near the mouth of the Mackenzie River.

In line with the department's wishes, the HBC obligingly closed its post at Cape Parry. The Roman Catholic mission was supposed to do likewise; instead, the priest moved back to Paulatuk, accompanying six families who refused to accept what amounted to deportation from the region.

The man who met us on the beach of the lagoon and inquired about our appetites introduced himself as Joe Thrasher. A leading member of one of the local clans, Joe became our guide and mentor.

"Come up to Auntie Jessie's tent. We have big feed and good talk. You guys tell us what happenin' in Cambridge and all them places."

Jessie Green was a woman of consequence in Paulatuk. Joe told us: "Husband he die about twenty year ago, leave her with two kids, two boys, so she go ahead and raise them on her own. Done it by trappin' and huntin' by herself. Jessie never got married no more. Maybe nobody ask her 'cause she always was a one to go her own way, and was better hunter and trapper than pretty near any man in the country.

"When the people was gettin' moved out of Cape Parry, Jessie say she won't go where they tell her. Goin' home, she say. When the fellow from government tell her she got to go to Tuk Tuk, she tell him, *'You* wanna go there, *you* go there! I goin' back to Ikarluak.' And that's just what she done, her and a bunch of other people."

Jessie Green was a smiling, sturdy woman with a wild thatch of sparse grey hair and a face the colour and texture of cracked amber. She was living in a weathered old tent while a small wooden winter house was being built for her nearby by Joe and several other volunteers.

"Goin' to be her 'come home' house," Joe explained. "Want to make it herself, but gettin' too old now so we do it for her."

After welcoming us warmly, Jessie wanted to know where we had come from, where we were going, and what we were doing in the country. Curiosity satisfied, she told us we were not the first visitors to Paulatuk that day.

"This mornin', them Reubens boys playin' on the beach see big dog lie up there. He very big...big...BIG...boys throw stone at him see if dead. Is *not* dead! He get up and shake and he a big brown bear. He look at boys. Boys look at him. He run away along beach *that* way...boys run *this* way. They come tell me, and I tell them, 'Don't you throw them stone at bear. That not nice.'"

Not smart, either, I thought. The barren land grizzly is as big and powerful as his western cousins and, I imagine, as jealous of his dignity. However, he is wise, which may be why, ninety-nine times out of a hundred, he will avoid an encounter with human beings. Perhaps especially with twelve-year-old boys.

Jessie apologized because the fire in her camp stove was out, and she had no fresh fish, but she led us to a nearby tent where Ida and Charlie Reuben took over as our hosts. Joined by at least a dozen adults and innumerable children, we feasted on boiled char, fried grayling, and strips of sun-dried caribou, washed down with gallons of tea.

Later, during what became a very long evening, most of Paulatuk's inhabitants gathered in, at, and around another tent for a party during which I played a tape recording of the drum dance at Coppermine. This delighted the audience although most were unable to understand the words of the Coppermine chants.

"Seems like our people forget how to talk own language," a stout little man said softly when the tape was finished. "Good thing Joe Tedjuk write stuff down or pretty soon we forget who we are."

Joe Tedjuk, I learned, was a man afflicted by writer's itch. Everywhere he went he carried a school scribbler into which each day without fail he entered an account of his life and of the activities of the animals and people around him. I dearly wanted to meet Tedjuk but, unfortunately, he was then at a coastal camp some distance to the westward. Several people assured me they would tell him of my visit and that I, too, was a writer. "Maybe he write you," Jessie said.

Over breakfast next morning Joe Thrasher talked about his and Paulatuk's prospects.

Joe had first worked for wages during construction of the station at Cape Parry, after which he had been employed by DNA at Inuvik, capital of the western Arctic. There he acquired considerable understanding of the new world which was exploding around him.

DNA send me back to Paulatuk, where I was born, to help set up some stuff here, like wooden houses they are making now in Aklavik, and maybe a new school. But I figure they don't really going to make a place for people here. Everything done too slow. So slow they never finish. They don't want people stay in Paulatuk. I figure they like to close it down.

Well, after I been back here a while, I make up my mind I'm going to stay anyway. I know what is like livin' outside! So does lots other people now. And the most of them don't like it one damn bit.

The old people and even lots younger ones figure things was better when everybody live on the land. Sure, there was tough times. But everybody pulled along of everybody else to get through, and the feelin' you got from doing that was worth a few tough times.

People used to stick together. You don't find too much of that no more outside. It's gettin' to be everyone for himself out there. So us Paulatuk people, we made up our minds to stay on here.

Word gets around, eh? There's families got sent to Tuk, even Aklavik and Cambridge, goin' to come back here now. They'll be surely welcome.

Paulatuk people goin' to straighten their lives out. Keep best of old ways and take on some new ones...do what suits us, not what some smart white guy says.

For example. There's only but one Ski-Doo here. When it breaks I don't guess we'll get another. Goin' back to dogs. Already got some of the best dogs you could find, and we'll breed lots more.

We know people can't live without some money, so we goin' to start our own co-op for huntin', tradin', and buyin' stuff from outside. We'll be bosses of all that, not the traders or the missions or anyone else.

Maybe tourists come fish in the Hornaday or Brock Lagoon. Maybe we have craft shop. Lots of stuff we can do right here. Pretty near everything we need is right close by.

Can take you to a coal mine in cliff west of Langton Bay where you can drive sled right under it and just shovel coal on 'til dogs can't pull no more. We even got a freezer don't need no electricity: big chunk of ice down under the ground. Never melt. We put a shed over it and keep meat there all summer.

I tell you, Paulatuk's goin' to last. People been here since a long, long time. Goin' to be here long time to come....

Joe Thrasher's vision has been largely realized. The Paulatuk Co-op Association opened for business in the summer of 1967 and as of 2002 remains a going concern, as does Paulatuk itself.

CHAPTER TWENTY-FIVE

Back to the Land

S EVERAL MONTHS AFTER MY RETURN TO SOUTHERN Canada a parcel reached me from Tuktoyaktuk. It contained a verbatim transcript of one of Joe Tedjuk's scribblers. There was no covering letter.

I found his account of the life of an Eskimo, as Joe called himself, fascinating, and felt it should be published. However I was unable to make contact with the author. When I began writing this present book I concluded that Tedjuk's memoir must have a place in it, so my assistant undertook a new search. Eventually she located the 79-year-old Joe Tedjuk living at Cambridge Bay.

He told me he had long since lost the original of his memoir. When I sent him a copy he responded by hoping I would be able to put it in my book.

What follows is my edited version of that journal.

This book was written in November, 1965, by Joseph Tedjuk, an Eskimo man age of 42 years old, and been to school before and got 6th grade....I write my books when my family is sleeping. I write all night sometime 'til 7 oclock in the morning. Day time when it's good weather, I go out to open water for sealing. Now is pretty soon trapping time coming, then got to travel a lot pretty soon, but I'll have time to write at night.

Well, this book was written at Clinton Point and I'm going to keep on writing so that one of these days I might pass away and then my children could have something to remember me, if they read my books, what I wrote of many things.

I born in 1923 in winter camp of Kogmalik, People of the River. People them time stay all year far inland, 100 or 200 miles from coast at Coppermine, 'til April when they come down to trade, with sleds loaded so high they have to help their wives to climb on top of the load and also us children. They bring skins like wolves, wolverines and caribou skins for trade because, boy that is good country for wolverines. Used to be many people come to Coppermine for trading; so many caribou tents along the river bank! Use to be nice living inland, lots to eat; dry-meat and caribou fat and fresh meat all the time; lots of caribou. They people then was doing pretty good....

At the age of seven, Joe tells us, he was separated from his people and, at the insistence of the Roman Catholic missionary at Coppermine, was sent to a residential school at Shingle Point in the Mackenzie River Delta. There he remained, winter and summer, for six years during which he never saw his parents, or his own country, or any of his own family. Like other native children, he was punished if he spoke his own language.

Boy, 6 years was too much there for a boy like me, so far from my parents, and after 6 years when I saw them, they look not like my parents when I get home. Everything look different than I thought would be; strange too, and the people they couldn't understand us kids been away, cause we forgot how to talk Eskimo. It all look funny, the people, the way they live and eat. It took me quite a while to learn my own language again.

The thirteen-year-old also had to learn how to hunt, trap, live, and work in the land of his fathers. He was a quick learner, but handicapped by his long absence. In a world where a man's hunting abilities were the measure of his status in the community, Joe was unable to compete for the kind of wife who was vitally essential to the survival of an Inuit family living on the land. He remained unmarried until 1955, when he gave up trying to live as his ancestors had done and moved into Coppermine settlement.

One day the Nurse and her husband from the Nursing Station went into my tent and started asking if I want to work at the Station. She want an interpreter cause not many of the Eskimos could talk English. I told them I don't mind to work at all, so they told me to come in the morning.

Well, I enjoyed the work for four years then I had to quit cause it was too much for me. Besides I seen a few people die at the Nursing Station and didn't like it.

Just when I start to work for the Nurse I met a widow, a woman older than me.

She wanted to stay with me. A nice looking woman too that even the white men in Coppermine they liked her. Then I make up my mind to stay with her but we never get married, just stayed together for 4 years. Then something happen. I did not like the way she was doing with some white men when I was away so we quit staying together and I went out to Fort Smith then down the Mackenzie to Inuvik. Went down there to see my sister and my brother that I never see since they went to residential school. I start work at building a new hospital there. For five months had good wages, room, and board, and ate at the mess hall with the white men. Then I quit and just roam around town at Inuvik spending money like nothing.

Now thirty-six years old, Joe felt he had little future in the new town of Inuvik where, like many of his peers, he drank far more than was good for him. When, in 1960, he was offered a chance to go whaling with two Inuit brothers at a place called Whitefish Camp at the mouth of the Mackenzie, he jumped at it.

We got a few white whales that summer. Then we went to Tuktoyaktuk and I went deckhand on the Hudson's Bay Company boat Banksland. *A nice boat, but when it got no load sure could roll, that boat, in rough water. That fall I went as a reindeer herder for two Eskimo partners, they got their own herd of reindeer. I herd for them for one year then quit cause the pay was small, but before I quit I met a young girl was staying at the herders' camp and we got together in 1961 and went to Tuk to stay. We got married in church and I start working on DEW Line for Federal Electric Company.*

But DEW Line construction was tapering off, and soon Joe and most of the hundreds of other Eskimo men who had come off the land to become wage earners found themselves without work. Life was hard in Tuk. Native unemployment topped 90 per cent. Living costs were very high, and because the local grounds were overcrowded the chances of being able to make a living by hunting or trapping were almost nonexistent. Like many others, Joe, his wife, and two small daughters could only get by with regular help from the welfare officer.

By the end of 1963, Joe Tedjuk had had enough of trying to live the white man's way of life. He began scrounging for dogs—any dogs that could haul themselves about. Early in March of 1964, he sold the last of the family's few possessions to buy dogs. By mid-month he had eleven. With two nondescript teams driven by himself and his wife, the little family set out to go back to the land.

Their destination was Coppermine, some 650 miles distant.

Was still pretty cold in March when we were travelling, too cold for the two children. Then finally we got to Atkinson Point where two Eskimo families working there at Dew Line site. We stay 3 or 4 days to rest the dogs, and cause our little girl was pretty sick.

Then we reach Cape Bathurst. There was a family living there, but was short of white people stuff. We had Easter there. Well, we had a nice feed of polar bear meat. It was a nice fat one, but not much bread or bannock; mostly what we had was tea and bear meat cause we was saving our flour for travel on.

In April we get to Cape Parry. There was about ten families of Eskimos at Pin Main; an RC mission, one priest.

Joe and his family had now been travelling for three weeks and had consumed most of their supplies. The missionary, who was doubling as welfare officer, refused to give them what they needed to continue on to Coppermine. *Ayorama*, they decided to remain in the Cape Parry district, which had always been one of the best places along the coast for hunting and fishing.

I went caribou hunting east of Horton River and I got two. Never eat caribou for five or six years I was at Tuk and Inuvik. We only eat reindeer meat there— taste a lot different than caribou.

Then in May we move across to Fish Camp, they call it, on Brock Lagoon near Paulatuk. We stay for winter at Brock Lagoon but never did too good for trapping and sealing and caribou there. Just about starve there at Brock Lagoon, nothing to eat and couldn't hunt cause we was losing our dogs. They was sick and dying 'til we had only three left. Well, it was the toughest winter of my life, last winter, cause once we never eat for 9 days. Just live on tea, with no sugar. That was around Christmas time. Can't even get seal cause the weather was bad, always blowing.

A plane was come from Inuvik but it unload at Cape Parry, so they got two men there with dog team to haul some food to us. They got there New Year's Day, then we had a nice feed.

Around March we went to Cape Parry for Relief. When we got there it was good open water for sealing so we stayed 'til middle of March, then we plan to go again on our trip to Coppermine.

Joe had considered remaining at Brock Lagoon but the hungry winter just past made him decide to pursue his original plan. If Coppermine should prove disappointing, he could always return to the Paulatuk area.

Stormy weather, the birth of another child, and the need to gather more dogs delayed the family's departure until the end of March.

We never made it to Coppermine. Our little baby boy was so sick we had to stop at Pin One radio site at Clinton Point. So I got some medicine from the Station Chief. He gave me some penicillin. Well, our little boy just about had it if we try to keep going, so we stop here and finally he get better slowly.

It so nice to travel with dogs when its nice and warm in spring time; best time of the year for travelling around. Get sun tan on your face, a nice brown. Get snow blind some time, but when we get snow blind we put on a pot of tea, make it real strong as can be, then put tea leaves on your eyes when you going to sleep. In the morning your eyes feel fine.

I think us was lucky to stop here. That was in May last year. Well, we had caribou all spring and summer, and we got a few ring seals and also some bearded seals. We sure worked hard to make dry caribou meat for winter food; and catch seals for dogs food. We get some ducks here, and lots of ptarmigans and a lot of ground squirrels around our place.

Sure a lot of caribou along that shore. You could shoot them just from our house. Just across Roscoe River is a little creek where I build our house at the mouth of it. In spring before the ice go, you could get seal right near the shore when the cracks start to open up. Seals, boy, lots of them on the ice! Boy, sometime in big bunches 60 or 80 together, sleeping away.

I went on the ice with my dog team, nine dogs I had now. Boy, did I ever had fun when I got close to the seals on the ice, about 40 or 60 of them and the crack was narrow. Some was having a hard time trying to get down and the dogs could not stop cause we were on ice with no snow. When they got to the seals two of my dogs bite a seal on the flippers and I shot and got 6 of them with my rifle.

One time on the ice 5 minutes walk from our house I get one of them bearded seals. I got him in the head and run to it quick as I could before it sunk, and hook it and hold on with one hand for long time, with my other hand cutting the skin to make a hole so I could tie a piece of rope. Then I try to pull it out, but it too heavy for one man to pull out of the water onto the ice. So I tie rope to big piece of ice and go home and get my 9 dogs and let them pull it out. No wonder I couldn't pull it out! It weighs about 1000 lbs. that seal. Me and my wife try to put it on the sled but we couldn't, so I cut it up and it took me two hours to skin it and cut the meat into four pieces. Boy, they a lot of feed on one of them bearded seals.

As long as I got enough bullets, and tea, tobacco, and flour for the kids, I'm happy to stay at Clinton Point. In wintertime wind always blow, but when you got enough driftwood it's a good place to stay right through the year round. Last year not much foxes for the trappers, but I hope this year is a good year for foxes and polar bears. Well, anyway, we will see how it is.

In winter time an Eskimo got to tough it out hunting and trapping, but fun though when you not short of food, and also got dogs. An Eskimo can't go without dogs. I think its more better to have dogs than a Ski-Doo. They cost too much and for parts and gas. Also when they break down 60 or 100 miles away from home, then a man got to walk home, but with a dog team, just ride on the sled. Them machines just good for around town. Or for fellows got steady jobs.

The one thing I like to have is a 5 1/2 horsepower kicker [outboard motor] and a good boat; that all I always dream to have up here for sealing in summer time and going to some place like Cape Parry. A small kicker, like 3 1/2 or 5 1/2 real handy; not like 50 horsepower kicker. They use too much gas, but lots of young men now they like Ski-Doos and real fast kickers just to fool around with. Can loose their lives like that specially with drunkenness.

Lots of young people drink too much now-a-days. Me, I was like that when I was pretty young. Use to be a heavy drinker. Boy, I use to be bad for drink; but now I'm older I'm thinky more of my family than drinky.

I try hard on my own this year, and then I want to write a book about it to the Government of Canada in Ottawa; some place like that. Send a book out, how tough it is to be an Eskimo now. I'm not proud of myself cause I'm an Eskimo, cause I'm not the only Eskimo that lives in the North, here, living on Relief most of the time. The thing we need is help to stay away from a town so we could be able to go out hunting instead of staying in a village just depending on Government. Oh yes, its good to get Relief, but they should give us enough to start with, then let us try by ourselve.

Anyway, I'm going to keep on writing for my children to have and to keep for my grandchildren to read. I'm not a good writer or a story maker but I could write how we are living and hunting and trapping, and other things what's going on at our land, and about my own people. Well, I wish every reader to enjoy what I wrote. My name again is Joe Tedjuk, an Eskimo man at Clinton Point.

CHAPTER   TWENTY-SIX

Tuk Tuk

GETTING AWAY FROM PAULATUK WASN'T EASY. OUR hospitable hosts seemed loath to see us go but, even more to the point, we didn't have enough gas. Doug radioed the military at Cape Parry to ask if we could buy a hundred gallons. A duty officer replied stiffly that they could not let us have any at all unless we had permission from DEW Line headquarters, which appeared to be in Washington.

I blew my stack at that.

"Frigging Yanks!" I snarled. "Think they own the goddamn country!"

Joe Thrasher overheard this outburst and grinned.

"Now you know how Eskimo feel about white man, eh? But don't you fellows worry none. We help you out."

He and Edward Reuben puttered off in a big outboard skiff. They were gone several hours but when they returned they brought with them two forty-five-gallon drums that they assured us contained avgas, though the identification marks on the drums had been obliterated. We asked no questions, but I would not be surprised if one of the emergency gas caches established by the U.S. Air Force had sprung a leak.

Our next destination was Tuktoyaktuk, usually called Tuk Tuk or simply Tuk. It lies on the eastern approaches to the Mackenzie River Delta some 230 miles west of Paulatuk.

Soon we were over Langton Bay at the foot of the Parry Peninsula. Ahead of us the Smoking Hills were living up to their name. Patches of lignite exposed along their steep seaward cliffs by a retreating ocean in ancient times were plumed with white smoke from fires, perhaps originally lit by lightning, which had been smouldering for God alone knows how long.

Steep coulees gouged into the hills by tributaries of the Horton River were limned with beds of red, saffron, and orange ash, the signatures of burned-out lignite fires. If much of the country we had overflown to the east of Paulatuk had looked like Hell without the heat, this country looked like Hell in the process of ignition.

By noon we were over Anderson River. Thereafter the country grew lower, softer, greener. I even spotted a few little patches of dwarf spruce crouching in river valleys. The autumnal frosts had flushed intervening stretches of tundra with a gold, scarlet, and sepia wash.

These were the fabled arctic prairies, but the apparent absence of animal life was disturbing for this ought to have been prime caribou country. Then, forty or fifty miles beyond the Anderson, I saw what appeared to be a herd of several hundred deer drifting across the tundra. I touched Doug's shoulder and pointed. He nodded and guided DCL toward the herd.

We flew over them at less than five hundred feet but they ignored us, placidly continuing to graze as if the thunderous monster in the sky did not exist. I was astonished...until the answer dawned on me. Too small and too pale as well as too docile to be caribou, these creatures had to be reindeer, doubtless offspring of a herd brought to the Mackenzie region in the early 1930s. There were no herders with this lot, but then I had been told that the whole enterprise had effectively been abandoned.

A vast, level, and saturated plain stretches 150 miles inland to the west of Liverpool Bay. It cradles the Eskimo Lakes, linked bodies of brackish water which by rights belong to the sea. In antiquity they formed the major outlet channel of what may then have been the greatest river in the world. The Mackenzie River has since lost much of its flow and has shifted its mouth farther west but its 2,600-mile length still makes it Canada's longest river, and second only to the St. Lawrence in the volume of water it carries to the sea.

Its ancient flood plain was a maze of ponds and muskegs dissected by slow-flowing streams and contorted meanders. It was also pocked with holes ten to twenty feet in diameter from which coal had once been dug. The identity of the diggers remains a mystery. Historians assure me they must have been modern since prehistoric man would have had little need of, or use for, coal.

Because coal is an almost sacred symbol of modern man's industrial achievements, it is not easy for us to credit our primitive ancestors with the wits to make use of its near-miraculous properties. Yet there are indications that some prehistoric peoples in the western Arctic not only cooked with coal and heated their homes with it, but may even have used it to smelt copper.

We encountered our first pingos just east of the Eskimo Lakes. Pingos are spectacular eruptions thrusting out of the flat tundra to heights of as much as two hundred feet. Some resemble volcanic cones; others, seen in silhouette and from a distance, bear an uncanny likeness to the pyramids of Egypt. Pingos are not, however, of man's contriving. They consist mainly of ice sheathed in a skin of gravel, mosses, and lichens.

The world's largest concentration of pingos (more than 1,450 of them) is in the Tuktoyaktuk region. Grizzly bears excavate dens in their steep sides and rough-legged hawks nest upon them, but men have paid them little heed until recently when the citizens of Tuk Tuk excavated a cavern in the heart of a nearby pingo to create a year-round curling rink. It would appear that pingos have now found a purpose in the human scheme of things.

They intrigued even our usually blasé pilot who, without being asked, brought DCL down close to deck level and circled some of the larger ones. His interest was reflected by Roy.

"Jesus! Don't it look like the whole goddamn country's bustin' out in boils?"

We touched down on the inlet of the Beaufort Sea, which forms Tuktoyaktuk's busy harbour, and taxied in to join three other float planes moored at one of several docks. DCL was no longer alone in the wilderness.

Tuk Tuk itself was a hodgepodge of shoddy shacks interspersed with shiny new constructions. Many years earlier, Tuk had usurped Herschel Island's role as the major transshipping point for the central and western Arctic, then the construction of the DEW Line turned it into a boom town. At the time of our visit, it had a resident native population topping four hundred, and the highest birthrate in Canada. Twenty-odd (and some were very odd) whites (mostly men, but a few women), including police, traders, teachers, and missionaries, were also quondam residents. Few remained longer than a year or two. During the summer an influx of technicians, scientists, government officials, prospectors, and construction workers swelled the population by several hundred. Tuk provided good earning opportunities for most of these transients—but not for its native inhabitants.

One of the first people we met was Dave Anderson, Tuk Tuk's principal entrepreneur and owner of the only hotel. We took rooms there because they provided the only amenities of which we had really felt deprived during our journey—hot water and showers. The hotel did not, however, boast a bar because Tuk was nominally a dry town. In practice this meant you could not buy booze over the counter, but you could import as much as you wanted and drink it when and where you pleased.

Anderson welcomed us to his establishment and poured complimentary beers with a generous hand. He told us he was awaiting the arrival of a DC-3 bearing a delegation of distinguished visitors led by the Honourable Arthur Laing, Minister of the Department of Northern Affairs.

"We've got a hell of a lot to show him," said our host. "Tuk's the fastest-growing town in the north. Got a million-dollar future!"

I asked Anderson how he happened to be here.

"Came up three years ago working for the government. I could see it was wide open for free enterprise so I married a local girl, quit my job, and got down to it.

"First thing I did was take out thirty-three business licences, though that's kind of narrowed down now to about nineteen. They cover the hotel, a restaurant, a store, movie theatre, water taxi that I haven't got yet but it's on order, contracting and construction, jukebox and shuffleboard agency, handicrafts, and fur trading."

I asked how many natives were employed in his multiple enterprises.

"Well, we've *had* up to three, but right now, none. It's hard to get locals at a price we can afford so we get by using family, like my brother, and my wife's folks. But I'm flying to Inuvik tomorrow to see if I can pick up some fellows there because they've got big unemployment in Inuvik."

There was big unemployment in Tuk but, according to Anderson, the local people would not work for reasonable wages because they had been spoiled by Northern Transportation, a Crown corporation which had for some years been the community's principal employer and remained the prime reason for Tuk's existence.

"I can't afford the people here. They put too big a value on themselves. More than they're worth to me."

Anderson intended to complain to the minister about the wage problem and about other difficulties he was experiencing. Chief among these was the area advisory council. It was composed entirely of natives and was as enthusiastic about cooperatives as Anderson was about free enterprise. As president of Tuk's Chamber of Commerce, Anderson planned to protest what he saw as unfair competition from co-ops. When I asked how many members the Chamber had, he grinned.

"At the moment there's just me."

After a shower and a change of clothing I went looking for the Anglican missionary, to whom I had an introduction. Tuk's main street was a waste of gravel, ruts, and rocks. The weather had been hot and dry, and a haze of yellow dust lay thick over everything. A construction company from Yukon Territory was busy moving Northern Transportation's plant from across the harbour into Tuk proper. Big trucks and earthmoving machines seemed to be everywhere. I dodged among them, noting a large RCMP barracks, a variety of governmental, scientific, and military installations, and three missions: Anglican, Roman Catholic, and Pentecostal.

The Anglican priest, the Reverend Douglas Stanley, was a pink-faced, youngish man with cautiously unorthodox opinions. He had been three years in Tuk, which made him something of an authority.

"I've heard it said," I told him over tea, "that Tuk people are exceptionally independent-minded. Is that so?"

"I suppose it *is* true of the white people here, and it *used* to be true of the natives but, to be honest, they are now very confused and, you might say, put down by the presence of so many people from the south.

They've been made so many promises about how things are supposed to be, and the promises have been so often broken. Now their confidence is pretty well shattered."

"What about the employment situation?"

"Well, you know, there's a great many more people living in Tuk than the local hunting and trapping can support. They're supposed to convert to a wage economy. But at the present time...Tuk is a welfare settlement.

"It's not that people don't want to work, it's that very few jobs are available. And their training for most jobs is poor. Education is undoubtedly the answer, but there's a certain amount of resistance, even aggressive resistance, to sending children away to school."

"Why would that be?"

"Well...I wouldn't like to say."

He would not enlarge upon this, but I already had some intimations of what he was hinting at—intimations which would be bleakly confirmed before many more days had passed.

Reverting to the employment situation, he told me that only *eight* native men in Tuk had full-time jobs. However, he added with a smile, *eighteen* native women were employed in a fur garment cooperative.

I made a point of visiting the fur garment project. It was housed in a brand-new structure in which six native women were enjoying a coffee break when I arrived.

Jessie Andreasson, middle-aged, with a broad face deeply creased by laugh wrinkles, took me into the co-op's little showroom-cum-retail store to see the co-op's products. These included sealskin cushions with intricate inlay designs; duffle-cloth socks richly embroidered in coloured yarn; sealskin boots; rabbit-fur slippers; and an array of stuffed toys. But the crowning glory was a rack of sumptuous knee-length parkas made of muskrat, beaver, and white fox fur.

"We use all kinds of stuff, you know," Jessie told me proudly. "Plenty seal, specially for boots. Muskrat for parkas. Deer hide sometime. Beaver, can we get some. Most come from fellows lives round here."

The most serious problem the co-op faced, Jessie explained, was a shortage of quality furs.

"One time lots trappers, but since a while many men quit trapping and come to Tuk to work if they can. If don't get work, can't go back out onto land then 'cause they got no dogs and traps and gear like that any more. So we don't get so much fur and skins here."

Charlie Smith, a young DNA employee who worked with the co-op, was resolutely optimistic.

"With enough throughput from the shop the co-op could pay top prices for fur—a lot better than the traders ever paid—and that'd encourage men to get back into trapping. They could be part of the co-op. Then everybody'd be working together and they'd be their own bosses again, like in the old days. Given a break, co-ops like this could make the difference for a lot of Eskimos."

"So why aren't there more of them?"

"White businessmen don't want it to happen...." He cocked his head at the discordant sound of twin aircraft engines overhead. "That'll be Laing's plane coming in."

The minister had indeed arrived, bringing with him thirty members of the prestigious Economic Council of Canada—industrialists, trade unionists, merchandisers, agriculturalists, and scientists being given what was, for most, their introduction to the north.

I made my way to the community hall where an open meeting between visitors and residents had been arranged. Laing and his companions were soon seated on a makeshift stage together with the president of the Chamber of Commerce and the few other local dignitaries. Folding chairs in sufficient numbers to accommodate most of Tuk's inhabitants had been set out in the body of the hall but only a few were occupied.

The meeting had been scheduled for 6:00 p.m.—at the end of the working day. But when the ministerial party arrived three hours early, Laing's aides had decided to shift the time of the meeting to 4:00 p.m. to give the travellers extra time for rest and recreation. Unfortunately, nobody had bothered to tell Tuk's residents of the change. When most people arrived at the hall at 6:00 p.m., it was to discover that the minister and his party had departed for Inuvik.

When I entered the almost empty hall, the audience was being addressed by the manager of Northern Transportation.

Northern Transportation was a good example of how government serves the public need when private enterprise cannot or will not do so. Surface transportation in the central and western Arctic prior to World War II had been virtually a Hudson's Bay Company monopoly. The enormously increased demand for northern transport during the war years, together with the post-war surge, faced the HBC with the prospect of having to spend a lot of money to improve and enlarge the transport system. Concluding there was little profit to be made from such an investment, the HBC pulled out of public transport. The federal government then had to come to the rescue by forming a Crown corporation called Northern Transportation to do the job.

NT now carried most of the freight in a region almost a million square miles in extent. By 1966 it was operating a fleet of 57 tugs and 109 big barges up and down the Mackenzie between Tuk and the railhead at Waterways in northern Alberta, an over-the-bottom distance of close to two thousand miles. Saltwater cargo ships and tankers sailing out of Tuk served the coast from Alaska east to Spence Bay.

If the corporation's performance as a public carrier was impressive, its record as a local employer was less so. I learned that during the sailing season (the ice-free period of about fifty days each summer) NT hired 122 people to operate its vessels—but of these only fourteen were natives. Most of the rest were brought in from the south in spring and flown out again in autumn. For nine months of the year, not a single native was employed at NT's extensive Tuktoyaktuk base.

When I asked why this was so I was told, "It is cheaper to fly trained men in and out from the south than train Eskimo and Indian people here. Besides, there is the matter of attitude. The natives are not very responsible. Smart, perhaps, but not trustworthy to work like white persons will. It is difficult to change such attitudes."

The antipathy to hiring natives was not all-embracing. Down at the harbour I found a big yellow machine driving pilings into the muddy shore. It was being operated by a native who, when he got down from his machine for a break, introduced himself.

Dark-skinned, squat and sturdy, John Steen was clearly someone to be reckoned with. He gave a friendly nod at my explanation of why I was in Tuk, then told me, "You wanna find out about what's going on, don't spend too much time talking to white guys. Listen to what we got to say."

The upshot was that I spent most of the night in the company of John Steen and two other members of the area advisory council, of which John was chairman. They were an impressive trio—two calling themselves Eskimos and one Indian, though all three bore European names.

Eddie Gruben, a man in his mid-forties, counted himself an Eskimo. He was also a maverick who was not about to let himself become a cog in the white man's machine. He made a living of sorts by hunting and trapping, supplementing his meagre income by guiding wealthy white trophy hunters and fishermen from "outside."

Manuel Felix, a Dene, was going another route. Small, with a pointed beard and a Fu Manchu moustache, he had worked for government agencies for the past ten years earning regular wages. Although he saw this as the best guarantee of being able to ensure a future for himself and his family, he had most emphatically not become a civil servant.

John Steen occupied the middle ground. Until his mid-thirties he had lived a traditional Eskimo way of life and had been happy with it. Then a shortage of foxes, a drop in fur prices, and the explosion of what he called "DEW Line good times" had disrupted the pattern.

"People weren't content no more. Even my wife, she wanted stuff I couldn't buy. Old story, eh? So I took a job on the DEW Line. Made money, and spent it just as quick. Got fired and hired lots of times, and learned a lot of stuff. Now I'm onto heavy equipment when I get the chance."

As we talked we nibbled on rancid potato chips that cost three dollars for each small bag at the HBC store. John's softly moustached and no-nonsense wife made coffee which we sweetened with a little rum. Kids ran in and out of the kitchen where we sat. As the evening wore on we were joined by several more, mostly silent, men who were not introduced by name.

There was not much overt show of emotions until I enquired how people felt about the aborted meeting with the minister.

Eddie responded angrily.

"Why those guys come here anyhow? Mountie tell me they come to listen to us people—find out what we need—find out how can help us. Shit! Big shots! Never stay long enough even give us the chance to say nothing. Most people still working when that plane leave again. I think

they just come by to say they been here, and talk to some white guys here."

"Oh, they talked *about* you," I said. "I went to the meeting and they talked quite a lot about you. They said quite a lot about the problems of labour availability, and productivity, and how they have to train the native people so you can take responsibility."

Eddie snorted. "Yeah, that's the way they look at us. Wonder how they think we look at them, eh? Whose country they think this is anyway? What happens we go down their country and talk about the people there like they do about us? They'd be some trouble then, eh John?"

John thought a moment before replying.

"It really bothers me when they say we don't act responsible. They're dead wrong. If they give us the responsibility we will use it. Take care of jobs. Take care of ourselves. Give it to us and we will take more interest in the work they want done. If people had responsible jobs they'd take more interest. Wouldn't quit so easy. When I see I got no chance to get ahead on my job because some white guy's going to get it anyway, I don't feel too responsible.

"Look at our advisory council here. Northern Affairs guys tell us to start one so we can be responsible about how Tuk is run. So we do it and, sure we can advise, but still we don't have no real say in how Tuk is run. That's done by Northern Affairs and NT and the other white people here. We aren't responsible enough. And about businesses. They tell us best way get ahead is get a business started. But they don't help us do that."

"That's right," Manuel interjected. "They treat us like kids and we don't like be treated like kids. Told we can't be trusted look after money. Huh! I try borrow some to start fishing lodge out on Husky Lake for tourists, you know, and got turned right down. Bank guy good as told me I don't know how to handle money. So what happen, eh? White guy gets money from that bank to build lodge and I can go work for him, maybe. Maybe not.

"They think I handle money okay when I pay for grub and stuff. How come pretty near any white guy come up here to start a business can get money from the government and the bank, eh?"

It was a rhetorical question.

"You know damn well," added Manuel in disgust, "business is for white man. Leave us do the shit work, 'cause that's all we're good for. They'll run the business, yeah, and make the money."

John took over.

"They won't let us into their businesses, but when we got nothing they don't want us to starve neither, so they give us stuff. Food, houses, stuff to wear. They give us what we got to have to keep alive. Then they call us welfare people! Say we can't look after ourselves. Not responsible! Me, I hate the welfare and so do most of the people…but we got to live.

"So what I say to you, Mr. Mowat, and I hope you say my words good and loud so other people down south can hear: Just give us people a chance! Just give us *half* a chance!"

CHAPTER TWENTY-SEVEN

The Reindeer
Herd

INDIAN SUMMER HAD COME UPON US. IT SEEMED appropriate, since we were about to enter the heartland of the Athapascan Indian tribes inhabiting the northwestern reaches of Canada's and Alaska's boreal forests. The sun was ablaze, the sky crystalline, and the temperature sixty-five degrees Fahrenheit when we took off from Tuk bound south to Inuvik with a planned stop en route at Reindeer Depot.

Because we wanted to see at least one of the several mouths of the Mackenzie, we first flew west. The coastal lowlands were strewn with silver-hued windrows of ancient driftwood brought down to the sea by the great river and cast up by storm tides at a time when the Beaufort's shoreline was higher than it is now. Such a plethora of wood (a substance which is a rarity in so much of the Arctic) spoke of massive forests lying not far to the southward.

East Channel is the river's premier mouth. It flows into Kugmallit Bay at Kittigazuit—a legendary Eskimo gathering place. During summers still vivid in human memory, it had hosted hundreds of Inuit catching fish and hunting beluga for meat, blubber, and muktuk. Those times were gone. Hardly anyone visited Kittigazuit now, although it had recently been of considerable interest to white men. During the early phases of the Cold War something called an I-site had been built here as part of the U.S. electronic air defence. However, the construction of the DEW Line had made the I-sites redundant, and most, including this one, had been abandoned.

Originally each site had sported a steel tower three hundred feet high surrounded by a cluster of metal-sheathed buildings, storage dumps, access roads, and a landing strip. Now the deserted sites were junk yards, their towers felled and lying sprawled across the tundra like the skeletons of gigantic serpents, their buildings succumbing to winter gales, their acres of steel fuel drums (full and empty) disintegrating beside dead trucks and other vehicles amid a welter of nameless debris.

All this material had been transported north by sea and air at enormous cost; then almost everything, even including damaged aircraft and still-serviceable bulldozers, had been abandoned because salvage would have been too costly. During our travels we flew over four ruined I-sites. As many as thirty are scattered across the Canadian Arctic, with more in Alaska. They are a foretaste of what to expect as the massive DEW Line system also becomes redundant. Many DEW Line stations have already been abandoned, leaving thousands of tons of litter as *their* memorials. Doubtless the rest will soon follow.

I once commented on this grim prospect to a senior officer of the U.S. Corps of Engineers. He hastened to reassure me:

"Don't you worry none. Nobody lives in them places. Nothin' there but caribou, they tell me. And I guess *they* won't be bothered by a little junk."

We turned south over the desolation of Kittigazuit to follow the course of the East Channel into the enormous Mackenzie River Delta, a vast fan of alluvial muskeg, a spongy maze of rivulets, ponds, and channels stretching a hundred miles from south to north and fifty from east to west.

This is fertile country. Ten miles after leaving the coast, we began seeing patches of birch, willow, and even spruce. Here and there were the ruins of little cabins built by muskrat trappers in the not-so-long ago, but now deserted.

We had reached timberline and were now entering the realm of northern forests.

The broad tundra plateau of the Caribou Hills to the east of the delta was swathed in dwarf birch, which had already been nipped by a hard frost and glowed like cherry brandy. The delta flats below these hills formed a kaleidoscopic pattern of greens and golds interspersed with labyrinthine swales and bogs glittering like metallic confetti.

We approached Reindeer Depot shortly before noon. It consisted of half a dozen neat frame buildings set high on the east bank of the Mackenzie. We buzzed it, but could elicit no signs of life, human or otherwise.

I particularly wanted to visit the depot because I had heard that the reindeer project centred on it was in trouble and that the Ottawa bureaucrats were intent on getting rid of it. It seemed as if they had already done so. We decided to fly on to Inuvik, where we could find out.

"Yes," I was told upon arrival there, "the whole scheme's being wound up, but there's still a herd, and the reason you didn't see anybody is it's roundup time. The herders and their folks are out on Richards Island at the mouth of the river, chasing deer into corrals for marking and culling. We just got a boatload of steaks in from there yesterday."

Unravelling the story of Canada's reindeer venture took time. In the late autumn of 1966, and again in 1968, I travelled widely in Siberia, visiting herders and reindeer specialists, and was astounded to find some twenty thousand of Siberia's native peoples raising and marketing domesticated reindeer. In 1966 their herds numbered just under 2.6 million animals annually producing about fifty thousand tons of high-quality meat.

Nor were the Siberians the only ones committed to reindeer husbandry. Norway, Sweden, and Finland continue to maintain base herds which together amount to nearly a million animals and provide primary income for many natives.

During the 1920s some white Alaskans heard about the Soviet success with reindeer culture and imported a few hundred of the animals from Siberia. The venture proved so successful that by the early 1930s about 800,000 reindeer were browsing the Alaskan tundra providing employment to more than three thousand Alaskan natives.

Also in the 1920s, Vilhjalmur Stefánsson, one of Canada's most energetic (and least appreciated) northern explorers, recognized the potential for reindeer in the Canadian Arctic. Largely due to his efforts, the federal government eventually purchased three thousand reindeer from Alaska and hired Andrew Bahr, a Sami (Lap) herder, to bring them north, then east along the coast of the Beaufort Sea to the Mackenzie River Delta.

The thousand-mile trek begun in the autumn of 1929 became a five-year epic as Bahr and a few Inuit and Sami helpers slowly shepherded the herd eastward. In February of 1935 the animals reached their destination.

A Canadian reindeer industry could now begin. The low-lying islands comprising the northern portion of the delta, together with a huge stretch of mainland tundra to the eastward, were set aside as a reindeer reserve. The federal authorities built Reindeer Depot on the banks of the Mackenzie to house more Sami herders brought to Canada to teach local natives the special skills required. Within a few years the base herd had grown to ten thousand animals, and the authorities were ready to begin moving "seed herds" farther east to establish an economic mainstay for other Eskimo groups.

Then disaster struck.

It was not natural disaster, but one contrived by man.

Reindeer husbandry in Alaska had become a major export industry with the meat finding a ready market in the western United States. The first refrigerated shipments to reach San Francisco caused a sensation, for the meat was delicious, nutritious, and relatively cheap. Demand for it grew with such rapidity that the beef barons of the American West became alarmed. Their lobbyists in Washington were set to work convincing legislators that Alaskan reindeer posed a threat to the mainland livestock industry. Not long thereafter the import of reindeer meat into the lower states of the Union was banned.

Alaska's nascent reindeer industry collapsed. Within a few years after the embargo was imposed, the herds had shrunk to less than thirty thousand animals.

Canadian cattle producers saw a similar danger to their industry and followed the U.S. lead, but chose a somewhat different path. An outright prohibition on the sale of Northwest Territories reindeer meat in southern Canada might not have been tolerated by the Canadian public, so the method used to protect Canadian livestock producers was to quietly throttle the Mackenzie reindeer project in its cradle.

Support for it became political anathema. Government

maintenance and development funds were cut again and again. Scientists were found who declared that the introduction of reindeer would endanger the native caribou through crossbreeding, overgrazing, and infestations by new parasites. Such hired-gun experts blandly ignored peer research from Europe and Asia, which had shown that domesticated reindeer and wild reindeer could and did successfully exist in the same territory.

Despite being out of favour in Ottawa, the Canadian Reindeer Project nevertheless managed to survive, if tenuously. By 1954 six small herds still existed in the Mackenzie River Delta region, giving employment to twenty-three Eskimo families and providing high-quality meat to residents of the Lower Mackenzie Valley.

The Reindeer Project was proving hard to kill, but a decade later the *coup de grâce* was administered when what was left of it was "privatized" and virtually given away to a white businessman.

By the time of my 1966 visit, perhaps three or four thousand semi-domesticated reindeer still survived, though many of these were reverting to the wild and were being absorbed into the caribou herds. Detailed information was hard to come by. Most government officials and their supporting scientists preferred not to discuss the matter. Their reluctance was understandable in view of a series of horrific disasters which had taken place in Keewatin during the 1950s resulting in the deaths of at least two hundred Eskimos, mostly from starvation and the consequences of severe malnutrition. There can be little doubt but that this tragedy could have been averted or, at the least, greatly alleviated had the Eskimos involved been supporting themselves with reindeer husbandry.

The Reindeer Project did not fail because, as has been said, Canadian natives could not or would not adjust to its demands. During a visit to reindeer herders in northern Finland in 1990, I talked with a Sami herder who had worked on the Canadian project. He described how, at every turn, the enterprise had been undercut, if not sabotaged, from above. According to him the natives had readily learned reindeer husbandry and had practised it effectively. But the wages paid them were abysmally low and, not infrequently, were not paid at all. Logistic support of food, supplies, and transportation often failed to materialize. In general, so many difficulties were placed in the way of those trying to make a success of the venture that most gave up.

Yet these people differed in no significant way from the Alaskan natives who had made an unqualified success of the business—so long as they were permitted and encouraged to do so.

The failure of reindeer husbandry in the Canadian north should be laid at the feet of those who really *were* responsible for its collapse: those who, to benefit themselves, stifled a project which promised so well for the future of the northern people.

CHAPTER TWENTY-EIGHT

Kidnapped

MOST OF THE SETTLEMENTS WE HAD SO FAR VISITED enjoyed at least some degree of harmony with their surroundings. Not so Inuvik. If ever a northern town was at shrieking odds with its natal womb, this was it.

We came upon the place suddenly for we had been flying low over the muddy waters of East Channel. Rounding a wooded bend we almost ran into Inuvik's eastern suburb.

Identical rows of spanking-new bungalows painted institutional turquoise, boudoir pink, soapy yellow, and ketchup red stretched before us like play blocks laid out by a kindergarten teacher.

Beyond this field of toys lay Inuvik's working centre, remorselessly geometric and filled with gaunt, low, cheerless buildings designed to house bureaucrats, school children, and businesses. There was also a very large Roman Catholic church intended, one would suppose, to resemble an Eskimo igloo, but which looked more like an enormous toadstool.

All of these structures were linked by huge boxed and insulated umbilici running over the stony surface of the ground. Carrying heat, water, and sewage lines, this high-tech octopus, called a Utilidor, had been designed to overcome the problems of making civilization viable in the high north, where permafrost lurks only a foot or two below the surface. The Utilidor tentacles made both foot and wheeled traffic through the town akin to a steeplechase. They also cost so much to install and maintain (and they failed so frequently) that they were not much admired. As one Inuvik resident told me, "It was tough enough living up here when all we had to handle was the weather and stuff like that. Now we got to live with the effing Utilidor too!"

The space pre-empted by Inuvik had been obtained by ruthlessly slashing and bulldozing a spruce forest bordering the river. Hardly a tree had been left standing. If ever we build a station on Mars or the moon, we will doubtless employ the same school of planners, architects, and engineers responsible for Inuvik.

Designed in the bureaucratic warrens of Ottawa, the new town was intended to replace the long-established community of Aklavik forty miles distant on the western side of the delta. Reborn Aklavik on the eastern bank, Aklavik would then become the administrative capital of the entire western Arctic and a shining example of what the Northern Vision was all about.

Construction began in the late fifties and no effort or expense was spared. Maps (including the aeronautical editions by which we were navigating) were printed showing Aklavik *already* transported to its new location. By 1958 the transition was nominally a *fait accompli*.

Not quite.

Due to some minor oversight, the acquiescence of the citizens of the genuine Aklavik had not been obtained. When the time came for them to be transported from their "muddy swamp" to the glorious new mini-metropolis of the north, most refused to go. Threats, cajolery, and bribes would not move them. Eventually the planners had to restore the name "Aklavik" to its rightful owners and find another for their new, model town.

They settled on Inuvik, which in Inuktitut means "Place of the People." Inuvik was not then, nor is it now, a true place of Inuit, Indian, or Metis people.

At the time of our visit, natives were indeed living in Inuvik but most of these were students at the new, government-built but church-run residential schools, while others were people in transit between their home settlements, and hospitals and schools in the south. A few were government employees. Among the latter was Elijah Menarik, an Inuk from the eastern Arctic whom I had met some years earlier. Elijah was managing the Canadian Broadcasting Corporation's Northern

Service Station in Inuvik. I had let him know we were coming, and he met us at the seaplane dock.

"You supposed to go to DNA office," he told me apologetically. "Want to see you right away. They don't tell me why."

They didn't tell me either—not in so many words—but from the time I was "paraded" into the office of the director, it was obvious I wasn't going to get VIP treatment. I was told that, since the minister and his entourage were in town, no accommodation was available for me or my crew nor, it was made clear, would I be a welcome visitor at any government establishment, all of which were far too busy to have time for the likes of me.

When I reported back to my companions, Roy snorted.

"Travelling with you, Farl, is like travelling with a clapped-out whore. Nobody wants you. Hell with 'em. We'll make out."

Doug and Roy found beds at the float-plane base; Pete went to stay with friends of his own. Elijah considerately let me have a couch in his tiny living room, though I saw little of it.

We had been in town only a few hours when the Honourable Arthur Laing took his place as guest of honour at a reception and "information" meeting attended by almost everyone of importance—and by some who were not so important. Among the latter were three young women who neatly winkled me out of the meeting before it reached its inconclusive end. They carried me off to a gathering of quite another sort in what was unmistakably the native quarter. Here were no Utilidors. The streets were roughly gravelled trails. The houses were small and mostly built of whatever materials their owners had been able to scrounge. A few were "government issue" prefabs, one short step up from the boxcar prototype.

The house we entered was full of natives who seemed somewhat surprised to see us.

"Jeeze, girls, never thought you'd do it," cried a buxom Dene woman with long pigtails. Then, to me, "Guess you don't mind too much, being kidnap by such pretty girls!"

I didn't mind in the least. Mary Carpenter, ringleader of the gang, had already explained the purpose of the exercise.

"People know you're a writer so the idea was we get you and bring you to our place so you would hear something except the bullshit shovelled out at Laing's meeting. Then maybe you could pass it on to Canadians in the south how we people really feel about what's happening in the north."

A very large man with a flaming-red face and a grip like a bulldog seized me by an arm and thrust a mug into my hand.

"Hey!" he shouted fiercely. "Made this stuff myself! Mounties know I got it but they too scared to bust me."

What ensued was no drunken party. My escort allowed me only a smidgen of alcohol before marching me off to a YWCA hostel for native students whose manager, a Metis woman, had been persuaded to turn a blind eye as twenty or thirty young people crowded into an unused dormitory for what amounted to an alternative to the official meeting being held in downtown Inuvik.

My captors were all named Mary. Mary Carpenter and Mary Jordan were strapping, black-haired young women, part Eskimo and part white. Mary Firth was part Loucheux Indian and part white.

At twenty, Mary Carpenter had already experienced most of the tribulations of being a native in the new north, as well as some of the problems of being one in the south, where she had spent a year. She had strong opinions about what was happening to the people and their culture. To *all* the people—for she made little distinction between Indians, Eskimos, and those of mixed race.

"We all got the same troubles. All us young people are a lost generation. White kids down south at least have the history of their people behind them in books and all that stuff, but we've got nothing written down. Nothing, only the stories the old people used to tell in our old languages that's been taken away from us by the education system of the whites. And the old people are dying off, so *our* history's lost. So most of us younger people have lost touch with who we used to be, and even with our own land..."

A young Dene man sprawled on a lower bunk interrupted fiercely: "We're being suffocated by your world with all its pressures and beliefs forced onto us. Us natives aren't given any time or help to ground ourselves or defend ourselves. We're just told this or that is good and right. That it's the only way. That what you white people say about everything is God's gospel! That we have to go your way—or else it's too goddamn bad for us!"

Mary Carpenter resumed: "Our way of life was built on trust, you know. So we trusted what the white man told us. But they came up here for *their* own good, not for ours, and it never bothered them to lie their heads off to us. They come up here now with their families even, to teach, do scientific stuff, run government jobs, be missionaries, and it's a big adventure for some and a holiday for some, and most get free housing, food subsidies, and what they call 'hardship pay' added to their salaries for the year or two is all they usually stay. They live like kings among a bunch of poor, ignorant natives. Of course, they tell us they are here for our benefit, to help us. The fact is we are just their excuse— their justification, you could call it. The fact is we're just being used.

"Here in Inuvik there's two communities. East end and west end. East end is white. West end is native. And where do you think the RCMP spend the most of their time? Look out the window. See that big police car with its lights on high cruising our street, just about blinding every-one walking? You step outside with a bottle in your jacket to go visit a neighbour, like natives do, and pinch, you're in the coop. Too bad for you! You lose your job next day 'cause you're in the coop.

"But over in the east end there, they have parties we can hear 'way down here! Bad as anything ever happens down here. Get so drunk at the Legion Hall they fall down and the RCMP have to pick them up, but they don't go to the coop. That's for natives. They get driven home and put to bed. Probably get a lullaby sung to them."

"This spring," said Mary Firth, "the RCMP grabbed an Indian fella on our street. Wasn't even drunk, just singing and laughing loud. They slammed him in their car, and in the coop, and broke his leg, and kept him there yelling for help for five hours before anything was done about his leg. He lost his job. Was in and out of hospital three months. His family still has to live on welfare. He was going to lay charges against the Mounties but some Indian fellows that work for the government, they told him, no, you can't do that. It'll make trouble. If you do that the welfare will stop."

It was Mary Jordan's turn.

"Mary Carpenter got interviewed one time by *Maclean's* magazine when she was down south and she told how natives got treated up here. Mary got hell when she got back. Some of our own people, *big* people working for government, told her she should shut up. When she said she wouldn't she got slapped around. It don't pay to make a fuss."

"It's old-fashioned race prejudice we've got," snapped Mary Carpenter. "Same as black people in the south. It's in the schools here. It's in business. In government offices...."

Up to this point the three Marys and one or two others had done most of the talking while the other young people listened, almost stoically it seemed to me. However, Mary Carpenter's denunciation of racism opened the floodgates. I heard, with mounting discomfort, a litany of accusations ranging from accounts of relatively minor humiliations to the horrendous story of what a Dene girl who had been only twelve at the time had endured at the hands of a white construction gang on a mining site the previous winter.

The girl's father had been unable to obtain credit from the local trader and had been refused welfare by a priest acting as government agent, on the grounds that the man and his family of seven no longer came to church.

"Cook of work gang, he offer my father twenty dollar if I spend one night at that camp. My father, he take that money and buy flour so family can eat something.

"That cook, he keep me in shack behind cookhouse for a week, and I guess the men, they pay him, and they come and screw me. If I yell or anything, there is no food and the cook beat me.

"One day that cook, he tell me go back to my hole now. Like I was a dog or something. When I get home I tell my mother. She tell me I should keep quiet. Those fellows, they *white* men, she tell me. 'You Dene. The Father, he won't want to hear you tell story like that. The trader don't want it. Police call you liar. You better close your mouth.'"

The reference to a priest unleashed another flood, which I made a fainthearted attempt to stem by suggesting that religion as a whole could hardly be blamed for the transgressions of individuals. Mary Carpenter would have none of it.

"Religion!" she almost shouted. "Worst thing of all. That's where the *worst* racism is! Brotherly love, my ass! Jesus was a white man, eh? Still is, and they don't let us forget it. We're lucky the missionaries are so busy fighting each other or it'd be worse for us.

"They do just about anything to get you into their church and away from the other ones. An Eskimo man at Sachs Harbour one bad year, him and his family was pretty hungry. He was an Anglican but there was no Anglican minister there that winter. So the Roman Catholic priest said, 'I'll let you use my motorboat to go fishing and sealing if you turn RC.' Did the man do it? What do you think? What else could he do?"

I admit to having felt somewhat relieved at this juncture when the hostel manager appeared and asked us to end the session.

"Too many police cars out there tonight," she explained. "Guess they don't want no foolishness 'cause of the minister. We don't want no trouble, so everybody better go on home or to their dorms."

Docility in the face of authority had been so ingrained into these young people by years of residential school discipline that there was no argument. The three Marys proposed we spend the rest of the night where we were to avoid the risk of encountering an overzealous police patrol.

"Wonder if you'll be like most white guys," said Mary Carpenter wickedly. "Try and screw all of us then look for more?"

Truth to tell I slept alone on this, the only night I have ever spent in a Young Women's Christian Association hostel.

Sachs Harbour was Mary Carpenter's nominal home. Three hundred miles northeast of Inuvik, it is the only human community on Banks' Island, which is no insignificant piece of real estate. A third again larger than the province of Nova Scotia, it appears not to have had a permanent human population during historic times, which may explain why, until quite recently, it was a paradise for non-human animals.

As with most arctic settlements, Sachs owes its existence to white men. In 1914 Vilhjalmur Stefánsson, Ole Andreasson, and Storker Storkerson travelled over the ice of the Beaufort Sea from the coast of Alaska to Banks Island as part of an epic exploration of the northwestern Arctic Archipelago. After the sea ice broke up that summer, they were joined by their support vessel, the auxiliary schooner *Mary Sachs*, which spent the succeeding winter at the little harbour on Banks' southwestern coast to which she gave her name. That harbour became the expedition's base and was later occupied by mainland Eskimos drawn there by Stefánsson's discovery of the amazing abundance of animals on Banks Island, especially of musk ox, white foxes, and wolves. The incoming people made Sachs Harbour their new home and prospered there.

By 1966 Sachs had a population of 115 native people, six Department of Transport employees running a weather station, two RCMP constables (this on an island where crime of any sort was virtually unknown), a Roman Catholic priest, and a husband-and-wife team of Glad Tidings Pentecostal missionaries from the United States.

The Anglican minister went away and never came back, Mary explained to me, but there's another white guy messing about there now worse than a missionary. He's a social anthropologist from some big university studying our habits. Those guys are everywhere in the north now, asking personal questions and busy taking notes like we was bugs for them to study. They crawl over us worse than lice.

Before the missions came, Sachs people were all one bunch. Everybody as good as everybody else. Kids ran all over the place and did whatever came naturally. Any kid was everybody's kid. Everybody was friends and everybody helped each other out when times were tough.

Then the Anglicans came and they built a little church and pretty soon everybody was Anglican, or said they were, because that made the white man happy. Then along came the Roman Catholics, and now the Pentecostals, and it's like war has come to Sachs. The Anglicans got knocked out pretty quick, but the fight is wicked between the RCs and the Pentecostals.

The worst of it is, there's no kids left now except a little while in summer. They're all taken out to the different church schools, come home for only a couple months in summer—if they're lucky. And they don't find it easy, coming home. I'm one of them, you know. I'd sure like to live on Banks again, but when I tried I found Sachs wasn't my place any more. I was a stranger in my own place and I couldn't take it. I'll tell you one thing—winter at Sachs without any kids running around is the nearest thing to purgatory you could ever put people in.

My dad, Fred Carpenter, was born at Sachs. His father was a white man working for Stefánsson who married an Eskimo woman. Dad had three wives—two died on him—and thirteen kids, and he looked after all of us kids real good. He trapped enough foxes so he could buy a schooner, the North Star, *and* summertimes the whole family lived aboard her. Winters, Dad would freeze her in someplace where he and the older boys could trap white foxes. Sometimes at Baillie Islands near the mainland east of Tuk, sometimes around Banks or Victoria Island.

He set up as a trader at Sachs because there was no trader there. He's kind of a hard man who works 'til he drops. He's a good man though—a good thinker, too, who hates welfare. He tries to keep the people at Sachs from going on welfare. There's one widow there now taking welfare and she's the only person who is. Dad tries to get people to help each other the way they used to in old times. He says once they get you on welfare you can say goodbye to your freedom.

I was actually born in Aklavik in the summer of 1946 when the North Star was in there getting supplies to take home to Sachs for the winter. For the next five years I lived free as the wind, just travelling around to wherever Dad thought there'd be good trapping. In wintertimes we kids used to ride on the dogsleds, right up on top of the loads, where we could keep a lookout for foxes and polar bears. If we spotted one we got a lot of praise. Summers was mainly at Sachs with a bit of travelling in the schooner to hunt white whales; do a bit of trading; or go hunting caribou, musk ox, whatever you needed.

Then one time the North Star was at Aklavik the Anglican minister came on board and told Dad all us kids had to go to residential school because now that was the law. Nobody wanted to go, and our parents hated to let us, but they had to do it. If we didn't go, the RCMP would fly in and just take the kids away to residential school.

I was five when I was put into the mission hostel at Aklavik. I never got back to Sachs Harbour 'til I was seventeen. All those years I didn't even get home in summertime. Instead, they kept me at the Anglican hostel in the summer. My mother was there in Aklavik in hospital for a while before she died with TB, and my father would sail in for two or three weeks during the summer, so I sometimes saw them but, you know, the hostel was so strict they would not let me spend the night with my father or my mother. I had to be back in the dormitory every night. I used to hide behind my father's legs and cry not to let them take me back. But I had to go.

There was both Indians and Eskimos in the hostel, but more Indians, so they were always the bosses and, you know, from old, old times Indians and Eskimos didn't get along too good.

There were four dormitories: A, B, C, and D. We were divided up according to our ages, the youngest in A dorm. After 8:30 at night it was like Lord of the Flies in any of them. Most of the supervisors didn't know what went on, or if they did they didn't care. And some were worse than the worst of the kids.

I remember when I was six, there was a girl near me who was so miserable she often wet her bed, so the girl who was boss of the dorm made all the rest of us line up and pee in her bed, then this girl had to sleep in it.

The dorms were packed. Fifteen beds on each side and about ten inches between the beds. There was no privacy. You owned nothing and you wore the same clothes as everybody else. We used the same toothbrushes and the same bathwater.

Things got no better when we moved up to B dorm. There was one girl that the boss girls really went after—used to beat her up naked in bed. Tie her up, her feet and her hands, and beat her with a wooden club and make her drink piss. If they didn't like you they'd put Sunlight soap in your behind and make you shit in a Coke bottle or a bean can.

There were lesbian types who would make like a man and a woman, and if we didn't watch them do it, they'd beat us up. You had to line up around the bed they was on and watch. The head girls took advantage of the young ones, mostly young Eskimo kids. If you dared to complain you could get beat up really bad.

The boys' dorms were in the same building and there was one boy was the boss of them all. They used to sneak into the girls' dorms and rape the girls, until one of the Indian girls got her courage up to tell the minister. Nothing happened to the boys, but that girl was sent away somewhere and I never heard about her again.

It was the monotony that was the worst. The food was mainly fish and tapioca. You couldn't talk your own language. If you did, and you were caught, you got a beating. Everything was in English. In the end, most of us lost our native language.

You want to know what I got out of my twelve years' schooling? I lost my Eskimo language. I lost contact with my parents, with most of my brothers and sisters, with the old people who were my relatives. When I left Aklavik mission school they sent me to Yellowknife. That was even farther from home. After Grade 12 they finally let me go home to Sachs at last. That was the first time since I was five. I didn't know the place. I didn't know what to say or what to do. I didn't know my parents. I couldn't talk Eskimo no better than one of the white missionaries!

But you know what was the worst thing of all? I didn't know who I was any more....

Ten years later Mary visited Claire and me in Ontario. She listened to some of the tapes I had made in 1966 but said little until I asked her what her current thoughts were about northern education.

"Isn't it goddamn obvious?" she replied with fierce intensity. "Learning useful stuff never was what it's all about. It's about breaking the connections that keep people together, that make them *into* a people. If natives stay united they're always going to be a problem and you probably have to kill them to get rid of them. But break up their society, alienate the kids from their parents, make a mockery of their beliefs, take away their language, turn the different generations against each other, graft a lot of alien ideas onto them, and pretty soon they'll be gone. Not dead...but gone. They'll fall through the cracks of your world. And you bastards won't even have to feel guilty, though you've destroyed them as sure as if you'd lined them up and shot them.

"Education!" She paused significantly.

"I call it eradication—and it was used deliberately on us by you people through your government with lots of help from the missionaries— not for *our* good, but for *yours!*"

CHAPTER TWENTY-NINE

Mudopolis

THE MORNING WE WERE DUE TO FLY ON TO AKLAVIK dawned grey and sombre with heavy rain. We flew very low over a hazy delta, flushing small gaggles of ducks and geese from countless ponds and meanders. The birds were the tag ends of immense flocks that had already gone south. Thousands of newly mudded muskrat houses and push-ups (piles of vegetation gathered by the rats for winter food) also testified that summer was near its end.

Aklavik looked as if it, too, might be near an end. It seemed to consist chiefly of disintegrating frame or log cabins squatting disconsolately at the intersection of two of the Mackenzie's silt-laden channels. Water was everywhere: on three sides of the settlement, in a vast bog behind it, and in a slough within its boundaries. It was also in the air. The rain pelted down as we landed and taxied to the sodden shore.

Roy almost mutinied.

"I don't wanna go ashore. That mud's gotta be so thick you'll sink up to your crotch."

Three people emerged from shelter and sprinted to the shore to help moor DCL to a rotting wharf. One of them was Lyall Trimble, a shaggy, youngish man who hustled us up the soggy bank into the patchwork structure which was Aklavik's one and only café. Lyall turned out to be the owner, cook, and waiter. He was also the elected member to the Northwest Territories Council for the Delta district, and self-appointed official greeter for Aklavik.

"Welcome to Mudopolis," he said as he poured mugs of strong coffee. "That's what the Inuvik bastards call it."

People (mostly male and mostly native) trickled into the café for a
look at the newcomers. Trimble introduced me as "a guy who's got no
use for Inuvik." That was a help, but the atmosphere was still cool.
These people had endured too many visitors spouting "expert" solu-
tions for their problems. My attempts to find out how they felt about
their lot were mostly met with silence. They sipped their coffee,
smoked, looked at the floor, and made me feel like the interloper I was.

Trimble filled me in on the history of the place.

Aklavik was founded, if you want to call it that, around 1912 by a Hudson's
Bay Company hustler. But, long before that, old-time Eskimos and Indians used
to meet here—the Eskimos called it Aklavuk, the Meeting Place—sometimes to
trade and sometimes to fight. The HBC guys' plan was to turn it into a regular
trading post and pull the Eskimos down from the coast and the Indians from
up the river. Wasn't long before whites changed the name to Aklavik, which
means Grizzly Bear Place, maybe on account of there was tough times here in
the early days.

Whatever. It soon got to be the busiest spot in the western Arctic, except maybe
for Herschel Island. Steamboats came down the Mackenzie to Aklavik all the way
from the head of navigation at Waterways in Alberta. Boats from Alaska going
east to Queen Maud Gulf met the riverboats here and exchanged furs for supplies.

It was headquarters for Loucheux Indians, Eskimos, and whites who trapped
beaver, rats, and mink in the delta. Lots of rats! One year 340,000 rat skins were
traded at Aklavik, not to mention plenty of other furs. Some folks called it Ratville,
and people living here were proud to consider themselves part water rat.

You needed webbed feet, but it was still the hell of a good place to live. The
Richardson Mountains caribou herd hangs out only fifteen or twenty miles to the
west and if it's ducks and geese you're after, or damn near any kind of fish, there's
no better place in the north. If you've got a taste for blubber, there's dandy white
whaling and sealing around the channel mouths. And we still have a reindeer
herd right next door on the delta's northern islands. All Aklavik ever lacked was
a licensed brewery and a distillery, but so long as it was getting plenty of fur
the place never went dry.

Until Inuvik got invented, Aklavik was the biggest town in the western
Canadian Arctic. Seldom less than seven hundred people. There's still nearly six

hundred—about half Eskimo, a third Indian, and the rest white—and the number is holding up despite everything Ottawa can do to choke us off.

We're the real melting pot of the north. We've got Loucheux, Eskimos, whites of all kinds, and every mixture in between. In fact, most people here, except the few came in recently, are mixtures and proud of it.

I'm one of the newcomers. Arrived in 1956 with the RCMP. Really liked the country and the people so I quit the force and stayed on.

Greatest little town on earth! She may look like a tattered old bag, but that's because she's had the hell of a hard time of it last few years. The clipboard boys from Ottawa tried to run her right out of the Territories. They scared some people into moving to Inuvik, and that left a bunch of buildings empty, and empty houses fall apart quick in this climate. Most of the people that went to Inuvik eventually came back, but by then their places were beyond repair. Those are the wrecks you see here now. But we're tearing them down and building new homes. The HBC is actually spending $100,000 on a new store, after tearing down the old one so they could move to Inuvik.

Once Ottawa decided to close Aklavik down, a good many places was left run to rot and ruin. Even the missions got into the act: closed most of the mission schools and the hospital and moved to Inuvik where the government built them dandy new ones.

Quite a few whites was willing to move—but not many natives. Most still won't budge. They know there's nothing much for them in Inuvik except welfare. No fur or game around there, just a handy place for a swanky town and a big airport for those can afford that sort of thing.

For sure it's no bed of roses here either but we've got a terrific fur garment co-op going. Then there's Allan McClelland. He's set up a sawmill and planing mill in the woods to the west. Allan designed a prefabricated house specially for this country. He built a prototype a couple of winters back, and experts from the south looked it over and said it was just what was needed. It's a two- or three-bedroom bungalow, ready-wired for electricity and piped for plumbing and so well insulated you can damn near heat it with a match. It can be delivered and assembled most anywhere in the west and central Arctic for about six thousand dollars.

It's a world beater compared with the God-awful prefabs DNA's been shipping up from Ontario, Quebec, and Alberta. There's just one rub. DNA says they'll use Allan's model if he'll move his operation to Arctic Red River. That's seventy miles *south of here and would put Aklavik out of the picture. Which may be what they have in mind.*

When the rain let up a little, Doug and Roy went back to the plane. Pete disappeared somewhere on business of his own. I went for a walk.

The downpour had turned Aklavik's normal quagmire into something akin to Saskatchewan gumbo, than which nothing in the world is muddier. But the sun came out and the white crests of the Richardson Mountains to the west flared against a setting sun. Waterfowl took to wing over the river channels and a trio of lordly ravens followed me about, commenting (lewdly, I suspect) on my antecedents as they flung themselves in and out of the poplars and birches that provided a park-like background for the often decrepit buildings.

My objective was the fur garment shop. It turned out to be elder sister to the one I had visited at Tuk and was an equally impressive example of what cooperative enterprise in native hands can accomplish.

The co-op manager was an intense young man called Freddie who bore the unlikely surname of Greenlander. Although he was mostly Loucheux, one of his forebears had come from Greenland. A son of this man had been part of the posse that, in 1932, chased the notorious Albert Johnson—the so-called "mad trapper of Rat River"—through the Richardson Mountains. Freddie's version of this episode differed so markedly from all other accounts I had heard or read that I spent most of my remaining time at Aklavik pursuing fading memories of that bizarre episode.

CHAPTER THIRTY

The Loner

ONE HOT, MOSQUITO-HAZED JULY DAY IN 1931 a motorboat bound up the Mackenzie from Aklavik nosed into the muddy bank below the little settlement of Arctic Red River. The boat had brought a small sack of official mail for Constable Ernest Millen, officer-in-charge of Arctic Red River's two-man RCMP detachment. The mail included a memo from Inspector E.N. Eames, commanding the Western Arctic Subdivision of the Force at Aklavik.

"It is reported that a strange man going under the name of Johnson landed near Fort McPherson on the evening of July 9. He apparently came down the [Peel] river on a raft of two or three logs....As far as can be learned he had no outfit, neither rifle nor dogs, but appeared to be well supplied with money. He purchased some supplies from the trader there and is supposed to have made enquiries regarding the route to the Yukon."*

Although the traveller, whomever he might be, had committed no crime (nor had any complaints been made against him), Eames seems to have decided that his conduct was presumptuous, if not suspicious, and he therefore ordered Constable Millen to patrol to Fort McPherson, a small trading post fifty miles to the westward of Arctic Red River on the tributary Peel River, and interrogate the newcomer.

* This and other quotations by policemen involved in the case are taken from RCMP reports made at the time, and from *Policing the Arctic*, Harwood Steele, M.C., Ryerson Press, Toronto, 1935.

Millen set out the next day by boat. At McPherson he found a stranger who called himself Albert Johnson.

Millen described him as being "145–150 pounds, wiry, slightly stooped, of about thirty-five or forty, say five-foot-nine, snub-nosed, with light brown hair, blue eyes, and good white teeth....He was extremely taciturn both with whites and Indians. When questioned he answered evasively in a faint Scandinavian accent."

Taciturn he may have been, but he did tell the Mountie he had come in his own canoe down the Mackenzie from northern Saskatchewan, and that on reaching the mouth of the Peel had tried to ascend that river. Somewhere deep in the almost uninhabited and largely unknown interior of the Yukon's Peel Basin, he had lost his canoe and most of his gear while tracking up a rapid. He had then built himself a raft and ridden the river back to Fort McPherson, the nearest place where he could replace his outfit. This much he told the inquisitive policeman, but as far as his personal history or his future plans were concerned he had little or nothing to say.

When Constable Millen's report of the encounter reached Inspector Eames in Aklavik, he was less than pleased.

"I am not," he wrote in another memo to Millen, "prepared to accept Johnson's reticence about himself....If Mr. Johnson's intentions are good, he can have scarcely objected to the Police knowing all about him."

Millen was ordered back to Fort McPherson to make a full investigation of Johnson's activities and antecedents and to report his purpose and intentions in travelling into the Mackenzie country.

This second attempt was no more successful than the first. The stranger took the position that so long as he obeyed the law, what he did and where he went were his business alone and the Mounties had no right to pry.

Baffled by such obduracy, Millen tried another tack. He told Johnson that if he intended to remain in the district he would have to obtain a trapper's licence, which required the applicant to answer a number of background questions. Johnson refused, on the grounds that he was not a trapper and did not intend to become one.

Millen was stymied. There being nothing more he could do he

returned to Arctic Red River and there wrote a somewhat plaintive report to Inspector Eames.

"He did not seem to want to give much information regarding himself. He said if he did not stay in this district we had no need to know all about him. He had not made up his mind yet, and might go over Rat River portage [to the Yukon]. He would not live at Fort McPherson because he did not want to be bothered and preferred to live alone.... The local trader said he was getting an outfit together, paying for what he wanted, and bothering no one."

There was nothing more Eames could do at the moment, but we can be sure he did not put the recalcitrant Johnson entirely out of mind.

Christmas of 1931 brought the usual crowd of trappers into Arctic Red River to trade and to celebrate. Among them was a man the police records identify only as "Indian Joe," who said that Johnson was living in a cabin he had built on the bank of the Rat River, which flows out of the Richardson Mountains into the Mackenzie about halfway between Fort McPherson and Aklavik. Indian Joe is supposed to have complained that Johnson was interfering with Indian trap lines in the Rat River area, but no specific complaint was laid and the consensus among the natives seems to have been that Johnson was simply trying to dissuade people from intruding upon his chosen solitude.

However, Inspector Eames seems to have seen the complaint as evidence of Johnson's contempt for the forces of law and order. He decided to put the uncommunicative stranger in his place by sending Millen's junior, Constable A.W. King, and Loucheux special constable Joseph Bernard to Johnson's cabin to demonstrate the determination of the police to do their job.

Driving a crack team of dogs pulling a carriole (a toboggan fitted with canvas sides) containing food and camp gear, the two men reached the cabin in two days. Bernard stayed with the dogs on the river ice while King climbed a steep overhanging bank to a small squat log structure set into the hillside and so snow-covered as to be almost invisible.

The policeman knocked sharply on the door. When there was no response, he knocked harder. He had almost concluded that the owner was absent when he glimpsed movement through the cabin's one small window. Again he banged on the door while ordering the occupant to open up.

Still there was no response.

Being young and somewhat unsure of himself, King was at a loss what to do next. He scrambled back down to where Bernard waited and, after some discussion with his special, concluded the best move would be to travel on to Aklavik and ask Inspector Eames for instructions.

Outraged by what he took to be Johnson's open challenge to authority, Eames reacted by doubling the strength of the patrol, adding to it Constable McDowell and Special Constable Lazarus Sittichinli, and by arming all four men with repeating rifles. He also supplied King with a search warrant and instructed him to use force if Johnson continued to deny entry to the cabin.

The reinforced patrol returned to Rat River on the last day of the year. New Year's Eve was only a few hours away, and the four men must have wished they were at home to celebrate it. But duty called. While the other three waited watchfully on the frozen river, King once more climbed the bank to the cabin; beat upon the door; and then, according to the official report, politely inquired: "Are you there, Mr. Johnson?"

Whatever actually *was* said triggered an explosive response. A bullet crashed through the door. King fell, but crawled away.

Constable McDowell immediately opened fire, drawing a volley from the cabin which sent the patrol sprinting to cover under the overhanging riverbank. In the silence that followed, Lazarus Sittichinli calmly emerged from shelter, walked slowly to King's side, helped the wounded man down the bank, and settled him into a carriole. Johnson made no attempt to interfere. The patrol was soon racing for Aklavik, some eighty miles distant.

The exhausted dogs drew up in front of the Anglican Mission's little hospital at 7:00 a.m. on New Year's Day. Roused from his post-party slumbers, the doctor patched up the policeman's injuries, which he described as "non-life-threatening." Eames, however, reported that the shot had "nearly killed the constable" and justified laying a charge of attempted murder against Johnson.

Some of Aklavik's residents felt this was overdoing it. According to Freddie Greenlander:

"Lazarus Sittichinli didn't think Johnson tried to kill anybody. Figured he just wanted to scare people away. He could've shot all them fellows easy if he'd a mind to. Lazarus said he wasn't afraid of being shot himself when he went to help King. Never thought he would be."

Nevertheless, a policeman *had* been shot, and Eames was grimly determined to bring the culprit in. He ordered Constable Millen and Special Constable Bernard to rendezvous at the mouth of the Rat, where Eames would meet them with a posse consisting of himself, Constable McDowell, three white trappers, and Lazarus Sittichinli. On board one of their four carrioles would be a canister of flares and twenty pounds of dynamite, together with fuses and detonators.

It was tough travelling. The temperature was forty-five below zero Fahrenheit and the Mackenzie's western branch, Husky Channel, was being fiercely swept by drifting snow. An attempt by the Aklavik contingent to find a more sheltered route through the fringing woods resulted in Eames losing his way. In consequence, the two parties did not meet at the mouth of the Rat until January 7, and two more days elapsed before they drove cautiously up the river to a point where Eames could get his first look at the cabin.

"It was situated on a promontory round which the Rat River ran so that cover from [Johnson's] fire was available only on the [rear] side....It was built of logs about 12" in diameter and was about eight by twelve feet in size...the roof constructed of heavy poles covered with frozen sod to a thickness of two feet....The walls were reinforced with extra logs and frozen sods....The cabin floor was sunk 38" below ground level."

Johnson had also cut loopholes in an upper row of logs. In effect he had created a classic strongpoint in the military mode. This was something Inspector Eames appears not to have grasped.

"By listening from a position under the riverbank we learned that Johnson was home, so I called to him to come out, and said we were determined to arrest him."

When this order met with no response, Eames decided to rush the cabin and smash down the door. This attempt at a frontal attack was met with a burst of fire which sent the attackers scuttling for cover.

Crouching under the shelter of the riverbank, Eames considered what to do next. Johnson seemed to be well supplied with ammunition.

It had to be assumed he was also well stocked with food, water, and fire-wood, and therefore prepared to withstand a siege.

Eames was not prepared to mount one. The posse had only brought along enough food to last dogs and men for a week, and most of the supplies had already been consumed. Time was now so much of the essence that Eames decided to risk a night attack.

While some of his party crawled close enough to fling sticks of dynamite at the cabin (with no significant results), others fired flares that bathed the scene in a garish light, thereby enabling Johnson to see what his assailants were doing and to reply "with well aimed shots." No one was hurt by this defensive fire but it turned back this second mass assault.

Eames was now growing desperate.

"At 3:00 a.m. the last of the dynamite, four pounds, was thrown against the front of the cabin. Immediately after the explosion Gardlund [one of the white trappers] and I ran toward the shack intend-ing to throw the rays of a spotlight on Johnson and endeavour to disable him with our revolver fire. Johnson evidently saw or heard us when we were within a few yards and commenced to shoot. Gardlund switched on his light, only to have it shot from his hands."

This demonstration of Johnson's marksmanship sent the members of the posse scrambling back to the shelter of the riverbank yet again.

Some of them seem to have been less than impressed by their leader's tactics. As Johnny Greenlander told it: "Johnson damn good shooter. Don't pay to push him too hard." Greenlander and other natives felt it would have been wiser to have blockaded the camp and so even-tually to have starved the quarry out. "That way nobody get hurt. Police don't want to do that. Want to grab that fellow quick. Pretty foolish. Like grab porcupine with bare hands!"

The failed night attack ended the episode. By 4:00 a.m. the posse was in ignominious retreat to Aklavik. However, on arrival there Inspector Eames seems to have had second thoughts. Next day he sent Corporal Millen and trapper Gardlund back to Rat River with orders to camp two miles from Johnson's cabin and keep him under distant observation while Eames assembled a new and more formidable posse.

This one included Quartermaster Sergeant Riddell and Staff

Sergeant Hersey of the Royal Canadian Corps of Signals detachment manning the wireless station at Aklavik. Riddell prepared for the task ahead by making a supply of fragmentation bombs from lengths of iron pipe filled with black powder.

By this time headlines were appearing in newspapers all across Canada, and even in the foreign press: TRAPPER HOLDS MOUNTIES AT BAY IN FROZEN NORTH...WILL THE FAMOUS FORCE GET THEIR MAN?...MAD TRAPPER OF RAT RIVER DEFIES RCMP.

On January 16 Eames, accompanied by a force of seven men, again set off for Rat River. Cautiously the posse approached Johnson's cabin— only to find it deserted.

Harwood Steele tells us the pursuers "discovered the flight was permanent, that the Force, putting the fear of God into Johnson, had him on the run—for he had taken all of his outfit with him—but they did not learn anything more. The cunning Johnson destroyed all papers, letters, etc., that might have assisted us in the matter of identity, antecedents, etc."

After spending three days blundering about fruitlessly looking for the fugitive in snow-filled ravines, the posse was again running short of supplies so Eames led three men back to Aklavik, leaving the other four to continue the search.

On January 30 Constable Millen, Quartermaster Sergeant Riddell, native trapper Verville, and white trapper Gardlund were cautiously following a snowshoe track up the steep valley of Bear Creek (a small tributary of the Rat) when they came upon Johnson's simple camp. It consisted of little more than an open fire and a lean-to shelter of spruce boughs, although the official report says: "Here they found the fugitive *ambushed* [my italics] in a thick stand of timber."

Quartermaster Sergeant Riddell wrote this account of what ensued:

"Gardlund and I went to a point on the opposite side of the creek... where we could see the camp. Millen and Verville came down the hill to the creek close to his camp. We could hear Johnson coughing. We heard him rattling his rifle. As Millen came past an opening in the timber, Johnson fired a shot at him. At this time Johnson could not be seen by any of us [so] some shots were fired blindly into the timber until no more shots came from there. We thought Johnson had been hurt.

Millen and I went up the bank to a patch in the timber and a shot was fired at very short range. I went back over the bank into cover. Millen, who was right behind me, remained on the bank....He fired two shots to my knowledge, and Johnson fired three. When I got to the top of the bank again at another point [I could see] Millen had been shot."

Johnson's first shot was evidently intended as a warning. It was taken as such by the soldier Riddell, but Constable Millen seems to have seen it as a challenge to be resolved Hollywood-style. That was a fatal error.

Johnson made no attempt to prevent Millen's companions from recovering the body, and they hurried back to Aklavik with it.

Having lost two of his total force of four policemen, Eames now had to conscript a posse consisting of himself, Quartermaster Sergeant Riddell, Special Constable Sittichinli, five white trappers, and three native men, one of whom was John Greenlander.

The weather remained so bitterly cold that it took three days for this motley crew to reach the place where Millen had been killed. Johnson was long gone by then. Eames describes what followed.

"We were now in the larger foothills, with numerous creeks in deep ravines and canyons. Between the creek valleys was the frozen tundra covered with snow made hard by the wind that seemed to blow without cessation, and always with a drift that obliterated snowshoe tracks or footprints very quickly....A patrol found his track, only a few hours old, on the Barrier Creek, but lost it again when it went up onto the tundra."

Eleven well-equipped pursuers with dog teams were making no progress finding one fugitive on foot equipped only with what he could carry on his back. Johnson seemed to have become a wraith as insubstantial as the snow-devils blowing off the crest of the surrounding mountains.

Eames once again reported to his superiors that the efforts of his men were being crippled by a shortage of food and other supplies. Yet without even dogs to help him, Albert Johnson was able to tote sufficient arms, ammunition, tools, bedding, camp gear, and food to maintain himself during more than six weeks spent in the foothills and coulees of the Richardson massif in the dead of a subarctic winter. And this he did without any resupply except for what small game—rabbits and ptarmigans—he could shoot or snare.

Why *was* Johnson still at large?

The answer seems to have been in part at least that most of his pursuers had lost enthusiasm for the chase, some because they feared their quarry, others because of innate sympathy for a man whose essential crime was that he had refused to knuckle under to authority.

We never hate that fellow, so John Greenlander told members of his family later on. *Some hope, maybe, he get away.*

The Force was determined he would not. The RCMP Commissioner in Ottawa now authorized the charter of a plane to help end what was becoming a severe embarrassment. Canadian Airways duly supplied a four-passenger Bellanca on skis. Flown by bush pilot "Wop" May and laden with weapons and munitions and another RCMP constable, the Bellanca made its way north from Edmonton in stages, taking three days to complete the journey, a record for those times.

Other reinforcements also arrived. On February 8 Constable S.W. May (no relation of Wop May) and his native special, John Moses, drove into the police camp on Rat River after five days' tough sledding up the Porcupine River and over Rat Pass from Old Crow in the Yukon.

Neither Wop May's aerial searches nor reinforced ground patrols seemed able to locate the quarry. John Greenlander remembered that the white members of the posse were less than resolute in pressing the pursuit.

Though it is nowhere explicitly stated in any of the official accounts of the affair, the Force had apparently concluded that Johnson could not survive much longer on his own in this desolate and formidable wilderness.

"They think the country finish him off" was how John Greenlander put it.

The police had abandoned "hot pursuit" in favour of trying to keep Johnson penned up in the harsh foothills country between a supposedly insurmountable mountain divide on one side, and the forces of law and order on the other. The inspector's little army occupied a blocking position near the mouth of the Rat while Eames himself flew back to Aklavik to wait for time and the elements to make an end of Albert Johnson.

Suddenly the situation changed.

On February 12 word reached Aklavik that a party of Yukon Indians hunting caribou on the Bell River, which flows down the *western* slope of the mountains past an abandoned trading post called La Pierre House, had come across the snowshoe trail of an unknown white man. In a land where almost everyone was known to everyone else, this was taken to mean that Albert Johnson had somehow surmounted the mountain barrier and broken out to the westward.

The official report that "plans were somewhat upset by the receipt of [this] news" is surely a masterful understatement. All hell seems to have broken loose at Aklavik with the realization that, if Johnson *had* indeed made it over the mountains, there was now nothing to stop him continuing west across Yukon territory into Alaska. The police detachment normally stationed at Old Crow, which might have been able to intercept him, was camped with the rest of the posse at the mouth of the Rat.

New orders were not long in reaching this camp. Dogs were hurriedly harnessed as tents were struck and gear flung into the carrioles. Soon five teams were racing up the Rat valley heading for the Pass, from which they would descend to La Pierre House where Eames was to await them, having been flown across the divide in the Bellanca.

On February 14 Wop May delivered Eames to La Pierre House, then made a scouting flight along the Bell, where he spotted snowshoe tracks which might have belonged to the fugitive. That same day the posse trailed in, to be told their quarry was probably several days ahead of them and striking south from the Bell *up* the valley of the Eagle into the enormous and little-known wilderness of the Porcupine Plateau.

Johnson *was* indeed travelling on the ice of the Eagle—but in the opposite direction. Avoiding Rat Pass, he had made his own way through the barrier peaks and was now heading *down* the Eagle toward the Porcupine River, which would lead him westward to the Alaskan border and beyond.

Since no other full account exists, we must let Inspector Eames conclude the story.

"We had broken camp [fifteen miles up the Eagle] before daybreak.... About noon of February 17th the patrol, consisting of 8 men with dog teams, with three [additional] men travelling on foot, were approaching a sharp bend in the river when Staff Sergeant Hersey, who was driving the leading team, saw Johnson coming down the river about 250 yards away. Immediately Johnson saw Sergeant Hersey he hurriedly put on snowshoes and ran for the river bank with his rifle in his hands. Sergeant Hersey opened fire, as also did Joseph Verville, who was driving the second team. They were quickly joined by Karl Gardlund and Frank Jackson and in a short space of time the whole party was moving upstream in more or less extended order; some on the river and others on either bank. Johnson had been firing rapidly but suddenly ceased firing and commenced to run back up the river. I saw that Staff Sergeant Hersey had been hit....Johnson, running in his own tracks, was actually drawing away from the posse....[He] was called upon to surrender but continued his flight, whereupon rifle fire was concentrated upon him which apparently caused him to throw himself down, and dig down in deep snow, after placing his large packsack as cover, though it is probable that he had just been wounded in the leg...Johnson resumed firing at the men on the river....However the men who had gone up the bank...from their position in the high ground quickly stopped Johnson's fire, and a few minutes later, at 12:10 p.m., it was found Johnson was dead, having desperately resisted to the last."

Sergeant Hersey survived, and the Mounties had got their man, though to this day neither they nor, it appears, anyone else knows just who he was; where he came from; or what his purpose may have been in journeying alone to the top of the world.

Wop May flew the shattered body of the man called Albert Johnson to Aklavik, where the authorities were in favour of burying it in an unmarked grave. But Aklavik people, among whom was John Greenlander, raised a simple cross over it. By the time of my visit, the cross had perished and nothing remained visible save for a slight depression in the ground.

Perhaps it was only in death that Albert Johnson could have found what he was seeking. Johnny Greenlander may have got it about right: "That Johnson was one of them loners. He just seem to want everybody should leave him alone...that's all he seem to want."

C H A P T E R   T H I R T Y - O N E

Here Are the News

FREDDIE GREENLANDER'S PRETTY WIFE GAVE US breakfast on the morning of our departure from Aklavik. The main dish was stewed muskrat bottled during the spring hunt. The meat had a queasy aftertaste, reminiscent of the castor oil I had been forced to take in my childhood. I thought Aklavik was rather pushing the muskrat motif.

Freddie beamed as he ladled a generous second helping into my soup plate.

"Sure glad you like that. You'll get plenty more in Old Crow. That's real Loucheux country. People there catch lots of rats. Won't let you go hungry there."

The community of Old Crow is Yukon Territory's northernmost settlement. It sits at the mouth of the Old Crow River, in the western reaches of the broad Porcupine basin. To reach it we had to cross the Richardson range, whose peaks tower to six thousand feet. Since this was Albert Johnson country, Doug undertook to give us an aerial tour via Rat Pass.

We flew south from Aklavik up Husky Channel, paralleling the mountains, which on this chilly autumnal day stood out sharp and clear, an ancient range whose massive bones have been ground down into sweeping slopes carpeted with tundra in their upper reaches and furred with spruce in the lower ones.

Half an hour's flying over the multicoloured palette of the delta brought us to the junction of Husky Channel and Rat River. DCL

259

banked gracefully to the right and began ascending the narrow, creeping crevice through which the Rat flows down from the Richardson massif. The worn stubs of mountain molars began boxing us in. The sky grew ominous, and racing black clouds drooped lower and lower until the steep and rocky slopes below us became frighteningly close.

I was straining for a glimpse of Johnson's cabin, the ruins of which were reputedly still visible, when the intercom crackled.

"Can't make it. The pass is socked in solid. Gotta go up and over."

The Wasp roared lustily as we climbed steeply into a grey obscurity. A quarter of an hour later we broke out into clear sky with nothing to be seen below except a seething ocean of cloud.

Doug apologized: "Sorry, guys. We'll be over La Pierre House soon but we ain't going to see it. I just hope this stuff thins out before we get to Old Crow or we may not see *it* either!"

The gods were kind. By noon the cloud deck was beginning to fray, allowing us to look down upon a magnificent panorama of taiga and tundra bordered by another mountain range rippling the horizon a hundred miles distant.

We were now well over the Porcupine basin, but unsure of our exact whereabouts. Rivers and streams abounded, as did sinuous chains of domed hills. We could identify none of them on our maps. Massive swathes of taiga rolling between ochre-coloured tundra plains offered no recognizable landmarks. Not a single indication of human activity, past or present, was to be seen. It was not hard to imagine that this enormous enclave was truly the north's last pristine refuge from modern man. If Albert Johnson had reached it, he might never have been found.

Eventually we came to the Porcupine itself, a broad serpentine river writhing across a thinly forested sweep of plain. We followed it westward to its junction with Old Crow River and our destination.

Straggling for the better part of a mile along a lightly wooded terrace beside the Porcupine, the settlement of Old Crow was a frieze of silver-patinated log cabins sunk deep into sand. Most were small; many had sod roofs on which grasses and mosses competed for space. This was truly a community of the Old North, with only a handful of relatively modern structures: a frail-looking little Anglican church; a no-nonsense nursing station; a two-room school; and a new white bungalow housing the RCMP.

Notably absent was the mushroom of new construction that characterized so many of the settlements we had already visited. But those had mostly been in the Northwest Territories and therefore subject to the enthusiasms of the Department of Northern Affairs, whereas we were now in the jurisdiction of the nominally self-governing Yukon, whose indigenous population still lived under the overlordship of the Federal Department of Indian Affairs, an archaic institution bogged down by *laissez-faire*.

The Porcupine was at low-water stage, exposing a labyrinth of sandbars and channels that only very shoal-draft boats could navigate. What appeared to be an old-time river steamer was hard and fast aground on a cutbank beside the village. Seen from the air she looked like the real thing but, close up, turned out to be just a big, box-shaped motorboat, dirty and unkempt. She bore the unromantic name *Brainstorm II*. When the water was high enough, she skittered between Yukon river ports and Old Crow, making two or three round trips most summers. This summer a drought had made it impossible for her to complete her second trip so she lay stranded, awaiting the rains of autumn to float her free.

DCL taxied to a makeshift wharf where a shy Loucheux man with a heavily pocked face helped us moor. He was Steven Frost, thirty-three-year-old father of seven children, all under the age of thirteen. He was also the agent for a Dawson-based flying service which, we had been told in Aklavik, might have avgas for sale. Steven confirmed that this was so and Doug and Roy began filling the Otter's tanks while Pete and I went walking toward the far end of the village.

Indian summer was upon the land. The air was still and warm and Old Crow seemed to be drowsing as we ambled along the dusty riverside path. We saw few signs of life excepting a couple of children and an old woman guiding, or being guided by, an equally old dog. Log cabins sprouted haphazardly beside the track; some had boarded-up windows and were evidently abandoned; some were so deeply sunken into the ground as to appear half-buried. Interspersed among a scattering of debris ranging from old oil drums to collapsed meat-drying racks were a few stained wall tents. Pungent spruce smoke drifted from tin stove pipes; otherwise there was almost no sign of the native inhabitants. Neither did we see any whites because, apart from a nurse, there *were* none then in Old Crow. The little church no longer had a priest; the trader was a native; and the RCMP constable and the two teachers were all "outside."

"Looks like the set for some old-time western movie," Pete mused, "with mangy dogs instead of mangy-looking horses. Wonder where the bad guys are."

The echoing crash of a rifle shot from behind us suggested an answer to his question.

We spun around to see a flurry of activity erupting near the now distant plane. People were boiling out of adjacent cabins but we were too far away to make out what the hubbub was all about. Then the Wasp belched into life.

"What the hell..." Pete cried, and we both began running.

The engine thundered. DCL drew away from the dock, went roaring down the river, climbed up on her step, and was quickly airborne. Without so much as dipping a wing in farewell, she climbed steeply and disappeared to the eastward.

Peter Benjamin, Old Crow's special constable, was waiting for us when, panting and bewildered, we arrived at the wharf. He told us what had happened.

After rolling some drums of gas to the plane, Steven Frost slipped off to his cabin a few yards distant. Minutes later, in the presence of his wife and several of his children, he shot himself in the chest with a .303 rifle.

The resident Department of Health nurse, who happened to be attending a patient in a nearby cabin, sprinted to the Frost home, assessed the damage (which was massive), ordered neighbours to carry the injured man to the plane, and ran ahead to warn the pilot.

"There were no 'ifs' or 'buts' with that lady," Doug told us later. "'Get your ass into the air. This boy's got to get to Inuvik! Jump,' she said, and jump we sure and hell did!"

Doug had left a message for us with Peter Benjamin.

"The pilot, he say tell you he come back when he can. Say you better wait."

There being no other choice we did as we were bid. Benjamin told us more about Steven Frost.

"Steve's father policeman from down south; was in Dawson a while. Leave the country long time ago. Never come back. Steve help his mother with her kids. Work hard too. Work hard for his own kids after.

"He get sick a lot. Some time because drink too much; like lots people 'round here now. Then he got some cancer too.

"He only been back home a week from hospital in Whitehorse. Doctors down there look at cancer on him and say maybe he get better, maybe not. I guess Steve don't think so. I guess he think pretty soon can't work for the plane company so won't have no job. Maybe hope you fellows had some booze he could get....Old Crow, she's pretty dry right now. Maybe that's why..."

Everybody in Old Crow soon knew our plane had become Steven Frost's angel of mercy. In consequence they could not do enough for Pete and me. We were taken to Chief Charlie Abel's house for lunch. When I casually admired a beautifully made bow and arrow set that had belonged to his grandfather, Chief Charlie promptly gave it to me. Only with difficulty could I persuade him it should remain with his people. Pete murmured that I should be careful not to admire the chief's wife, a rotund and jovial woman who must have weighed well over two hundred pounds.

Aided by several neighbouring women, Mrs. Abel fed us an enormous meal which included blueberry bannocks, caribou marrow, smoked caribou tongues, caribou liver, and boiled caribou ribs. Muskrat was not on the menu.

While we were stuffing ourselves, Chief Charlie, an introspective-looking middle-aged man, said very little, but when I expressed an interest in Loucheux history he became animated.

"Most don't care about that old stuff no more. Kids forget about it. White people never know anyway. Pretty soon all be gone. We go talk to Joe Kay. He know all about them times."

Old Crow people seemed notably large, powerfully built, and handsome. Joe Kay at eighty-five was no exception. He stood very straight and tall. Only the deep corrugations in his face betrayed his age. His command of English was limited but, helped by Chief Charlie and Peter Benjamin as interpreters, he took us back into another time.

The first thing I learned was that "Loucheux" was not the people's own name for themselves, but one bestowed upon them long ago by French-speaking fur traders. Predictably it was derogatory—meaning slant-eyed.

Properly the Loucheux are Gwich'in (Kutchin in English), which simply means The People. Although they speak Athapascan they use a dialect different from the Dene of the Mackenzie Basin. To me they seemed different from the Dene in other ways: bigger, bolder, better-looking (according to most observers), and rather dashing in their behaviour. They also possessed the overt good nature and joviality (and probably some of the genes) of their neighbours, the Inuit, who live not far to the northward.

Gwich'in country originally seems to have included most of central and northern Yukon and the adjacent interior of Alaska. Relatively recently some Gwich'in crossed the divide into the Mackenzie delta, but since time immemorial their heartland had been the basin of the Old Crow River—a huge expanse of bogs, muskegs, streams, and ponds, which was also home to astronomical numbers of mosquitoes and to myriad muskrats.

Prior to the fur trade era—which did not begin in this region until the latter part of the nineteenth century—the Gwich'in lived in clans composed of several related families moving about seasonally within a traditional territory according to the availability of food, especially caribou, fish, and berries.

The fur trade brought changes but, at least initially, these were not disastrous. During the trapping season (late fall, winter, and early spring) family groups within each clan separated to go in search of fur—mainly marten, lynx, and fox—but drew together again in spring to hunt muskrat, beaver, and mink. Throughout the summer they lived a leisurely existence; fishing for salmon, whitefish, and trout; berry-picking; gathering plants and succulent roots; hunting caribou on the tundra, sheep and goats in the mountains, and moose in the willow swales by the rivers. Small parties made long journeys by water to trading posts on the Mackenzie, or along the Yukon, to bring back a modest supply of such alien goods as powder and shot, flour, tea, tobacco, metal tools, needles, and calico. Families also travelled widely to visit friends and relatives, using flat, wooden poling boats or moose-hide-covered canoes.

The Gwich'in of the Old Crow and Porcupine basins lived good lives well into modern times. Mostly they were spared the destruction inflicted on land and people during the viciously disruptive Yukon and Alaskan gold rushes. Avoiding the worst consequences of the invasions by white interlopers, they continued to enjoy a robust existence in a wilderness so remote as to have been beyond the ken of most of the rest of the world. Their contentment showed. One of the few whites who did visit them during this period commented admiringly on "their colourful dress, proud bearing, and their delight in feasting, dancing and singing."

Old Crow village, Old Crow River, and the enormous, sodden Crow Flats stretching northward to fill a basin more than fifty miles in diameter, all derive their name from the man who was chief of the eastern Gwich'in before the turn of the nineteenth century.

Chief Walking Crow had also been Joe Kay's grandfather.

He remember long time back. Tell lots of stories about Eskimos. They come south in winter to get wood and hunt caribou. Gwich'in go north to get Eskimo dogs. Those Eskimo peoples they show our peoples how to make those long dogsleds; how to make bows and arrows stronger than ours.

These peoples mostly get along pretty good, but sometimes not. Long-time-ago winter two Gwich'in brothers take families north of Crow Flats to big hills near the ocean to hunt caribou.

In the night one brother say Eskimo coming. Nobody listen. Then Eskimo walk right into tent with bow and big bag of arrows. Pretty soon another, and another comes in and after a while there is big fight. The brother who heard the Eskimo, he had a big knife and he cut his way outside tent and run away. Eskimo shoot lots of arrows at him, but never hit.

That night he gather up Eskimo arrows and take a bow from an old cache and sneak back to that big tent where Eskimo men having good time with Gwich'in women. Dogs see him but don't say nothing 'cause they know who he is.

He throw big stone at tent. When Eskimo men run out, he shoot so fast they all fall down. One get killed. But that brother, he let two Eskimo go with arrows stuck in them so they could tell the rest they better leave Gwich'in alone.

Was no more fights after that.

Me, Joe Kay, when I boy walk to north coast with uncle to trade for dogs. Lots of Eskimo on coast them times. Treat us very good. Take us with them when they go with sleds to Herschel Island. I see those big boats there, and white people. They give us lots of stuff. Then those Eskimos take us back to our own country. I remember all pretty good…sure liked those Eskimo girls.…

First white man in our country come from Hudson Bay Company on Mackenzie River. French man called LaPierre. Long time ago come over mountains through Bell River pass and build LaPierre House. After a while he quit Hudson Bay Company, marry a Gwich'in girl, and live here until he die, a nice old man. He teach us trade for ourselves.

LaPierre seems to have set an example which was still being followed. Old Crow was the first and only settlement we visited where trade was entirely in the hands of a native—Joe Netro by name.

Joe Netro's store was an old log building distinguishable from neighbouring houses only by its somewhat greater size. Chief Able introduced us. There was no need to ask Joe questions. He was as naturally garrulous as a Canada jay.

Hello. My name Joe Netro. That mean wolverine. Born in Old Crow in 1897 and still alive here yet!

Never no white man live here my time 'til 1912. Then Billy Moore come up from Fort Yukon in Alaska and make a store. Them time was no law here. No policeman, nothing. Some white trappers from Alaska come in too, 'cause this very good fur country. All kinds fur. Coloured fox, white fox, mink, marten, and all. Them fellows, they kill just about everything. Use poison, put it all around and kill off just about everything. So after a while no fur for anybody. So they go 'way again. Billy Moore, he go 'way too.

Fur come back after, and about 1920 Hudson Bay Company—they got a post at Rampart on the Porcupine—start outpost here at Old Crow, but the people don't get along with it so that company pulls out too.

Then everybody say: why we don't have our own trader like LaPierre in old times? So I fix this place up. Make deal with Harry Anthony in Fort Yukon. He send up a steamboat-load of supplies and after that we do our own trade here.

Got no trouble 'til after the war, 1947, then Northern Commercial Company in

*Whitehorse, they come in and build store here. People don't deal there so they
don't do much. In 1952 Northern Commercial asks, will I buy them out? I say,
give me store and stock and in three years I pay twelve thousand dollar, and that's
just what I done. So Old Crow still got her own store. Got her own boat, too, that
Brainstorm we buy from fellow in Fort Yukon, so can haul our own freight when
she working. Still, there's some troubles, 'cause so many things change all the time.*

Charlie Able had something to say about change.

*I been chief six years. People vote for chief now. Used to be they just gathered
and everybody kind of decided. Now they got to vote on paper.*

*Hard job being chief now. Hard for make a living for everybody now. Myself, I
work a little for the white people, but still mainly trapper. Got good trap line about
hundred mile up the Porcupine. Me and my partner, cousin of my wife, charter
float plane take us in there in the fall. Take dogs, sled, grub, everything we going to
need. Stay all winter then come back out with dog team for spring muskrat hunt on
Crow Flats. Trap mostly marten in the country 'cause that's about only fur worth
anything these times.*

*Last year we took $1,600 worth of fur. That's between two of us, and the plane
cost $500. My partner, he's single, but I got to look after wife and four kids so I
work for wages in the summer if I can. There was an oil company come prospecting
last year and I work for them, but this year they left the country. Supposed to be
another one coming in, but nobody know when.*

*What money we make trapping don't go far. That's why hardly anybody left
trapping now. Don't hardly pay for your outfit. Trouble is, not much else to do
around here. One time could cut wood summertime for the steamboats. But no more
steamboats since the war time. Police and school still buys a few cords firewood,
and that's all there is for people to do.*

*Some go out to Dawson or Whitehorse look to work, but it cost $55 to fly to
Dawson. If you lucky you might get work for a couple months out there. Maybe
couple weeks. Maybe nothing. Pretty discouraging when that happen.*

*We can get welfare from police, but nobody likes that. So far there's only few
old people here on steady relief, out of nearly two hundred people live at Old Crow.*

*What we want is work. Young people around here, they got a few years' school,
enough so they don't know how to trap or hunt, but no work around for them. If
they go outside maybe they get work, maybe not. Maybe they end up in jail 'cause
nothing to do but drink. They didn't even get married no more. Last wedding we
had was six years ago. They didn't get married 'cause got no money to live.*

If government could help build new houses, that would make some work. Most houses are pretty old, you can see. Most was old when I was a boy. They leak pretty bad. When it goes down to sixty below they pretty cold.

We still eat good though. Lots of caribou, and they nice and fat in the fall. This people look after their meat too. Don't waste a bit of it.

Drinking is getting real bad. We don't have no white constable right now. There's just Peter and he's only a special so he can't do much to stop the drinking. It gets pretty rough sometimes when booze comes in on the plane.

The Indian agent flies in once in a while, but it don't seem like he can do much. We like to see more government people know about this place. Things was not so bad when Yukon part of Northwest Territories. Now Yukon got their own government in Whitehorse, seems like they forget about us people more and more.

How the government of the Yukon Territory could possibly forget about Old Crow was a puzzle since the village was the home of a woman famous throughout the northwest, and not unknown in the south.

Edith Josie was a solidly built, broad-faced Gwich'in woman of my own age. Unmarried, but with three children, Miss Josie, as she refers to herself, was, and remains, the Old Crow correspondent for the *Whitehorse Star*, the *Fairbanks Daily News*, and the *Edmonton Journal*. On occasion she has reported on the Canadian Broadcasting Corporation's news network. Her columns begin with the signature phrase: *Here are the news from Miss Josie at Old Crow.*

I found her entertaining a lady friend of her own age on a patch of grass outside her old log cabin. The two women, wearing bright kerchiefs over their greying hair, were squatting on their heels. A piece of oilcloth on the ground between them served as a tablecloth. On it were two china plates, two teacups, two saucers, and a tin of condensed milk. Each of the ladies had a long, sharp knife with which to spear morsels of boiled caribou out of a pot simmering over a small fire beside them.

I introduced myself and was graciously invited to join the party. We sipped tea and nibbled bits of caribou while Miss Josie and I interviewed each other.

"Most what I write is about visitors," she told me. "Put that in my news. And also about the people in Old Crow, about hunting and fishing, and cut-wood they got for sale. And sometimes I write about old-timers like my mother. She in the cabin right now. Eighty-three, and only got one eye, but see pretty good enough do some washing dishes and help in the house. Right now she making caribou sinew thread. After she doing that she sell it Joe Netro store."

When I complimented Miss Josie on the excellence of the meat, she pointed to the river running shoal and brown below us.

"Boat down there. My son William boat."

I had already seen and admired a square-ended, flat-bottomed sliver of a thing about twenty feet long and four wide. Although it had a 10-horsepower outboard mounted on its stern, it was designed to be poled up and down the Porcupine and its tributaries. It lay with its nose up on the muddy foreshore, full of roughly butchered caribou haunches and briskets glowing red under garlands of green branches protecting the meat from the sun. Three caribou heads with spectacular spreads of antlers had been arranged on the tiny foredeck in such a way that they looked like a tripartite figurehead.

"William, he catch lots caribou. Very fat right now. What you eating come from him. Today anybody in Old Crow need a little meat going to get good feed from my son. That's how it is with this people. We like give everybody what we got.

"I born at Eagle [in Alaska]. Raised there. Things sometimes tough down there so when I around eighteen years old we come to Old Crow. Was pretty quiet here so we stay. Hunting, trapping, and cut wood in winter. Springtime, around March, go out to Crow Flats and hunt muskrat. That's how the most of this people made his living. Everybody live pretty good, them times.

"Not no more now. Not much fur. Not much cut wood. But still have to get more money all the time. Hard to keep the money 'cause things just cost too much. Every time, more of this people got to take relief. Now I don't know what going to happen to this people. I guess we just go on, from time to time, and hoping things got better."

Things did get better for Steven Frost.

Dusk was veiling the Porcupine valley when DCL reappeared out of a darkening eastern sky to make an abrupt landing on the river. Wearily Doug came ashore and told his story.

"The poor guy was a mess. Roy and the nurse worked like hell to stop the bleeding, but couldn't do too much. I goosed the old girl at full throttle, and by the time Inuvik was in sight the tanks were just about empty. We came in fast and the ambulance was waiting, but we couldn't hang around to see how things turned out—not if we wanted to get back here tonight—so we gassed up and took right off."

The four of us were having a late supper with Chief Charlie when a radio message arrived from the nurse, who had remained at Inuvik.

Steven was out of danger.

Charlie Able put down his knife and slowly rubbed a hand across his eyes.

"This happen too many time. Mostly young fellow. Shot their self. Drown their self. Drink their self foolish and freeze to death...."

Miss Josie's interview with me was printed in the *Whitehorse Star* for Thursday, September 1, 1966.

Aircraft was coming from Inuvik [sic] and four passengers came, here are the names: Farley Mouat, Peter Murdock, Doug Lamb—pilot, Roy Boys—Engineer.

Soon as the plane land they met Miss Josie so Farley Mouat went to Josie house and make one whole tape. For the people how they make their living.

They all seen three oceans, Atlantic, Arctic and Pacific Ocean. 10,000 miles they travel.

Sure glad to met them, and very nice to be here. While a man murdered himself....Steven Frost shot himself and took him to hospital.

Lucky they took him to hospital so Doctor is there and we hear he feeling better.

Too bad this accident happen in Old Crow. As I know this news could go around Canada and States so please prayer for Steven.

He wounded himself but not so bad.

Steven should get marry in Old Crow but he got marry to one of the girls in Fort Yukon.

So his mother-in-law Abbi and Philip Peter if they hear this news...I hope God will be with them and make them happy every day.

This is the end the news.

CHAPTER THIRTY-TWO

The Captains
and the Ships

THE WEATHER ON THE DAY OF OUR DEPARTURE FROM Old Crow for Dawson City was not propitious. Pete and I felt it might be better to wait until next day but, being young men, Doug and Roy were anxious to see the bright lights and taste the high life that had made Dawson famous in song and story. So off we went.

A direct flight would have taken us 250 miles due south through the heart of the Ogilvie range, some of whose peaks soar higher than seven thousand feet. Considering the uncertain state of the weather, Doug opted to fly only a few miles south from Old Crow before turning west over the range at Salmon Fork Pass, which was a mere 4,500 feet high. Thereafter we would follow the valley of the Yukon River to Dawson. This flight plan entailed crossing the international border between Yukon and Alaska and flying briefly through U.S. airspace; but since we had no intention of landing, this incursion seemed to us to be of no consequence.

DCL rumbled over Salmon Fork Pass with about six hundred feet between us and the rocks below, and about the same distance between us and heaving grey clouds above. The Ogilvies were safely behind, when Doug's earphones crackled and a no-nonsense voice peremptorily ordered "the unidentified aircraft" that had just entered Alaska Air Defence Identification Zone to identify itself at once before proceeding directly to the nearest USAF base. The stern dispatcher did not add "Or else!" but he might as well have done.

Doug's reaction was a classic for brevity with passion.

"Holy shit! The guy means *us!*"

Doug had not bothered to obtain official clearance to cross the U.S. border. As he later explained, "Could have taken a week and we didn't have the time. Anyhow, I figured we'd be well below their radar, so who in hell would ever know?"

They knew. What was worse, we could not even try to talk our way out of this contretemps because, although we could receive radio signals, the surrounding mountains prevented *our* transmissions from getting out.

"I didn't figure we stood much of a chance with a bunch of U.S. Air Force fighter jocks," Doug recalled later, "so I figured to get the hell out of there!"

DCL banked sharply back to the east and began to climb. Not far away were five- and six-thousand-foot mountains concealed in a winding cloth of clouds. We fled directly into those clouds, and by them were enveloped. They comforted us with the promise that not even a fighter jet with all its electronic gadgets could winkle us out before we regained the safety of our own Canadian skies.

Regain them we did, to find their security came at a cost. Heavy cloud enwrapped us. After glancing at the mountain-mottled map, Doug concluded we would be unwise to look for landmarks. As he put it, "One of those bejeezly mountains would likely have found us before we found it."

The alternative was to put DCL into a long climb to the eastward, from which she finally emerged into flawless blue skies at sixteen thousand feet. Not a fighter aircraft anywhere in sight. Nor, alas, anything else which might have offered a clue to our whereabouts.

"Not to worry" were Doug's comforting words. "We'll home in on Dawson radio. Fly down the beam."

The outside air temperature was ten degrees Fahrenheit and the cabin heaters were not functioning. The windows began frosting up. Roy opened his, but the bitter blast was not to be borne for long. There was really no choice but to descend into the cloud again in search of warmer air.

Descend we did, *very* gingerly. DCL sank through several layers of clouds and then, with horrifying suddenness, we became aware of the black loom of mountains. *Big* mountains. On all sides!

DCL reacted like a yo-yo, bouncing up to nine thousand feet to find clear air between two cloud layers. The windows began frosting up again but a call to Dawson brought reassuring word that the ceiling there was five thousand feet, ample to allow us to land beneath it. *If* we could find the place.

It was now late in the day and the light was failing fast. Several windows were open and I was freezing. I was also, for the first time on this journey, seriously frightened. When Pete uncorked a bottle of rum and passed it around, I had no scruples about drinking and driving. But then, of course, *I* wasn't driving.

There was nothing we could do but go down again feeling our way through the murk, vision straining for the blackness which would be our only warning of a wall of rock.

The blackness did not come. Instead, the gloom began to lighten. Rifts appeared in the clouds, allowing us to catch glimpses of mountain titans rearing to port and starboard...but not, thank God, directly ahead. We were dropping into the steep-walled Tintina Valley through which the Yukon surges north toward a distant sea.

Overgrown trails, old placer gold workings, even abandoned farm clearings began appearing along the heavily forested slopes. Doug let down until we were flying only a few hundred feet above the river's roiling surface. We roared past the bank-side Indian village of Moosehide and, at 8:30 p.m., splashed down in front of what had once been the gold capital of Canada, if not of the Western world.

Although Dawson City in 1966 looked like a semi-abandoned nineteenth-century village fighting a losing battle against the encroachment of time and the forest primaeval, we were so happy to be down that for the moment it seemed like paradise regained.

Word had got around that an inbound Otter in difficulties was arriving, and a small reception committee had gathered on the floating dock. Foremost in its ranks was a stocky, broad-faced man of sixty-five who introduced himself as Alan Innes-Taylor and explained he was doing the civic duties of mayor because Dawson *had* no such dignitary. "Or any other kind of a stuffed shirt," he added cheerfully. "D.O.T. operator says you seem to be in trouble with the Yanks. Says they're looking for you chaps from Nome to the Arctic Ocean. But here you are, safe and sound in dear old Dawson! Come and have a drink. It's not every day we get to hoist a few with someone who's pulled the Eagle's tail."

Alan and his daughter Kathy took charge of us. Having settled my crew in an apartment in the old Whitehorse Hotel, they took me to their snug, if somewhat dilapidated little house on the outskirts of the village.

I spent much time in Alan's company in the ensuing days, listening to his stories about the region, and about himself.

I was born in England in 1900, but came to Canada an orphan at the age of five to live with a dissolute old uncle at Bobcaygeon in Ontario. At seventeen I added a year to my age and joined the Royal Flying Corps, but by the time I was trained to fly the war was over. So there went my chance at the Great Adventure. I went back to Bobcaygeon pretty downhearted and all I could find to do was hired hand on a worked-out farm at ten dollars a month. I itched for action so in 1920 I joined the North West Mounted Police; trained in Regina; did a short stint in Victoria during the difficulties with the Wobblies—Industrial Workers of the World—with whom I sympathized; and got posted to the Yukon for my sins.

The Yukon suited me just fine, but I wasn't cut out to be a policeman so in 1925 I left the Force and went to work for the British and Yukon Navigation Company as purser on their steamer Whitehorse, *which ran the upper river between* Whitehorse *and Dawson.*

The Yukon River stretches from its southern beginnings, just fifteen miles above tidewater on a skinny finger of the Pacific Ocean called the Lynn Canal, north and west about two thousand miles to empty into the Bering Sea at Norton Sound. It was the heart and soul of human life in interior Alaska and in Yukon Territory both. Always had been, I guess, since the first ancestors of the Indians came paddling or poling their way along it. Before roads, cars, and airplanes, the Yukon was the central highway for all comers, and it still was when I joined the Whitehorse. *Everything man-made or man-wanted that came into the country or went out of it had to travel by boat on the river the Kutchin people call Yukon—the Great One.*

There were two types of steamers on the river—upper-river boats and lower-river boats. All were stern wheelers patterned after those used on the Columbia and the Mississippi. The upper-river boats had a draft of three feet maximum; lower-river boats could draw more because their stretch of the river was deeper.

Fuelled with cord wood, those boats could run from Whitehorse downstream to Dawson in thirty-six hours, usually pushing a barge nearly as big as themselves— but going back upstream took three and a half to four days. On a round trip the Whitehorse would burn 100 to 120 cords—"long" cords—four feet wide by eight feet high by eight feet long. The wood was cut and stacked along the banks of the river during the wintertime by anyone and everyone who needed work or a grub stake.

As purser, I would get hauled out of my bunk any hour of the day or night to tally a load of wood coming on board, and to pay the wood chopper.

There was one wood chopper I particularly remember, fellow by name of Ladue, at the mouth of Kirkman Creek. That was a nasty place to land, especially if you were pushing a barge, so the boats mostly used to pass it by. Ladue would stand there on the muddy shore, shaking his fist and hollering, "When are you bastards going to take my wood?" One summer he must have had twenty cord piled up waiting for a buyer, and no takers.

We were the last boat out of Whitehorse that year. The water was low, and when we got to Kirkman Creek, damned if we didn't get stuck on a bar. Old Ladue came poling out to us in his boat, whooping like a maniac. Charley Coughlin was our captain, and when he stepped out on the wing of the bridge, Ladue let him have it.

"You wouldn't take my wood, you old bugger, so I've put a curse onto you and your boat! I'm the seventh son of a seventh son, and you're going to stay on that bar 'til next spring!"

Well, we stuck there waiting for a rise upriver, and all the time we had to keep steam up in case the rise came. Pretty soon we were out of wood. So then we had to buy Ladue's pile and ferry it out to the steamer in our skiff. And Ladue raised the price from nine to twenty dollars a cord. We burned the twenty cord he had stacked, then we had to buy green wood from him, fresh cut, for forty dollars a cord. Captain Charley was fit for a straitjacket by that time. Was all for going ashore and shooting Ladue, but was afraid to do it. Charley was Irish and, big man as he was, he was afraid of the fairies—and of seventh sons!

One morning Ladue comes out to us again. "All right," he tells the captain, "I've got enough money now for a good grub stake at the gold diggings this winter, and I'm sick of cutting wood. So you can go." And you know, that day it started to rain. It poured down, and next day the river rose and we floated off. Long as I was aboard of the Whitehorse after that, Charley never missed making a stop at

Kirkman Creek and I believe he used to sneak a bottle of whiskey ashore there in the mail bag.

When we'd dock at Dawson I'd go down to the Bank of Commerce and the Bank of Montreal to take delivery on a pile of heavy-laden leather bags filled with gold dust and nuggets. Might be ten, fifteen, twenty thousand dollars' worth. I had an old safe in my office aboard ship, and a rusty Colt revolver that probably wouldn't have fired.

Not that there was ever any need of it. When tourists wanted to see what the gold looked like, I'd be happy to open the safe and show them.

There was almost no big-time crime in the country in those days because, for one thing, there was nowhere a criminal could go except upriver or downriver. You couldn't hide, even though the country on either side was as big as time. Somebody, an Indian or a prospector, would be sure to see your smoke or come across your trail or your camp.

The captains were God Almighty aboard the boats. People respected a river-boat captain more than any policeman or even a preacher. One of the most famous pilots ever on the Yukon was Captain Reid. When I joined the Whitehorse *in 1925 he was in his seventies. He'd been at it since the earliest days and was still as good for it as ever. He was just a little fellow—I don't think he'd have weighed 115 pounds soaking wet, but Lord, the way he knew that river! I can still see him bringing the boat down the thirty-mile stretch from Lake Laberge to Hootalinqua, one of the roughest runs on the Yukon, full of rocks and whitewater, especially in the fall of the year when the water was low.*

He'd tie up at the foot of Lake Laberge in the morning, waiting for the mist to lift. When it got high enough so you could just see the waterline at the banks, he'd holler, "Let her go!" and off we'd go downstream under a full head of steam so she'd have plenty of steerage way and be quick to answer her helm. I'd come on deck to see this little old man at the wheel there in the last of the mist; him barely high enough to look over that big wheel and the Whitehorse *going like a bat out of hell through the narrows and rapids, usually pushing a barge ahead of her, and she'd never so much as scrape a splinter off of her or the barge. I tell you, that old chap was a magician.*

Then there was Kid Marion—I sailed with him a good many times. At the turn of the century Marion had been a dog driver carrying the winter mail from Skagway to Whitehorse when he decided being a river-boat pilot would be an easier job. So he thought. He piled up one steamer on a rock before he found out different. After that he got very good at the job.

He was a master storyteller—could make you believe anything. One time we were bound downstream with a bunch of tourists up in the wheelhouse watching the goings-on, and the Kid told them: "You know, in the early days we had no fresh beef here and no milk at Dawson so it was decided to bring in a herd of sixty Holstein cows from Vancouver. They were brought overland from Skagway to Whitehorse and we got the job of barging them down to Dawson.

"When we were going through the Thirty Mile I was at the wheel and as we were making one of the bends I ran the barge ashore. The barricades on deck broke; the herd stampeded off the boat and scattered into the woods. We went after them, of course, but never found a one.

"A few years later people began to notice a peculiar kind of moose in the country—black and white instead of brown, so, of course, we figured what had happened. The woods was full of Holstein Moose."

Now among the ladies listening to this was a teacher from Birmingham, Alabama. "Captain Marion," says she, "you may take me for a fool, but you are the fool. That story is nothing but a wholesale lie!" with which she stomped off the bridge.

The Kid was pretty cut up. Nobody had ever called him a liar in his own wheelhouse before. That evening he asked me what I thought he should do about it.

"Well," I said, "I know where there is a Holstein cow. Pete MacMillan, the telegraph operator at Carmacks, has one. I suppose it's the only one on the Yukon."

"By God, yes!" yells Marion. "The minute we get ashore in Dawson you run for the telegraph office and send this message to Pete: PLEASE TAKE THE MOOSE ANTLERS OFF THE FRONT OF YOUR CABIN AND LASH THEM ONTO YOUR COW AND TURN HER LOOSE WHEN YOU HEAR FIVE BLASTS ON MY WHISTLE THURSDAY MORNING DOWN BELOW SHIRTWAIST BEND." Well, I did what the Kid said and a telegram comes back from Pete:

I'LL DO IT BUT ONE OF US IS CRAZY I HOPE ITS YOU.

On the way back upriver the Kid made some sort of excuse to get the Alabama lady back to the wheelhouse. I think he told her he couldn't sleep nights, he was so sorry for what he'd done, and wanted to apologize.

Anyway, when we got to Shirtwaist Bend he hauled down on the whistle lanyard and blew five good blasts. Everybody wondered what was happening and ran out on deck. We came around the bend and there in the long meadow grass by the shore about a quarter mile off was this poor old Holstein cow with the moose antlers tied to her horns. She was trying every which way to get rid of them. She just was jumping up and down. So was the lady on the bridge!

"Oh, Captain!" she cries. "It's me should be sorry for calling you a liar!"

The Kid didn't hear. He was too busy in the wheelhouse, bawling down the speaking tube to Larson, the engineer.

"For God's sake, Swede, open her up and get us out of here! If that damned cow shakes off her antlers, I'm done for!"

How did it end? Well, one fall when I was going out on the train from Whitehorse to Skagway, I met the Kid. He fumbles in his wallet and pulls out a newspaper clipping. Seems the lady had given a lecture on her trip to the Yukon to the local ladies society, and the Holstein Moose had been the hit of the show. She could have gone on the lecture circuit after that and made her fortune.

Captain Marion never lost a chance to take off a tourist. Every spring he'd get a pair of big old dirty moccasins somewhere. He'd put a stick into each one of them first trip of the season and when we came to the Indian cemetery on the edge of the flats at Lake Laberge, he'd row ashore and jam the sticks into the cutbank with the moccasins on the end of them.

Next time we came by with a load of tourist ladies on board, he'd draw their attention to the moccasins.

"You see that fellow's feet sticking out from that cemetery?" he'd ask. And the horrified ladies would say, "Oh my goodness! How terrible!" And the Kid would say, "Not at all, ma'am. That's the way we have to bury 'em. The summer gets powerful hot in this country, you know, and that's the only way a deceased can keep his feet cool."

One day Alan took me out on the Yukon in his little boat. About a mile and a half downstream on the left bank was a broad "flat," thickly over-grown with willows and poplars. I glimpsed wooden structures through the tangle and thought we were approaching an abandoned village until Alan put me right.

"This is a graveyard," he told me as we scrambled ashore. "A steam-boat graveyard. Used to be where steamers and barges were hauled out for the winter. In fact, some were even built here at the 'left limit' as it used to be called."

We poked about, pushing through the luxuriant new growth, everywhere encountering the mouldering remains of once proud and mighty river steamers. They loomed above us like the remains of titanic dinosaurs.

Alan knew them all by name.

"That's the *Julia B*," he said, pointing to a hulk whose collapsing wheelhouse still bore traces of ornate scroll work and gilt paint. "She was the last lower-river ship to go into storage here, in 1924, and she never came out of it. Those two big ones over there you can just see through the trees—what's left of them—they're the *Seattle No. 3* and the *Schwatka*. Two of the biggest boats ever to sail the lower river. They were hauled out here the winter of 1917 and never were launched again. By then the river fleet was dying off like flies.

"See there? Those great big capstans—big as small houses—they used to be turned by teams of horses to haul the big boats up. And over there, the wooden ways, built with logs three feet in diameter to take the weight of the biggest boat on the river. Another ten years and you won't be able to see any of that under the new trees growing up.

"Hard to imagine these old boats were part of a fleet of more than two hundred steamers not long after the turn of the century when the gold boom was coming to its peak. Most of the rest of them lie rotting on the beach at St. Michael near the river mouth.

"They were great boats to travel on. You could go aboard the *Julia B* and travel first class from Dawson to San Francisco via St. Michael for $125, including sixteen hundred miles down this river. And first class on the steamers *was* first class. They served four full meals a day. The cooking was superb. The cabins were clean and bright and as big as a man or woman could want. The service was as good, and as friendly, as if you were a millionaire in your own house. If you had one of those boats on the river today you could fill her full as a tick with tourists willing to pay thousands of dollars to make that trip. But it's all gone now.

"There was just one problem; the boats were dry so you had to bring your own booze. But there was a fellow in Dawson, Stanley King, who met all the boats. He had a wheelbarrow and he would take orders for booze, go to the government liquor store, load up, and wheel back to the wharf. They say his wheelbarrow made a rut so deep some chap fell into it and broke his leg. I *do* know, because I was there, one time him and his wheelbarrow made fifteen trips between the store and the *Whitehorse* to satisfy the thirst of a crowd of miners heading for Skagway and outside.

"Stanley's chum was a man called Edwards. He was Dawson's undertaker and he was a cadaverous-looking individual. He had terrible hot feet and used to sit in front of his business premises on summer days soaking his bare feet in a bucket of water. I think it was seeing him that gave Kid Marion the idea to stick those moccasins in the riverbank.

"Edwards was no stranger than many people in Dawson. He had a fantastic talent for forecasting who was going to die each winter. He needed to be right, because you can only dig graves in summer when the permafrost has softened. So Edwards would dig a certain number of graves each summer, and corpses and graves would balance out before spring came.

"Just once that I know about did Edwards miss. One September the *Whitehorse* was the last boat to leave Dawson. Everybody in town came down to the dock to see us off because they knew that, except for a stagecoach that lurched and bumped along the frozen Yukon from Whitehorse maybe once a month in wintertime, there'd be no freight or passengers coming or going until next June.

"I was on the top deck with Captain Charley Coughlin watching the last passengers come on board. One was an old-timer from the creeks, long, white, scraggly beard, not as much meat on his bones as a lost dog. Right beside him was Edwards, shouting at the old fellow, who was pretty deaf.

"'I don't see why you want to leave now, Bill, just when everything's all set. I'll see to it you got lots of grub, booze, whatever you need. Why don't you stick around?'

"Just then Charley leaned over the rail and bellowed down, 'Edwards, you old mortuary bastard, you've got a grave dug for Bill! Too damn bad! Bill, you get aboard or I'll drag you on.'

"So the poor old fellow climbed the gangplank and that was one winter Edwards had a grave left over.

"The river was surely the blood of the country in those days. Still is for some of us. Almost every day I meet Charlie Isaac, son of Chief Isaac of the Han clan at Moosehide. He used to be one of the Indians worked on the *Whitehorse.* The other day he said to me, 'Alan, you and I are the only steamboat men left. Why can't we go on the river again like we used to?'

"'Well,' I said, 'we can't, because the captains are all gone.'

"'Yes,' Charlie said, and he looked out over the river for the longest time. 'Yes, Alan, the captains and the ships…all gone.'"

CHAPTER THIRTY-THREE

Last-time
Box

A T FIRST ALAN WAS RELUCTANT TO TALK ABOUT THE aspect of Yukon history best known to the world—the Great Klondike Gold Rush at the turn of the twentieth century.

"Seems to be that's all you outsiders want to know about us," he reflected with some annoyance. "Klondike. Bonanza Creek. Eldorado. Gamblers. Dance hall queens. Men rich as Croesus or poor as dogs 'moiling for gold,' as Robert Service put it. A sort of arctic epic of human courage and endurance against the brute ferocity of nature."

He shook his head. "Well, I know, and you know, Farley, that wasn't the real story. No, not by a damn sight. Low-down *greed* was what it was really all about. Pure and simple greed that ruined thousands of human lives and some of the loveliest places on earth. I only saw the tail end of it but even that was enough to sicken anyone on human nature."

When Inspector Constantine of the North West Mounted Police got here in 1898 he took a good hard look and reported that the gold rush people "appeared to be the sweepings of the slums and the result of a general jail delivery." Maybe he was a bit hard on them, but they surely weren't all diamonds in the rough the way most storybooks and histories like to tell it.

Of course there were honest men on the creeks; good and generous men too. You have to admire them for their guts, but as for what they did to this land, to each other, and to themselves…well, I'd sooner not think too much about that.

There weren't many folk around, then or later, who cared to see what was really happening. Most everybody was blinded by gold dust. One chap who did see it straight was an Episcopalian missionary called Hudson Stuck.

A chap who never wanted anybody to call him Reverend, Stuck must have been one of the greatest travellers in the northwest. All winter long for decades he was on the trail travelling by dog team from one end of Alaska and the Yukon to the other. Then all summer he'd be on the rivers in a little gasoline launch called the Pelican. *I guess he drove that poor little thing up every stream in the country that had as much as two feet of water in it, and some with a whole lot less. He didn't miss much. Whatever was going on, he saw it, and his sight was clear as crystal.*

I met him just once, but I've got his books. Here's one he wrote in 1915 or 1916. Got a lot in it about George Carmack.

I've always felt it was tragic that Carmack, a white man who'd spent years trying to be an Indian because of his admiration for them, should have been an instrument of their destruction. Married to a Kutchin woman, father of her kids, an adopted member of the Han clan, it was Carmack who opened the floodgates to hell on the Yukon. Sooner or later somebody would have done it, I suppose, but he was the one.

Him and two Indian companions were net-fishing not far from here for winter dog feed when a white prospector came along and talked them into seeing what they could pan on a little pup—a tributary—of the Throndig River that comes into the Yukon just above Dawson.

That pup would soon be called Bonanza Creek, and the Throndig would become the Klondike...but here, let Stuck tell you about it.*

In August, 1896, George Carmack and his companions panned some gravel and found remarkably good prospects....The news spread up and down the Yukon, and Bonanza Creek and all adjacent creeks were soon staked from end to end. The local excitement grew as the richness of the ground appeared and in January of the next year men on the Pacific Coast began to learn of the "strike" and to start for the new goldfields. But it was not until August, 1897, when a ship came into San Francisco harbour with something like six hundred thousand dollars worth of gold on board that the excitement went world-wide.

Men of adventurous disposition and unattractive prospects began migrating to the New Eldorado; small shopkeepers sold their shops, clerks, bookkeepers and salesmen realized their savings, mortgaged their homes...professional men,

---

* Hudson Stuck, *Voyages on the Yukon and Its Tributaries*. New York: Charles Scribner's Sons, 1917.

physicians, lawyers, engineers and even ministers of religion abandoned their avocations and joined the ever increasing throng....From the British Isles, from every country on the continent...men crossed the Atlantic on every steamer, bound for the same goal.

Close behind the army of gold-seekers was the army of camp-followers who expected to grow rich catering to them; road-house and restaurant people; tradesmen of all sorts hauling little stocks of goods with them; liquor sellers; tin smiths; tailors; bakers and barbers.

And the parasitical class kept the caravans close company; women of a certain kind with their bullies; gamblers; crooks; confidence men....The shipping of the Pacific coast was insufficient to meet the demands, and steamboats were hastily sent around Cape Horn from the Atlantic, while every ship-building yard in the Pacific worked at full stretch.

In the fall of 1897 the stream began to beat upon the barriers of the land, but it was in the spring and summer of 1898 that the great rush came. They started, and then swamped, the towns of Skagway and Dyea on the coast; they swarmed like black ants up the snow-covered passes of the coast range, laden like beasts of burden. Many turned back but many pressed on and with infinite toil reached the headwaters of the Yukon, made and launched their rude craft, and descended the Yukon to the Klondike.

The Klondike Stampede was without precedent. Never before had a new gold region been so remote and inaccessible; never before had such masses of men... flung themselves into an arctic wilderness devoid of human sustenance, as most men use those words.

They had neither time nor opportunity to learn anything and they pitted their inexperience and ignorance against the savageness of nature in her sternest moods and most naked fastnesses. Hundreds of them perished. They died of exhaustion, of starvation, of pneumonia. They were drowned, were frozen, were smothered in snow slides, they lay in log cabins rotting with scurvy. And those that reached the camp at what would become Dawson herded themselves together and fouled their own surroundings with such disregard for health and decency that an epidemic of typhoid fever swept away many of them.

The great stampede to the Klondike brought nothing but harm to the native people....The navigation season of 1897 came to a close with many steam boats... far short of their destination. Capt. Ray of the U.S. army who was sent to investigate conditions, reports 350 white men wintering at Fort Yukon and is not at

all complimentary in his references to the character of many of them....These were
the days when there was no government at all in Alaska. Although the country had
been for thirty years in the possession of the United States, our inelastic system had
not permitted the setting up of any attempt at governing the Territory.

Given a large number of men with little or nothing to do, quantities of
whiskey—and there were quantities—and a timid and docile native people, it is
not surprising that there was gross debauchery and general demoralization. It took
a long time to recover from the evil living of those winters and the evil which
followed.

At Dawson the adventurers built a city. The flat on which it stands was partly
made by a landslide from Mooseide Mountain and partly by the swift little river
that comes into the Yukon with its swampy, sandy mouth—a little river famous
throughout the world, called Klondike.

I know not how to describe Dawson as I first saw it in 1904 when...it was
already past its prime. That was the year of the "rush" to Fairbanks [Alaska], and
boatload after boatload of people was leaving for that new gold camp a thousand
miles away, never to return. That is the sad thing about any mining town. However
it may grow and flourish; however comfortable its homes and however attached to
them its people; however, year by year as its market-gardens and hothouses become
more productive, conditions of living more pleasant, the whole thing is without
substantial foundation...and by and by the gold will be gone.

Then there is only one thing to do, get out while you can....

Kathy and Alan took us to see the sights. It was a strange experience.
Dawson was effectively a ghost town, albeit a well-preserved one in which
most of the few remaining inhabitants were playing at being citizens of
the Dawson of another era. We took a look at the last more or less intact
river steamer, permanently hauled out on the waterfront and tarted up
into a tourist attraction. We went to the Floridora saloon, saw the
Gaslight Follies, and visited various other tourist traps decorated with
Gold Rush memorabilia. We met a man who was treating a wolf pup to
beer in a bar, and another man in another bar exhibiting a glass eye in his
umbilicus. Natives were cadging money for drinks on the street.

Roads and the automobile had reached Dawson, so we rented a car
and Alan guided us around the district.

On Bonanza Creek we climbed over the last of the massive gold dredges owned by the iniquitous and ubiquitous Guggenheims, who, early in the twentieth century, established a virtual monopoly on placer mining in Alaska and the Yukon. This particular monster seemed as big as a city block. It squatted in a stagnant pond in the bed of one of Klondike's pups, having floated itself for miles down the valley on a lake of its own making, ravaging its way by means of a gigantic bucket-line. Now it was a mausoleum of rotting wood and rusting iron inhabited only by ravens, a pair of whom had built their nest atop the dredge's towering derrick.

This mechanical obscenity and its fellows (all owned by Guggenheim's Yukon Consolidated Gold Corporation) had devastated almost every gold-bearing creek in the Yukon watershed, ingesting and excreting the land and heaping the valleys with giant mounds of sterile sand and gravel that looked like casts left by titanic worms. The dredge diggings and the raw wounds still being inflicted by hydraulic miners disfigure tens of thousands of square miles of the Yukon basin. Seen from the air they give the landscape the appearance of having been hideously afflicted with leprosy.

But mining is only one of the atrocities this land has endured at the hands of modern man. Far too much of the country had been blackened by forest fires resulting from carelessness, ignorance, or attempts to expose the overburdens to make mining easier. We were told that half a million acres between Dawson and Whitehorse had been swept by fire during the preceding year alone.

Much of the country looked like what might remain after a monumental funeral pyre. Alan Innes-Taylor considered this to constitute indisputable evidence of modern man's inability to live in harmony with the world that gave him birth.

The thousands of human beings entering the Yukon during the gold rush days had a tough time of it, certainly, but the cruelties they inflicted on the animals dragooned into their service almost beggar description. In his book *Klondike*, Pierre Berton gives us this glimpse of the hell on earth for animals created by the gold rush stampeders.

"During tedious delays [on the trail over the coastal passes]...the wretched horses had to stand, often for hours, with crushing loads pressing down upon their backs....An animal might remain loaded for 24 hours and this was one reason why scarcely a single horse survived of the three thousand that were used to cross the White Pass in '97....By the time they reached the summit horses that had fetched $200 in Skagway were not worth 20 cents, for the Klondikers felt impelled to get across the mountains at any cost—and the cost always included an animal's life."

Samuel H. Graves, one of the Klondikers, would never forget the day he passed a horse that had broken its leg a few minutes before. "The horse's pack had been removed, and someone had knocked it on the head; then traffic resumed across the still warm body. By that evening there was not a vestige of the carcass left, save for the head on one side of the trail and the tail on the other. The beast had literally been ground into the earth by the human machine."

Major J.M. Walsh of the North West Mounted Police crossed the White Pass that autumn and reported: "Such a scene of havoc and destruction...can scarcely be imagined. Thousands of packhorses lie dead along the way, sometimes in bunches under the cliffs where they have fallen from the rocks above, sometimes in tangled masses filling the mud holes and furnishing the only footing for our poor pack animals, often, I regret to say, [the fallen horses are] exhausted but still alive, a fact we are unaware of until the miserable wretches turn beneath the hoofs of our cavalcade."

Jack London, one of the few chroniclers of the stampede who actually saw it, wrote: "The horses died like mosquitoes in the first frosts, and from Skagway to [Lake] Bennett they rotted in heaps. They died at the rocks, they were poisoned at the summit, and they starved at the lakes; they fell off the trail, what there was of it; in the rivers they drowned under their loads or were smashed to pieces against the boulders; they snapped their legs in the crevices and broke their backs falling backward with their loads; in the sloughs they sank from sight or were smothered in slime; and they were disembowelled in the bogs when the corduroy logs turned end up in the mud; men shot them, worked them to death and when they were gone, went back to the beach and bought more. Some did not bother to shoot them. Stripping the saddle off and leaving them where they fell. Their hearts turned to stone—those that did not break—and they became beasts, the men on the Dead Horse Trail."

For Alan Innes-Taylor, the treatment meted out to animals by the Klondikers epitomized the depths to which human beings will descend in their pursuit of wealth.

The trails to the headwaters of the Klondike from Dyea and Skagway over White Pass and Chilkoot Pass were slaughterhouses. It's my best guess that as many as five thousand horses, a thousand oxen, perhaps two thousand mules, and God alone knows how many pack dogs, died terrible deaths to feed the greed for gold of the stampeders. I'm glad I wasn't there. I might have shot a few of those human monsters myself, and done the world a good turn.

The real stampede didn't come for a couple of years after Carmack made his strike in 1896. When he paddled down to the settlement of Forty Mile, where the mining commissioner was, and registered his claim, it was a matter of hours before that little town was deserted. Nobody left in it but an old Indian woman and her dog. Miners who had been lying up there drunk all winter were loaded into boats for ballast, and everyone went to what became Dawson.

But it wasn't until '98 that the real avalanche began. Then people just poured into the country. Down the Yukon. Up the Yukon. Down the Mackenzie and across the mountains, up the Peel, or over Rat Pass and down the Bell into the Porcupine—some of the unlucky ones that went that way took two years to make it in from Edmonton—those that did make it!

It's estimated that one way or another about 60,000 got to the Yukon out of perhaps 150,000 that got as far as Lynn Canal, or St. Michael. At the peak of the stampede Dawson had about thirty thousand people; Bonanza about ten thousand; and there were at least another ten thousand scattered about on adjoining creeks. Today there might be three hundred people left in Dawson and hereabouts, and a good part of those are what's left of the natives, down at Moosehide village.

The Klondikers came and overran the country like a bunch of lunatics. Then, a few years later, they were mostly gone. I've spent years moseying around by boat and canoe in summer, with my dogs in winter, and everywhere I come across traces of those vanished people. You find an isolated mound and, when you clear the scrub off, realize it's a grave. You go ashore in a place you'd think there's never been a living soul, and back in among the trees you stumble on the remains of an old, rotting-down cabin. The stove is there; sometimes even the kindling in it, just the way the owner left it.

I was paddling up Hunker Creek not long ago and wandered off on one of the pups and found the remains of an old cabin. There was a marker behind it and I thought it was somebody's grave. It was a wooden cross with a plate on it made out of a flattened tin can, and punched into it was this message:

"HE WAS MY DOG AND THE BEST FRIEND I EVER HAD."

I understood, because dogs were always a big part of my life in the north. And out of it too!

In 1928 the British and Yukon Navigation Company sent me to Vancouver to look into buying a new steamboat. The BYNC manager there called me into his office and said some American fellow named Byrd needed forty or fifty dogs and a dog driver to take with him to the Antarctic. Could I get this fellow what he wanted? I said I could try.

I won't go into details but I scrounged up forty dogs and took them along on Byrd's expedition to the Antarctic. I spent three years Down Under, including a spell on a whaling ship, dogs and all, and finally brought the better part of the pack back to Dawson.

A lot of people had left the country before I went south, and a lot more left during my absence. They've been leaving ever since. Now you can travel down the river from Whitehorse to Dawson and hardly see a living soul, not even an Indian. And that was all prime Indian country. There were a great many of them, and they were a great people.

When I first came into the country a very famous Indian known as Jim Boss lived on Lake Laberge. He was over six feet tall and could pack three hundred pounds of flour over a portage.

Jim was one Indian nobody took advantage of. He stood up for himself and his people. When the stampede started, he got in its way as much as he could. It's said he charged the stampeders for crossing Lake Laberge, because it was Indian country. Frankly, I hope he did and don't blame him if he did, but he was lucky he didn't get a bullet in the back from one of the desperados in the rush.

I was still in the Mounted Police when, one winter, I happened to be in Taylor and Drury's trading post at Whitehorse. Bill Drury called me over. Bill had the most enormous feet of any man I've ever seen. He hardly needed to wear snowshoes. Anyway, he said: "Alan, Jim Boss is in from Laberge. Come back into the fur grading room with me; he wants to talk to me."

We went back and there he was—what a big man! He looked like a king. Very dignified and imposing. Bill said to him: "Glad to see you, Jim. What was it you wanted to see me about?"

"I tell. Me get old. Someday me die. Me want last-time box."

"Last-time box? Oh, you mean a coffin?"

"Yes. Last-time box. Me chief, so me want best last-time box. Like white men got. White silk inside. And me want different box, too. Me want lid with mirror inside. Looking glass, so can see."

"Well, Jim," Drury says, "we can get you a box like that, but we'll have to send out to Vancouver. It'll take quite a time. Do you think you can wait that long?"

The old chap was offended.

"Me live long time. Me live 'til Bill Drury wear out bear paws got for feet."

Drury didn't like that, but he sent the order out to Vancouver for an oak coffin lined with white silk, the under part of the lid to be a full-length mirror. The coffin arrived the following summer and Bill sent word up to the police post that I should hurry down to the store because Jim Boss was there to get his last-time box.

Old Jim had showed up with a big crowd of his people, but made them wait outside. Bill had the box in the fur-grading room on a couple of sawhorses with the lid standing up against the wall, the mirror facing out. Jim came into the room. He looked at himself in the mirror. Looked at the box. Felt the silk. Then he spoke: "Look good. Me try."

"Well," says Bill, "those moccasins…you'll get the silk all dirty, you'd better take them off."

Jim looks at Bill then turns to me and I swear there was just the hint of a smile on his grim old face.

"No good try steal my moccasins, Bill. Too small for you."

He took them off and we helped him into the box. He lay down and squirmed around a bit, getting himself really comfortable, you know, then he says: "Bill Drury, you put top on so chief can see."

We put the top on, but then of course it was pitch dark inside. Jim was furious. He was bellowing so loud we thought the other Indians would hear and come running in. We heaved the top off and helped him out and he was the maddest Indian I ever saw. He was so mad he couldn't get his moccasins on. He hopped out the door yelling, "No good last-time box! No good! Nothing!"

Bill ran after him, trying to quiet him down.

"All right now, Jim. I'm sorry about this. But you come back tomorrow and it'll all be fixed just the way you wanted."

As soon as Jim was gone Drury sent for Sydney Simpson, the village carpenter.

"Simmie," he said, "this is an emergency. Here's Jim Boss's last-time box and you've got to put skylights in it—little glass windows to let the light in so he can see himself when he gets in there."

"You goin' to bury him alive?" Simmie asks, real interested.

"No, you idiot. So he can see himself now."

"I dunno," says Simmie. "Don't like fooling around with stuff like this. Well, I suppose I'll do it."

Simmie let two sidelights in each side. I got in and tested it and I could see myself in the mirror all right, though it was kind of a gruesome sight.

Jim Boss came for his box next morning.

"You fix?" he demanded of Drury.

"Yup, we fix. You try."

So try he did, and he was satisfied. Two of his young bucks came in and carried the coffin away to Jim's cabin down the lake.

Some years after, when I came back from the Antarctic, I dropped in to see Bill Drury. I asked him if Jim Boss was still alive and he said, "God yes! Old bugger will live to be a hundred!"

A while later, going down the lake, I stopped to visit the Indian village and the old chief. I was curious about his last-time box, but you don't like to ask a man what he's done with a thing like that. Anyway, I saw no sign of it. As I was leaving his cabin, he said he'd get me a slab of smoked moose for my canoe trip downriver to Dawson.

"Me got in cache," he told me. "You come. We get."

Well, the cache was his last-time box, hoisted up on posts and full of old traps and other junk, and about half a moose. It didn't look too clean any more, but it still seemed pretty sound.

Time went by and it was several years before I could pay him another visit. By then he must have been nearly ninety, but I'd heard he'd sired another baby. I went into the cabin and there was his great big iron bedstead, a gramophone, and all the rest of his stuff. We were sitting there while his wife gave us tea and bannocks, talking about the old days, when a baby started crying.

"Got another baby, Jim," I said politely.

"Me got. You want see?"

I nodded and he limped across the room to where a blanket was nailed in a corner, pushed back the blanket, and there it was.

The last-time box had become a cradle for Jim's newest and, as it turned out, his last offspring.

Two years later Jim died—a good friend, a good Indian. He was buried at the foot of Lake Laberge in his box—mirror and all, though the glass was cracked some by then.

That's not quite the end of the story. I was in Whitehorse a couple of years back to see a friend in hospital, and a nurse's aide came through the ward. I thought she looked kind of familiar. My pal saw me look at her.

"That's Sarah Boss," he said. "Jim's youngest. She's working to be a nurse so she can go out and help what's left of her people. I think she'll make it, too."

Well, old Jim's generation is all gone now. But, you know, maybe the natives have turned the corner. I keep thinking of old Jim in his last-time box, and of that young woman as a baby in her first-time box, and I hope to God it all works out. Because you know, Farley, the north is their country. Maybe it never belonged to them in the way we whites use the word...but they sure as hell belonged to it.

I doubt we ever will.

Envoy

ONE NIGHT THERE CAME A SHARP FROST AND IN the morning a skim of ice covered the pools beside the Yukon, warning us we were in danger of overstaying our time.

We fired up the Wasp and headed south. It was our intention to pause at Whitehorse just long enough to refuel, then fly westward over the coast range and the infamous White Pass and land on saltwater at Skagway in Alaska so we would be able to brag that DCL had wet her pontoons in three oceans. But at Whitehorse we heard the U.S. authorities were still on the lookout for us.

So from Whitehorse we flew east and south to Watson Lake, Fort Liard, Hay River on Great Slave Lake, Uranium City, and finally The Pas, stopping only to refuel and to sleep a little along the way. Three long flying days after leaving Dawson, our stalwart Otter wearily came home to a familiar mooring at Lamb Airways.

I don't remember much of what was said in the way of goodbyes, but I do recall one phrase of Peter Murdoch's.

"We've surely listened to a lot of voices on this trip, Farley. Likely we'll hear echoes of them for quite a while."

I shall hear them always.

Index

🐦